Growing Up Red

Growing Up Red

✦

Outing Red America From the Inside

By Tim Schilke

iUniverse, Inc.
New York Lincoln Shanghai

Growing Up Red
Outing Red America From the Inside

Copyright © 2005 by Timothy Schilke

All rights reserved. No part of this book may be used or reproduced by any means, graphic, electronic, or mechanical, including photocopying, recording, taping or by any information storage retrieval system without the written permission of the publisher except in the case of brief quotations embodied in critical articles and reviews.

iUniverse books may be ordered through booksellers or by contacting:

iUniverse
2021 Pine Lake Road, Suite 100
Lincoln, NE 68512
www.iuniverse.com
1-800-Authors (1-800-288-4677)

ISBN: 0-595-34613-8 (pbk)
ISBN: 0-595-67138-1 (cloth)

Printed in the United States of America

Contents

Introduction: An American Shade of Red 1

CHAPTER 1 Born on the 16th of January 5
- *Flip Flopping Evolutionary Creationism* 5
- *God, Country and Republicans* 7
- *Tossing Babies from their Incubators* 11
- *"Give Peace a Chance"* 13

CHAPTER 2 Growing up Red 16
- *Tears over Jimmy* 16
- *Red House Values* 18
- *The Reagan Revolution* 19

CHAPTER 3 Facing Red House Ghosts 24
- *Moral Relativism in Suburban America* 24
- *The Intercessor's Elephant Gun* 26
- *It's Not Torture Unless We Say It's Torture* 31
- *Sodomy of the Mind* 37
- *Real American Values* 41
- *The New Morality* 44

CHAPTER 4 War and Country and The American Media 49
- *Media Complicity* 49
- *Rescuing Jessica* 55
- *Deducing a Draft* 58
- *Saving Private Face* 61
- *Armstrong Williams and Pay for Play* 63
- *Sinclair Broadcasting: A Liberal Media Case Study* 65

- *Seeking Out Varied Opinions* *69*

CHAPTER 5   America On a Bumper 72
- *Bumper Sticker Politics* *72*
- *Safe from the Evildoers* *75*
- *Who's Your Daddy?* *78*
- *Doomed to Repeat* *81*
- *Educating to Comply* *83*
- *You Have the Right to Go Back to Class* *87*
- *Teaching Directly to the Tests* *89*
- *Don't Challenge Me, Please!* *91*

CHAPTER 6   The Reality-Based Chapter 95
- *Marketing America's Army* *95*
- *Long Term Avoidance* *100*
- *Hard-Coding Saddam to the PTSD* *103*
- *Homers and Pills and Shots in the Ass* *108*
- *Have Faith Young Man* *111*
- *Finding Truth on a Turkey Farm* *114*
- *The Fallback Reality* *119*
- *Blame the Trial Lawyers* *122*

CHAPTER 7   The Dawn of Fear 125
- *Pilfering Playboys* *125*
- *Learning to Fear* *127*
- *Sunday Drivers on a Beautiful Tuesday Morning* *129*
- *No Really, You Will Never Forget* *130*
- *Don't Mess with Texas* *131*
- *The War On Mud Huts Continues, News at 11* *133*
- *Puppets and Their Pipelines* *135*

CHAPTER 8   Fear's Agenda Takes Hold 139
- *Waves of Fear* *139*
- *Safe and Warm In the Suburbs* *143*

- *Winning over the Security Moms* *147*
- *Legislating Patriotism* *148*
- *The Anti-Patriots Proliferate* *154*
- *Affronting the Real Patriots* *156*
- *You Don't Need These Anymore Do You?* *158*
- *Freedoms Lost—Patriot Act Case Studies* *160*
- *Loyalty Oaths and the Republican National Convention* *163*
- *The Next Generation of Patriots* *165*
- *Sitting in the Family Section* *169*

CHAPTER 9   Most of History's Lessons are Never Learned 171
- *Napping Through History Class* *171*
- *The Alien and Sedition Acts of 1798* *172*
- *Espionage and Sedition Acts of WWI* *174*
- *Temporary Insanity for Temporary Safety* *177*
- *Fascism in the United States?* *179*
- *Looking Back at the Present Day* *184*

CHAPTER 10   On the Front Lines of Class Warfare 187
- *Thriving in Middle America* *187*
- *Tax Breaks for the Middle Class!* *191*
- *Following in Reagan's Footsteps* *193*
- *George Bailey Democrats* *196*
- *Off-shoring the American Dream* *200*
- *Denouncing My "Fiscal Conservativism"* *203*
- *My "Free Market" Coworkers* *206*
- *The Nicest Buildings in Every Small Town* *208*

Epilogue: Bigger Than You Can Imagine 211
- *The Castle on the Hill* *212*
- *About the Election* *221*
- *Letter to the Red States* *225*
- *Blueness is a State of Mind* *230*

- *America the Beautiful* *232*
Notes and References 237

Acknowledgments

For my wife, who was my ultimate "idea bouncer", and never-wavering supporter. For my two small children, who inspire my continued Patriotism.

For my skilled editor, Judy Devlin. I promise to never use contractions again. Thanks also go to my other chapter and content editors, Cliston Brown and Daniel Wilkinson.

For my mother and teacher, for teaching me to read at age three and to think like a writer from the day I was born. And for my father, for being my primary motivation and subject matter, all rolled into one.

Introduction: An American Shade of Red

Moderator: "Please stand up, state your name, and how long you have been blue."

Me: "My name is Tim Schilke, and I have been Blue for 14 years now."

Group: "Welcome Tim."

Yes, I voted for Democrats in 2004, in a densely Republican community. I spent the greater part of the past year alienating myself amongst friends, coworkers, and family members. Just about every suburban professional is a staunch war hawk and Red Elephant these days. In the weeks before the vote, I confronted many of them on their political views, and convinced only a few. The topics of debate ranged from Iraq to the War on Terror to the deterioration of civil rights through the Patriot Act; from the dumbing down of America, to the eventual need for a military draft and the questionable morality of using fear to win elections.

One of my coworkers was still waffling on whether or not to vote and he was still somewhat undecided. In my many conversations with him, I tried to answer his most pressing issues with direct answers, and I always provided supporting evidence where possible. I shared various documentaries and editorial columns with him, and we would discuss some of them at length. Over time, I saw him noticeably changing his approach to current events and news articles.

He was starting to make sense, because he was starting to think critically. He implied that he could never vote for President George W. Bush based on his actions of the last four years. Ultimately, he said he was either going to vote for John Kerry or he was not going to vote. On Election Day I stopped by to see him, and jokingly asked him if he did the right thing. I was so happy for him and proud of our political process. Things were going to be okay after all. His answer still rings in my ears like a hollow echo…

"I just couldn't vote for Kerry. My dad would never speak to me again. I voted for Bush."

My fellow American Red suburban professionals are not stupid or ignorant. They want pretty much the same things that every American wants. They want to provide for their families and keep their children safe; maybe they are a little over the top about it but it is not intentional. If they can, they want to stash away some cash and pay off some debt. They want to watch football on the lounger with a cold one after a hard week at work, or they just want to play with the kids, doing nothing in particular. They like the status quo and they like to buy stuff. They go to church on Sunday and they go to the park with the family. They drive sport utility vehicles with Support the Troops ribbons in yellow or the increasingly popular red, white, and blue. But they are definitely capable of extremely deep thought and reasoning. I know this to be true; I have heard many of them slice into a Green Bay Packers' defensive scheme for hours. And really, how can they give up a 4th and 26 against Philadelphia in the playoffs?

In the coming pages, I will try to explain my Midwestern Red suburbanite friends, neighbors, and family members. When we are done, I want you to understand them as I do, through their eyes, and through mine. I know these people inside and out. I grew up with them for over thirty years. As I go through events of our common past, I will attempt to frame them in my perspective, and contrast my view with the significant slant of my Red house ghosts.

While writing this book, I came up with the title, *Growing Up Red*. I spent some time researching, and I found that Red was not always the color used to represent the Republican candidate on the electoral map on election night. But the more I thought about it, the more it fit. Red *is* the color that represents the incumbent party on the electoral map. Red represents the consensus thought, the majority, and the status quo. I certainly grew up with all of these things shaping my suburban life, and not coincidentally, I was also raised to be a Republican.

In the early morning hours of November 3, 2004, I declared a personal Civil War on Bush voters. No more free passes on political emails. No more free passes on nationalistic or religious self-righteousness or moral relativism. And growing up in a Red house? That is not a free pass either. It is time for the good people of America to reclaim our country, while we still have a Democracy to defend.

Enjoy.

1

Born on the 16th of January

"Twenty years from now you will be more disappointed by the things that you didn't do than by the ones you did do. So throw off the bowlines. Sail away from the safe harbor. Catch the trade winds in your sails. Explore. Dream. Discover."
—Mark Twain

"You must unlearn what you have learned."
—Yoda

FLIP FLOPPING EVOLUTIONARY CREATIONISM

When I was eighteen years old, I temporarily left my Red house behind to attend college at Valparaiso University in Indiana. For a kid from a Red neighborhood this was a pretty rough transition, but not for the reasons that might be assumed. My father has often stated that he wants his tuition money back, since he "did not send me to school to learn to become a Liberal". Unfortunately for my dad, there will be no refund check in the mail. The great metaphoric irony of my "Liberal Arts" education is that there was nothing blatantly Liberal about it. My education taught me how to approach complex situations in complex ways, like any good education. In doing so, I learned that I am in the minority in today's America.

My Freshman year started in 1990. George H.W. Bush was President, and our country was in its tenth straight year of Republican rule. My roommate Jeff was a Republican from Rockford, IL. His parents were like mine. He was on the swim team, and I was on the cross country team. He was shy around girls, and I could not even talk to one without choking on my own tongue. He was from the suburbs, just like me. We were identical in nearly every way. The two guys in the room next door were much the same. One was also from Illinois, studying to be a Lutheran pastor, and the other was a Minnesota native headed for a degree in Engineering with a minor in Going to the Chapel Every Sunday.

In high school I got good grades without trying too hard. But my Freshman year in college was different. I got a 2.6 GPA, the worst in my life, thanks largely to my Freshman English class. One assignment in the first few weeks was to write an essay, in which I had to debate myself on a controversial topic and come to a conclusion based on the facts. At age eighteen, there is not much controversy for a kid from a Red house. Honestly, the most controversial issue I was aware of was the debate between the theories of evolution and creation. So I tackled the topic in a ten page paper, and I came to the following shocking conclusion:

"God created the world to look like it had evolved."

Yes I know; I was the original flip-flopper, trying to please everyone. The Creationists would love my paper because "God created the world", and the Evolutionists would love my paper because "the world evolved". I was very proud of this paper, and I was sure it was going to put my grade over the top in that class. I spent days on it, phrasing it just perfectly. A few days later I got the paper back with the following comment:

"The assignment was to explain your conclusion based on facts. Grade: D"

I was flabbergasted. At least three different teachers in grade school and high school had taught me the theory of Evolutionary Creationism as fact. A pastor had backed them up! My whole life, I had heard the theory of creation. Then one day in science class I learned about evolution. The two theories were in such conflict. I asked so many questions and there were no good answers. Then, one day the pastor came to visit our class. Someone asked him about evolution, and he said, "God does many wonderful things to challenge our faith. Why would he not *create the world to look like it evolved?* That is the explanation I find most credible." I remember this very clearly, because I was so happy to hear this explanation. It made sense to me at the time.

The English professor said I used no facts? I would show him facts. After class, I went to see him. Surely he would see the brilliance of my pastor's argument. I stated my case, and he tore so many holes into my paper that I almost had nothing left to throw away when I got back to the dorm. This guy went line by line through my paper expertly shooting down each one of my arguments. I wish I had not thrown that paper away because I would love to read it today. As I recall my strongest supporting argument was "God can do anything, so why could he not make the Earth to look like it evolved?" Where did I get *that* theory from? Needless to say, I ultimately ended up with a C minus grade in Freshman English. I could write just fine, but I could not reason.

Since I am on the topic, if God still does mysterious things to test our faith, could he possibly drop some Weapons of Mass Destruction into Iraq to make it *look like* they were there all along? My faith is being tested on that particular issue.

GOD, COUNTRY AND REPUBLICANS

Right around the time I was debating my English grades, Saddam Hussein was invading Kuwait. Shortly after that, debate began about the possibility of an intervention to liberate Kuwait, led by the United States. Talk of war was common in the dormitory. A nervous energy permeated these conversations. But to my surprise the energy did not originate from fear or uncertainty, but from genuine *excitement*. Every one of the Christian men on my floor was nearly drooling with anticipation of the coming attack. As the days wore on so did the level of excitement.

In Washington, debate raged over the merits of liberating Kuwait. The war hawks argued that the United States had a moral duty to defend Kuwait. Saddam Hussein was frequently compared to Hitler, and he was classified in the same realm as a neighborhood bully. When confronted, I failed to see the logic in this argument. Kuwait was a tiny country, with enormous oil profits. I did not think that we would have retained much interest in joining the conflict if that murky black substance of wealth, oil, was not also involved.

In January 1991, President George H.W. Bush issued *An Open Letter to College Students on the Persian Gulf Crisis*, in an attempt to win support for the coming war. In the letter, he said, "If armed men invaded a home in this country, killed those in their way, stole what they wanted and then announced that the house was now theirs—no one would hesitate about what must be done. And that is why we cannot hesitate about what must be done halfway around the world [in] Kuwait."

On the evening of January 16, 1991, I heard hoots and hollers from a room down the hall. With each red flash from a Coalition for Peace bomb hitting Baghdad there was clapping and cheering, and boisterous "Oohs" and "Aahs". This was shock and awe at work in the Heartland, even before it had been given the official moniker. Even now, most people remember where they watched the first night of bombing of Baghdad. It was certainly memorable. Even the news anchors on the major networks were simply giddy—beside themselves with glee.

The guys in the room down the hall actually had the lights turned off and the sound cranked up through the stereo speakers, just like they had watched the movie "Terminator" the night before. Each bomb flash lit up the walls with reddish orange colors, and the colors flickered in and out like a demented Fourth of July fireworks show.

It was 1991, and I was just eighteen years old. I had really never spoken out against (or for) anything in my life, because I never wanted to cause any trouble. It was at that precise moment that I realized I was different from the other guys in the room, the others on the floor, and most others in the dormitory. Instead of cheering, I was literally overcome by rage against the country for that I had waved the flag with so much pride for my first eighteen years of life. For the first time in my life, I was questioning my country, and it was a truly horrible feeling for a Red-tinted kid. It was as though I had grabbed my own heart, torn it out, and it was beating right there in my hand in front of me.

I walked into the room. There were at least eight guys sitting and standing, crowded around the television, still making a ruckus. I did not even like these fucking guys. I mean, what kind of sick bastards would cheer for war and death? I was nothing like these guys, and I could not wait to prove it. At that moment I instinctively said the first negative thing I ever said about my country.

"You know, there are innocent people dying," I said. "And I'm not really sure why the hell we are there anyway. I don't think it's very cool to be cheering right now."

I was shaking uncontrollably as I said it. I hated saying it. It was the proudest and yet the most miserable moment of my life. What had I just done? Would God strike me down? The Redness oozed out of me and onto the carpet, where it just lay there, rotting and stinking.

In the summer of 1990, I had seen the movie version of Ron Kovac's story, called *Born on the Fourth of July*. I was a train wreck after watching that movie, which portrayed life in America for a soldier returning from Vietnam. Like most Red house kids in the 1980s, my previous exposure to war was entirely from history books. In the official version, there were heroes and there were evildoers. The school book accounts contained no gray areas. The official factual version did not mention soldiers returning from war with catheters and flashbacks, and missing limbs. This event now unfolding in Iraq was real. It was not on the screen and not on the pages. The bombs were falling on real buildings, real people were dying, and there I was with my racing heart in my hand.

The silence in the room was palpable as the bombs continued to fall and the walls continued to flicker red and orange. After a long uncomfortable silence, one of the guys in the room stood up, picked me up by my shirt, and threw me up against the wall. He held me up there, our faces bathed in reddish orange light, for at least thirty seconds. He was breathing heavily, the anger and testosterone and Christian values dripping in and out with each breath. I swear I could hear his thoughts. "God and country and Republicans, you Liberal Fuck. God and country and Republicans, you Liberal Fuck. Did you forget to pray for our troops?" I thought he was going to kill me.

Finally he spoke. "You are going to support your country and the troops that are over there, or you are going to leave this room." He put me down, still breathing venomously. A few others came and grabbed him and pulled him back away from me. They were staring at me like I had leprosy. I could swear that I saw fear in their faces.

On that winter evening in 1991, I left the room with my tail between my legs. And I regret it to this day. If I had it to do over again, I would fight back—until I had no fight left in me. My brain was finally awake to the reality of war, and there was no turning back.

TOSSING BABIES FROM THEIR INCUBATORS

A few months earlier in October of 1990, a Human Rights Caucus had been formed in Washington in order to discuss accusations of human rights violations which were committed by the Iraqi occupiers in Kuwait. The United States was very split on the issue of Iraq, and the war hawks underwent an enormous public relations effort to convince the Congress and the American people that there was a good reason, other than just oil, for the United States to liberate Kuwait.

The most compelling and emotional testimony came from a fifteen-year-old Kuwaiti girl named Nayirah. The girl told a tear-jerking story of what she witnessed while working at a hospital in Kuwait City.

"I volunteered at the al-Addan hospital," Nayirah said. "While I was there, I saw the Iraqi soldiers come into the hospital with guns, and go into the room where…babies were in incubators. They took the babies out of the incubators, took the incubators, and left the babies on the cold floor to die."

This young girl's story instantly became the rallying cry for war advocates everywhere. The evildoers are killing babies in Kuwait! They took them right out of their incubators and threw them on the cold floor! Bomb the bastards!

Pro-Life political activists could not sleep for weeks, so great was their excitement about the pending invasion to slaughter the evil baby killers. Amnesty International issued a scathing report on the incident, stating that "In addition, over three hundred premature babies were reported to have died after Iraqi soldiers removed them from incubators, which were then looted."

There was only one slight problem. Cute little Nayirah was either lying or greatly exaggerating. And cute little Nayirah was not exactly anonymous.

In the three months between the baby killer testimony and the start of the bombing, this story was told repeatedly by President George H.W. Bush, used in UN Security Council meetings, and used in other Congressional testimony. It was a discussion topic on nearly every radio and TV talk show. But Little Nayirah the anonymous, whose identity was supposedly kept secret to protect her family in occupied Kuwait, was actually the *daughter* of Kuwait's ambassador to the US, Nasir al-Sabah, who sat listening to her testimony in the hearing room.

John MacArthur, author of *The Second Front*, later noted the following:

> "The Human Rights Caucus is not a committee of congress, and therefore it is unencumbered by the legal accouterments that would make a witness hesitate before he or she lied...Lying under oath in front of a congressional committee is a crime; lying from under the cover of anonymity to a caucus is merely public relations."

Hill & Knowlton, the world's largest PR firm at the time, had actually coached Nayirah and prepared her in advance for her testimony. After the war, Nayirah herself was never able to be reached for comment. In 1992, it was finally discovered that she was the daughter of the Kuwaiti ambassador to the United States. When reporters asked the ambassador for permission to speak to his daughter about her testimony, he angrily refused.

"This is the first allegation I've had that she was the ambassador's daughter," said Human Rights Caucus co-chair John Porter. "Yes, I think people...were entitled to know the source of her testimony."

Despite the suspicion of a possible public relations stunt, most of the American press was extremely reluctant to reconsider the facts of the testimony, with one exception. Shortly after the war ended, in March 1991, a reporter from ABC News interviewed key Kuwaiti hospital officials. These officials acknowledged that some infants had died due to the chaotic hospital conditions around the time of the invasion, related mostly to staffing problems. According to the officials, there were no babies dumped from incubators onto the "cold floor" by Iraqis.

The only mainstream news organization other than ABC to carry this important follow-up to the original story was Reuters. Amnesty International sent its own investigators to the hospital and subsequently issued a retraction on its earlier report, and even Kuwaiti investigators later confirmed that the incubator testimony was false.

On January 12, 1991, after three days of debates and much more talk about three hundred and twelve Kuwaiti babies thrown from incubators, the war gained approval by the United States Senate, by a vote of 52-47. If just three Senators had voted differently, it may have forever changed the landscape of the United States and our perception to the world. Is it possible that just three out of one hundred Senators believed the fifteen-year old Kuwaiti daughter of the Kuwaiti Ambassador? Not just possible, but probable. Any good PR guy from Hill & Knowlton could tell you that.

"GIVE PEACE A CHANCE"

Back on campus in the Midwest, days after the start of the war, I learned about a planned March for Peace when I overheard some students joking about it. "Fucking hippies. What do they think this is, Vietnam?"

On the night of the March for Peace, I picked myself up out of the murky swamp of my Red house upbringing and went to the meeting place. I felt like a traitor, to God and to my country. Even out in the middle of campus, I felt like somebody still had me by the shirt and was holding me up against the wall. I was doing something that was completely against my deep Red heritage. In my mind, it was so contrary to my love of my country. It also felt so appropriate that I had to continue.

There were only about forty marchers, and we marched around the center area of campus with candles, singing "All We Are Saying, Is Give Peace A Chance". A few of the marchers carried signs stating "No Blood for Oil". It was an incredibly cliché anti-war demonstration and it was completely meaningless. Only about twenty people saw us and the ones who did were pretty oblivious. Most of the marchers were, frankly, hippies. And I bet I was the only one in the bunch who came from a Red house in a Red neighborhood.

Meanwhile the guys down the hall were also taking action. The "video game reality" haze that surrounded our bombing of Baghdad was just getting started in the halls of commercial America. In 1991, Topps Corporation offered three sets of Desert Storm trading cards. The third set was the "Victory" set, and it included the cards "Bombs-Eye View", "These Colors Don't Run", "The Burning Fields", and "Iraqis Surrender". Thinking back on events from thirteen years ago, I thought I surely must have imagined this. Gulf War trading cards? No corporation or consumer could be that callous. But sure enough, it is still right there in Technicolor on Topps Web site in the "Flashback" section. Not only did Topps offer these tasteless cards, but apparently they are still proud of their despicable actions to this day.

I marched right in the front of the group that night. I had no sign, but I can imagine the message my face must have conveyed. "No Cheering for War Death, You Hypocrites." I was so damn proud to be an American. When we turned the corner and passed the chapel in the middle of campus, I instinctively turned my head. The hypocrisy of my neighbors in the dorm still sickened me. Every one of those guys marched down to the chapel every Sunday morning and sang hymns about forgiveness and joy, all the while hoping for the service to end so they could head back their rooms, crank up the volume, and cheer for the death with the red flashes of the television numbing their minds.

Even in 1991 in Valparaiso, Indiana, there was a Vietnam veteran in a wheelchair who had positioned himself along the march route, fully decked out in his army fatigues with medals attached. As we passed, his fingers solemnly lifted in a sign of peace. He did not say anything, but his eyes said plenty. I was not alone in my apprehension. I was not alone in my questioning. As the march progressed, the manifestation of my passion for America had transitioned from blind acceptance to curious doubt; from nationalism to patriotism. And the memories of the Fourth of July parades from my childhood in Hales Corners, Wisconsin drove my actions.

2

Growing up Red

> *"I do not know what I may appear to the world; but to myself I seem to have been only like a boy playing on the sea-shore, and diverting myself in now and then finding a smoother pebble or a prettier shell than ordinary, whilst the great ocean of truth lay all undiscovered before me."*
>
> —Isaac Newton

TEARS OVER JIMMY

One of my earliest memories took place in November, 1976. I was four years old. I wandered into my parents' bedroom late at night and encountered both of them in an extremely distraught condition. This was the first time I had seem them so upset about anything. Wondering what was wrong, I approached them.

"Ford lost the election. Jimmy Carter's our new president." My mother's voice trembled, as though she could hardly bring herself to say the words.

"What does this mean," I asked.

"Our country is in big trouble now," said my father. I lay in my parents' bed staring up at the ceiling. A feeling of despair that I had never before experienced came over me. Our country was in big trouble? I wanted to stop Jimmy Carter. I was only four and I wanted to grab the grown ups and shake sense into them, so engrained were country, religion and Republicans in my four year old mind.

From the day I was born, these three things went together like milk, cookies, and Sesame Street. At church there were Republicans praying, smiling, and shaking hands. At the Fourth of July parade there were Republicans waving, smiling, and shaking hands. What did I see and hear from the Republicans themselves? Patriotism and Religion, over and over. Democrats were unpatriotic from their objections against the Vietnam War, and Jimmy Carter was immoral for his interview in Playboy magazine during which he confessed his sins of the heart. Some things never change, even after twenty-eight years and seven presidential campaigns.

Looking back on the Carter presidency, it is somewhat ironic that my parents opposed him so vehemently from the start. Carter was known for his strong morals and his strong linkage to religion in the office of President, while President Ford was best known for pardoning Nixon. Carter's presidency was admittedly not economically strong. By the time he left office, interest rates hovered around twenty percent. But, after all, he was a good Christian who loved peanuts.

With this exchange, politics entered my life for the first time. Among the few memories I have from the Carter years is a dream that I had when I was about five years old. In my dream, Jimmy Carter came into my room. Laughing maniacally, he stole my favorite truck, and tied it up in the hallway.

I used to play baseball with imaginary players in the driveway of my suburban home. In these baseball games, Paul Molitor and Robin Yount faced off against Jimmy Carter. Carter lost every time, usually because he slipped on some peanut shells while running to first base. In my five year old mind, he truly was an evil, evil Democrat.

Such was life in the small suburb of Hales Corners, Wisconsin. Hales Corners had about seven thousand residents, and at least seventy-five percent of them were Republicans. Almost all of them were Christians. Ninety-seven percent of them were white, and the children grew up watching Sesame Street together.

RED HOUSE VALUES

The Fourth of July was always something to remember in suburban Wisconsin. We would get the family together and walk down the road to the Hales Corners Independence Day parade with our lawn chairs and cooler full of soda. I always wanted to get a bomb pop from the ice cream truck that was parked nearby, but I had learned not to ask. The answer was usually no, and it really did not matter anyway. The marching bands and the fire trucks were the highlight for me, and the colors lit up the street while the sounds overwhelmed my ears. Every local church had a float with "God Bless America" blasting from a boom box, and some youth group mom would dress up as the Statue of Liberty and march alongside, waving her big green arm.

The highlight for my father was always the politicians. He would grab me by the arm and say "Look Timmy, it's our state representative." I would wave and gawk out of admiration, probably mostly because of the look of respect in my father's eye. "I can't believe he came to *our* Fourth of July parade. There are so many others he could attend, but he always chooses ours." My dad was not alone with his excitement. As the politician would walk along the parade route, people would actually stand up, applaud, and not sit down until long after he passed. Of course, they were all Republicans.

As night fell, we would head for the park with a blanket and mosquito repellant, and we would lay on our backs and look up as magical explosions filled the sky and patriotic music played somewhere in the distance. Already at the age of six years old, Independence Day defined America to me. It still does. God, Country, and Republicans still course through my veins while watching the color guard pass by, with guns ablazin'.

Thirty years later and fifty miles away, I sit watching a carbon copy of those Fourth of July parades with my own kids. The first few minutes the parade gives me that same old feeling again, but then I remember that everything has changed. As the Statue of Liberty lady walks by, on stilts now, I find myself suddenly choked up. F-15's fly over the parade route and everyone cheers wildly. But I sit silently, looking at my son and daughter, wondering what America will mean to them by the time their childhood is over, or by the time they are parents, or when they are elderly.

Almost as if on cue, a chorus of boos begin to rain down from the parade watchers. The Kerry for President group is walking by, and it consists of a handful of moms pulling their kids in wagons, and about a dozen Vietnam vets. They hold signs which read "A New Hope for America." As they walk by, they hang their heads and avoid eye contact. The boos become even louder now, and I yell out, "No booing vets. It's the Fourth of July, damn it." But it is useless. This is an eighty percent Red county in the suburbs, and anyone who disagrees gets booed, even Veterans on the Fourth of July. Things are changing quickly, and there is no going back.

THE REAGAN REVOLUTION

My first memories of Ronald Reagan can best be compared to miraculously seeing the face of Jesus appear in the burn marks on a piece of toast. To my Red house, Reagan was literally the savior of America. He would swoop out of the California sky with his movie star good looks and charm, and rescue America from the immoral mind of the evil Jimmy Carter. After all, Reagan was all-American, and Carter was an immoral man who lusted after women in his heart. It also did not hurt that Reagan did not like the Soviets, he wanted to cut taxes, and he was a Republican.

Reagan's first political involvement came as president of the Screen Actors Guild in the 1940s, during the time of alleged communism in the film industry, that originated through the insanity of McCarthyism. At the time, even Captain America was dedicating comic book story lines to flushing out the bad guys, preaching, "Beware, commies, spies, traitors, and foreign agents! Captain America, with all loyal, free men behind him, is looking for you."

It was mostly during this time of his life, that Reagan's actions earned my utmost respect. During a period when actors in Hollywood were caving and chirping at every opportunity to avoid prosecution, Reagan stood up to the House Committee on Un-American Activities. When testifying before the committee on October 23rd, 1947, Reagan said:

> "I will be frank with you that as a citizen I would hesitate, or I would not like to see any political party outlawed on the basis of its political ideology. Because we've spent 170 years in this country on the basis that Democracy is strong enough to stand up and fight for itself against the inroads of any ideology, no matter how much we may disagree with it."

After many years as Governor of California, Reagan easily defeated Carter in 1980, and all was right in my Red-tinted world. I remember when Iran freed the fifty-two American hostages, and I can still see them getting off the plane. If I was not wearing my American flag tank top on that day, I am sure I put it on. And I remember the buzz about the tax cuts and the excitement over "Reaganomics". The day Reagan was shot by John Hinckley Jr., I prayed for hours that he would survive and become the greatest President ever. He did survive, but the second part of my wish did not come to be. I guess God does not always answer prayers in exactly the way that we ask him to.

Strangely, I remember no conversation at all in my house about the Iran-Contra affair, but I do remember Oliver North plastered all over the television set and on the nightly news. My parents knew it was going on. I asked them once if they remembered the scandal, and they said that they did remember Ollie North, but they could not remember the details. Ultimately, investigators concluded that Reagan was possibly involved at an approval level, but he pleaded ignorance. To my Red parents, this was certainly a case of hearing what they wanted to hear, and ignoring anything that did not fit their perception of the Reagan mold.

The U.S. economy was in recession when Reagan took office. According to Reagan's economic advisor John Rutledge, Reagan said in 1981, "Look guys, I don't like taxes, I don't like inflation, I don't like the Russians. Work something up."

At the same time President Reagan was raising defense spending by $100 billion to intimidate the Soviets, he was also slashing taxes. Over the next few years, the national deficit nearly tripled. In retrospect, I find this to be a rather interesting synergy with the current Bush Administration, which has followed the Reaganomics model quite closely. The later years of Reaganomics were not a stellar economic success for America.

"He, in fact, tried to recoup it over the succeeding years with a series of tax increases which were necessary to bring the budget back at least into decent position." said Fred Bergsten, with the Institute of International Economics. "I think the budget deficits and the trade deficits that came along with them were seriously debilitating to the economy for about ten to fifteen years."

Even David Stockman, Reagan's budget director, said, "It leaves behind a profound fiscal policy failure and imbalance."

As with most Americans, my strongest memory from the Reagan years was the nuclear build-up and the acceleration of the Cold War with the Soviet Union. Reagan called the Soviet Union an "evil empire" and began to fund the Star Wars program, a multi-billion dollar project to build an outer space shield against nuclear weapons.

Along with the rest of the country, I was terrified of the Russians. The Cold War was the lead story nearly every night on the news. We were regularly updated on the current stockpile rankings of various types of bombs on both sides of the Iron Curtain. Missile exhaust trails across the sky overhead were standard images in my imagination as I grew up in the midst of the Cold War. I sat in the classroom dreaming in terror about the movie *Red Dawn*, where Commies dropped out of the sky and American kids took up arms against them. Fear was a daily undertone, never much spoken about directly, but it was always there.

As the stability of Communist Russia started to break apart and some of the satellite countries began to declare independence, I rejoiced with the rest of America. We were finally on the verge of ending the arms race and winning the war of warheads with the Soviets. *Red Dawn, War Games, Miracle Mile,* and the other sensationalistic Cold War movies of my youth had never come to pass in reality.

With the Soviet threat diminishing, the stage was set for a great civilization. America of the 21st Century has great potential, and Reagan was attuned to this possibility. As he began his second Presidential term, he said, "My fellow citizens, our nation is poised for greatness. We must do what we know is right and do it with all our might. Let history say of us, 'These were golden years when the American revolution was re-born, when freedom gained new life and America reached for her best.'"

By the end of his second term, Reagan's public approval rating was higher than any other modern president. I was sixteen-years-old, starting to get focused on the mile run for my High School track team, and I was glad to see another good Republican take over in the person of George H.W. Bush.

In 1989, when the Berlin wall tumbled down in a sea of rejoicing people, I watched on television with great national pride. I wanted a brick or even a piece of spray-painted concrete. In my mind, I jumped for joy along with the raucous teenagers on both sides of the wall that day. However, as the scene calmed, and the cameras were turned off, I felt empty and confused. I thought, what will we do now that we don't have a real enemy? What is it like to live in a world where we are the only superpower? Will we lead responsibly, or recklessly?

I never would have guessed just how soon I would get the answer to all of my questions.

3

Facing Red House Ghosts

"The idea that religion and politics don't mix was invented by the devil to keep Christians from running their own country."
—Jerry Falwell

"A tyrant must put on the appearance of uncommon devotion to religion. Subjects are less apprehensive of illegal treatment from a ruler whom they consider god-fearing and pious. On the other hand, they do less easily move against him, believing that he has the gods on his side."
—Aristotle

MORAL RELATIVISM IN SUBURBAN AMERICA

If you have ever seen the classic television show, *Leave It to Beaver*, then you have seen my upbringing. Ward, June, Wally and the Beav were my favorite family growing up—both on TV, and inside the four walls of my own house. My mother and June Cleaver have a few things in common. She volunteers at church and teaches Sunday School. She and my dad go to visit lonely elderly people in their homes. She is a perfect model of a Christian woman.

Given this saintly image, the biggest challenge for me has been attempting to reconcile these two disparate things: my mother's goodness to her very core vs. my loathing of her political views.

How could there be such a disparity? How could a kind, loving, compassionate Lutheran woman, through her vote, support the ruthless perpetual war machine of President George W. Bush?

Indeed, when it comes to the morality of war and Neo-Conservative foreign policy, my own deeply-religious family is apathetic on potential moral conflicts. I have asked my family many times about the possibility of one hundred thousand civilian deaths in Iraq, both offhandedly and directly. The answers are always the same.

"That's the cost of war. War is just awful. Just look at Hitler!"

"But guys, Hitler posed a legitimate threat to our national security, it's been proven that Saddam and Iraq had no connection to 9/11 or Al Qaeda. Even the *9/11 Commission Report* admitted that this connection did not exist."

"Oh I know but Saddam is evil. Don't you think he's evil? Saddam was out to get us!"

"They never found the weapons of mass destruction. They never will. There were no weapons."

Silence. "Well I don't know. I just know that President Bush is a good person and he knows what he is doing."

"He is not a good man. Give me a break." I have to laugh a bit at that one. Even for a Red house it is a bit over the top to claim that Bush is a good man.

"I don't like to see you get so worked up about this, Tim. Why don't you take some time off from politics for a few weeks and just relax and spend some time with the family?" Translation: Just drink this kool-aid and you will feel better about things. Just turn on the TV and stare at the red flash of the bombs for hours until you are numb to the hypocrisy.

No matter how hard I try to bring the conversation to some logical conclusion based on fact, the ending is always the same. It is like the Grade C paper from my Freshman English class all over again. Only this time the topic is hypocritical morality, and the essay writers are my Red family and friends.

"War is bad. War is tough."

"Facts are usually fuzzy when it comes to starting a war."

"People die in wars, even innocent people."

"At least there is a better life for us in Heaven. In the meantime, all we can do is pray."

"You can't believe everything you read on the Internet."

"It's unfortunate that people are dying, but we are at war. You can't be truly innocent if you are an evildoer. And they aren't intentionally targeting civilians."

"Saddam would have killed twice as many civilians. Soon they will have Democracy and it will all be worth it!"

"Once wars start they are difficult to end."

And the kicker: "If we didn't do this to them, they would have done it to us."

All of these rationalizations are based on moral relativism, and this type of reasoning is inexcusable in an educated society. Even for a Red house, no, *especially* for a Red house, this is a mountain of hypocrisy to swallow. In many families across America, morality is a core family inheritance. Unfortunately, the relative imbalance of the prioritization of moral values is also passed along from generation to generation. Part of this imbalance is grounded in the Old Testament of the Bible.

The Intercessor's Elephant Gun

When I was brought up in the Lutheran Church—Missouri Synod, I was consistently taught that the Old Testament was essentially superseded by the New Testament. The Old Testament was still part of the Bible, but purely for historical reference. The God of the Old Testament is the famous God of Fire and Brimstone. As the story goes, the sacrifice of Jesus ended this age of vengeance against man, and a kinder, gentler God emerged in the New Testament. Strangely, the passages normally used by my Christian relatives to justify the actions of the Bush Administration are almost all from the Old Testament.

Emails are already circulating with great fervor around some parts of the Christian community about the need to bring back "Imprecatory Prayers". Apparently, these are prayers that are intended to ask God to crush one of "his enemies". Some examples:

> *"Break the teeth in their mouths, O God; tear out, O Lord, the fangs of the lions! Let them vanish like water that flows away; when they draw the bow, let their arrows be blunted. Like a slug melting away as it moves along, like a still born child, may they not see the sun. The righteous will be glad when they bathe their feet in the blood of the wicked."*
>
> —Psalm 58.6-10.

> *"Pour out your wrath on them; let your fierce anger overtake them. May their place be deserted; let there be no one to dwell in their tents. For they persecute those you wound and talk about the pain of those you hurt. Charge them with crime upon crime; do not let them share in your salvation. May they be blotted out of the book of life and not be listed with the righteous."*
>
> —Psalm 69.24-28.

With these texts in mind, I am drawn to another term which is used frequently in Red-tinted suburban America, "Jihad". Is there much of a logical difference between this type of attitude from Christians in America and the highly condemned principles of Jihad in the Muslim world?

The same people who came in droves to make *The Passion of the Christ* the number one grossing movie of all time apparently forgot the meaning of THE passion of THE Christ before they got home from the theater.

After all, the New Testament paints a very different picture of religious "morals". The passages from the New Testament tell us of a Jesus who was clearly a Democrat, at least on most modern political topics. In Matthew Chapter 5, Jesus says, "Love your enemies. Blessed are the peacemakers. If someone strikes you on the right cheek, turn to him the other also." And in Matthew Chapter 19, he says, "Truly, I say unto you, it will be hard for a rich man to enter the kingdom of heaven. I repeat what I said: it is easier for a camel to pass through a needle's eye than for a rich man to enter the kingdom of God. You cannot serve both God and Money." It sounds suspiciously like Jesus may be warning against the dangers of moral relativism, in both foreign and domestic policy.

Howard Dean also pointed this out during the Democratic Primary campaign in late 2003.

"Christ was someone who sought out people who were disenfranchised, people who were left behind. He fought against the self-righteousness of people who had everything."

I can hear the voices of my Red relatives in reaction to this quote. "Howard Dean follows the teachings of that Jesus guy? Doesn't he know that Jesus was just another long-haired peace-loving hippie freak? Dean should stop acting like a commie wimp and get with the program—Jesus is so last week. Dean needs to read up on Yahweh and his smiting down of the infidels. Child sacrifices for everyone. That is the real Christian God."

Of course, they would never actually say that Jesus is outdated, but their actions speak those words and many more. Self-righteousness is what moral relativism is all about. For the most part, Christians strive to be "good folks." They inherently want to believe that their country's leadership and its actions are "good" as well. Riding on the heels of the desire to be "good" people, I find many Christians to be politically condescending and disconnected from reality, even as so-called Christian leaders carefully tweak their perceptions for political gain of a morally bankrupt agenda.

I once mentioned the increasing Iraqi civilian death count number to a precociously Red acquaintance, and I prefaced it with the sarcastic comment, "Let me guess, most of them would have become terrorists anyway?" The predictable response was, "You said it, not me." This is not the expected Christian response, but it is the expected conditioned response based on the cognitive dissonance of a well-trained moral relativist.

Jerry Falwell may have expressed this attitude best on CNN on October 24, 2004, when he said "If it takes 10 years, let's blow them all away in the name of the Lord." Can I get a Hallelujah please? When another guest on the show pointed out that the September 11th terrorists did not come from Iraq, Falwell said, "I don't care where they came from."

That is an example of Christian Jihad on national television, and Falwell is certainly not alone in his justification of war, any war, as long as it involves the killing of Muslims.

Henry Blackaby, president of Blackaby Ministries International, said that those who oppose the war to liberate Iraq need to read God's Word. "There is no question that the current war to liberate Iraq is a 'just' war—according to biblical standards," said Blackaby in an interview with Agape Press. Blackaby also prophesizes that any who resist Bush's authority bring God's judgment on themselves.

Charles Stanley of In Touch Ministries also defended the "War on Terror" on his national television broadcast. "Throughout Scripture there is evidence that God favors war for divine reasons and sometimes uses it to accomplish His will. He has also given governments and their citizens very specific responsibilities in regards to this matter." He also spoke out against protest, saying, "How can we justify the protests and marches against war? I understand that, in America, for example, we have a right to express our different opinions. However, there comes a time when our personal opinion is not a priority. The only reason we have the freedom to protest in this country is because thousands were willing to die for that liberty in the past." Apparently, both Blackaby and Stanley believe that free speech is great, except during times of national crisis, when it is most sorely needed.

The lengthy list of pastors and televangelists speaking out in favor of the War on Terror and the invasion of Iraq is truly terrifying. There is no Just War when it comes to invading a sovereign nation who did not attack us or anyone else. In retrospect, it is clear that Iraq and Saddam had no illegal weapons and no connection to al Qaeda. The underlying and unspoken defense of our country's actions is a Holy War against the Muslim community as a whole. That is a defense which comes straight out of the Old Testament.

Lest I forget my favorite bloodthirsty compassionate Republican, testosterone-charged political commentator Ann Coulter also weighed in on revenge and its non-specific nature. In a eulogy for Barbara Olson, who died on the plane that hit the Pentagon, Coulter said:

> "This is no time to be precious about locating the exact individuals directly involved in this particular terrorist attack. Those responsible include anyone anywhere in the world who smiled in response to the annihilation of patriots like Barbara Olson…We should invade their countries, kill their leaders and convert them to Christianity. We weren't punctilious about locating and punishing only Hitler and his top officers. We carpet-bombed German cities; we killed civilians. That's war. And this is war."

Upon advice from relatives, I stopped by a local Lutheran church on Christmas Eve in 2003. I was told that the pastor was a Vietnam veteran and a compassionate man. During the prayer that night, he said "And God, please bless those who are overseas defending our country." *Defending our country.* Even this cliché carries strong political undertones. There is a big difference between defending America and defending our self-proclaimed oil. Even if the official justification for attacking Iraq is now humanitarian, this still does not qualify as defending our country. If the goal was to liberate the Iraqi people, this still does not qualify. There were no WMDs, there are no WMDs, and there was no connection between Iraq and al Qaeda. Feel good platitudes like "Liberty" and "Freedom" contain very little actual substance. Therefore, to believe that American soldiers are protecting American suburbanites by fighting in Iraq is to believe in Christian Jihad, plain and simple. There are no other facts left to back up this position.

IT'S NOT TORTURE UNLESS WE SAY IT'S TORTURE

For many suburbanites, the moral justification of prisoner abuse in the War on Terror accompanies the routine rationalization of killing in the name of platitudes and falsehoods. Most Americans saw at least one picture from Abu Ghraib prison at some point during 2004. Maybe it was the picture of the hooded man standing on a small box on one foot, with wires attached to his genitals, ready to shock him if he fell. Or maybe it was one of the pictures of prisoners being forced to simulate sex acts with each other, while their captors laughed and tormented them. More likely it was one of the tamer pictures, with blurred out naked men standing around with hoods on their heads.

According to a report written by Major General Antonio M. Taguba and obtained by the *New Yorker*, the following cases were all noted:

> "Breaking chemical lights and pouring the phosphoric liquid on detainees; pouring cold water on naked detainees; beating detainees with a broom handle and a chair; threatening male detainees with rape; allowing a military police guard to stitch the wound of a detainee who was injured after being slammed

against the wall in his cell; sodomizing a detainee with a chemical light and perhaps a broom stick, and using military working dogs to frighten and intimidate detainees with threats of attack, and in one instance actually biting a detainee."

During a time that we were trying to convince the people of Iraq that they had been liberated, this is not very "liberating" behavior. Most of these actions violate the Geneva Convention, which was designed in part to protect prisoners of war from mental or physical abuse. For example, the Geneva Convention specifically prohibits "outrages upon personal dignity, in particular, humiliating and degrading treatment."

Army reservist Aidan Delgado was deployed at Abu Ghraib for a year-long tour of duty between 2003 and 2004. In a January 2005 interview, he talked about what he witnessed. "We talk about the Geneva Conventions a lot, but most people haven't read the Geneva Conventions and don't know what they say. [One thing] they say [is] that prisoners can't be held in an injurious climate. Abu Ghraib was extremely cold, and one of the ways guards used to control prisoners was to remove their clothing and tents, leaving them exposed to 30-degree weather. That's a violation of the Geneva Conventions."

However, according to the new Attorney General of the United States, former White House counsel Alberto Gonzales, the Geneva Convention may not apply in the "War on Terror". In fact, according to Gonzales, parts of the Geneva Convention are "quaint." Specifically, Gonzales said:

> "The nature of the new war places a high premium on other factors, such as the ability to quickly obtain information from captured terrorists and their sponsors in order to avoid further atrocities against American civilians...In my judgment, this new paradigm renders obsolete Geneva's strict limitations on

questioning of enemy prisoners and renders quaint some of its provisions…"

Gonzalez endorsed an August 2002 Justice Department memo, that implied abuse or torture of military detainees might be justifiable under certain circumstances. The memo stated that the captors could only be proseczuted if the pain inflicted was "equivalent in intensity to the pain accompanying serious physical injury, such as organ failure, impairment of bodily function, or even death."

If the Geneva Convention does not apply when we take prisoners, then it probably does not apply either when our troops are taken prisoner by the enemy. After all, that is the beauty of the Geneva Convention. Or is there an expected double standard at work here? The two warring sides agree to hate one another, but they also agree that there are limits to that hate when one side holds all of the power (as in a captive/captor scenario). Prisoners, with no way to defend themselves, must be protected from excessive abuse. This agreement only works if it is respected by both sides.

Senator Joe Biden said, "There's a reason why we sign these treaties: to protect my son in the military. That's why we have these treaties—so when Americans are captured, they are not tortured."

In preparation for his Attorney General confirmation hearings, Gonzales toned down his stance on torture. The new statement begins, "Torture is abhorrent both to American law and values and to international norms." No kidding. First of all, what about harshly-administered abuse? And second, where was this statement two years earlier?

Numerous right wing commentators have said that "terrorists don't follow the Geneva Convention, so neither should we." There is a serious flaw in that argument. The vast majority of prisoners held at Abu Ghraib, where the worst of the abuse took place, were rounded up for non-terrorist related activities. Many of them were common criminals. Many were simply in the wrong place at the wrong time, rounded up for simply being *near the scene* of an attack or driving through a security checkpoint out of fear for their families. Many more of them were rounded up for *suspected* involvement in insurgent activities.

Delgado confirmed that most detainees certainly could not be classified as "terrorists," or even enemy combatants. "I ended up reviewing the prisoner records and looking over the offenses of the people who were in Abu Ghraib prison. I found out that most of them were actually not there for anti-coalition offenses. They weren't insurgents. Most of them were there for petty theft, drunkenness, forged documents, really minor crimes. We were the depository for the Iraqi justice system; they didn't have their own prisons. Iraqi judges would sentence criminals, and a lot of them would end up coming to Abu Ghraib prison. The military would also do random sweeps if they received fire or were attacked from a certain area; they would just arrest everyone of a certain age in that area and take them to Abu Ghraib for questioning. Most of them would be cleared, but the process took so long that you'd end up being in Abu Ghraib for six months to a year before being released."

A group called the Christian Peacemaker Teams conducted interviews with prisoners' families and prisoners who were released, during thirteen months between late 2003 and late 2004. In an interview with BBC News, American CPT volunteer Peggy Gish reported, "We began to hear stories of a very violent interrogation process. Men would report being kept in very painful positions for hours at a time, being deprived of sleep and water and food, some kept out in the hot summer sun for hours. We also heard about sexual abuse and beatings when they were being questioned. If they did not give information about an explosion or something they would be knocked down, kicked in the groin, and hurt in other ways."

The interviewers also asked questions about why the prisoners were detained, and the circumstances of their capture.

"Many men are held because they happened to be on the street, even blocks away, from an explosion," Gish said. "The U.S. military would round up hundreds of men in the area to try to find the few that caused the blast. In fact, we came to the conclusion that eighty to ninety percent of the prisoners had never been involved in any violent action. A common reason for men to be detained is because an informant in the neighborhood has given their name to U.S. military and claimed that they are part of the resistance. Informants get money for each name they give, and many people have told us that informants use the system to revenge personal grudges."

Private First Class Lynndie England took much of the legal heat for perpetrating the acts of abuse, mostly because she showed up in the most widely-distributed pictures. In a May 11, 2004 television interview, England said that she was instructed by "persons in my higher chain of command" to commit the acts of abuse for interrogation purposes. Under the Charter of the Nuremburg Tribunal, following orders is not a valid defense for war crimes. Ultimately, soldiers are responsible for each of their actions, and they have the legal right to refuse orders that violate the Geneva Convention, and their own ethical limitations. But the next logical question still becomes, did the order really come from up the military food chain? And if so, who issued the order?

Army Spc. Charles Graner, Jr. was the first to be court-martialed over the incidents of abuse. Called the "ring-leader" of the abuse at the prison, Graner said that he was corrupted by superiors who ordered him to sexually humiliate and otherwise mistreat detainees. Graner was found guilty on ten various counts of assault, maltreatment of detainees, committing indecent acts, conspiracy, and dereliction of duty. On the day of his sentencing, Graner spoke of the orders he received. "If (military intelligence) asks you to do this, it needs to be done. They're in charge, follow their orders."

The ACLU thinks it knows where the order ultimately originated. Through a Freedom of Information Act request, the ACLU obtained multiple internal FBI email threads discussing an "Executive Order", authorized by the President. The Executive Order referred to in the email explicitly permitted techniques which are clearly forbidden by the Geneva Convention.

The FBI email memo, dated May 22, 2004, states:

> "We are aware that prior to a revision in policy last week, an Executive Order signed by President Bush authorized the following interrogation techniques among others: sleep 'management', use of MWDs (military working dogs), 'stress positions' such as half squats, 'environmental manipulation', such as the use of loud music, sensory deprivation through the use of hoods, etc...As stated, there was a revision last week in the military's standard operating procedures based on the Executive Order. I have been told that all interrogation techniques previously authorized by the Executive Order are still on the table, but that certain techniques can only be used if very high-level authority is granted."

According to these emails, there was an Executive Order in place when the Abu Ghraib scandal broke, and parts of it were modified (i.e. toned down) after the scandal gained international attention. Indeed, it seems hard to believe that the widespread level of abuse going on at Abu Ghraib and other prisons was not understood and authorized by those responsible for the prisons. And likewise, it is hard to imagine that those responsible for the prisons would not tell their superiors, and so on up to the President. Far too many people were aware of the prison conditions and tactics for the abuse to be kept in complete secrecy, from either the American public or the military chain of command.

According to the Bush Administration and the mainstream media, the abuse at Abu Ghraib was the result of a "few bad apples" in the military. Like any other walk of life, we were told, there are people in the United States military who make bad decisions and commit crimes. But the FBI email combined with common sense seems to indicate that the United States' moral authority may have already crumbled. Geneva Convention violations are not acceptable under any circumstances, regardless of what name we decide to give our pre-emptive aggressions.

SODOMY OF THE MIND

On Election Day, 2004, Americans did not pass appropriate moral judgment against elected leaders based on the documented justification of prisoner abuses conducted in our name. Instead, they chose a slightly different set of morals on which to vote. In the days following the election, I saw a picture of an eight-year-old girl standing in front of a polling place holding a sign. Her dad was standing next to her with his own sign, simply beaming with fatherly pride. The sign read:

"Sodomy is not a Civil Right."

Did I mention that this was an eight-year-old girl? Do you think dad bothered to define sodomy? "Well you see, Violet, when one man likes another man very much, sometimes they want to express that love…"

Suffice it to say, this is not my idea of sharing one's values with your kids.

In a voter study taken just after the elections in November 2004, twenty-seven percent of all voters said their top issue in the presidential race was "Morals". This was the top issue in the list, even beating Iraq, at twenty percent. But the now-infamous moral high ground of the strongly Red states has a number of notable inconsistencies.

First, of the ten states with the highest divorce rate (Nevada, Arkansas, Oklahoma, Tennessee, Wyoming, Indiana, Alabama, Idaho, New Mexico, Florida), nine of them voted for Bush in 2004. Of the ten states with the lowest divorce rate (Massachusetts, Connecticut, New Jersey, Rhode Island, New York, Pennsylvania,

Wisconsin, North Dakota, Maryland, Minnesota), all ten of them voted for Kerry.

In Churchill County, Nevada, voters chose Bush overwhelmingly (71%). But they also voted in favor of a referendum to keep prostitution legal in brothels (63%).

Most of the values that drove Conservative voters to the polls during the 2004 campaign were individual values, such as abortion, gay marriage, stem cell research, etc. But ultimately, every single conservative values issue, with the exception of gun ownership, falls into the category of *restricting* or limiting someone else's individual rights. Conservatives are no longer protecting what *can* be done, but instead they are attempting to set a legislative bar for what *cannot* be done by individuals.

For example, I often wonder if pro-lifers are really pro-life. Or are they simply "pro-birth"? Most of them don't support welfare or health care for the poor, because they don't want the government engaging in "socialism". So the baby must be born, but after the maternity ward it is every kid for himself. It is a dog eat dog world, kiddo, and your mom is not of the proper social class to obtain the assistance of the pro-life lobby. It seems like most of them are also in favor of the death penalty, and that is actually an anti-life position. A complete reversal of *Roe vs. Wade* would probably also include restrictions on abortion in medical emergencies during pregnancy, where the life of the mother is at risk. But lest we forget, "W Stands for Women". Security moms unite!

I lived with two gay guys for over a year. They were great guys. One of them was a little bit sloppy and the other would get so stressed about life that he would start to shake. But ultimately, if one of them wanted to marry a man, I would have no objection. As I said before, they were great guys. I heard a talking head say a few weeks ago that "Gay marriage destroys the foundation of normal marriage." This logic has no basis in logic. To me, there is not enough information to come to a conclusion one way or another, because there is by definition no relationship between gay marriage and traditional marriage.

The Supreme Court seems to agree, as they rejected in November 2004 a challenge to the Massachusetts law sanctioning gay marriage. The defense in this case argued that the people who filed the suit (representing heterosexual couples) could not demonstrate that they had suffered an injury. Indeed, no one is injured by the Massachusetts law.

Embryonic stem cells have the ability to grow into almost any other cell in the human body. Most scientists believe that the ability to grow human tissue would result in amazing advances in the treatment of cell-based diseases, such as Parkinson's disease and Sickle Cell Anemia. My grandfather died from the effects of Parkinson's when I was small, and I will never forget how he changed in his final months and years. I am, of course, in his genetic line, and I have an extremely vested interest in finding a cure. I am in favor of researching stem cells through whatever means are technologically possible; not just for myself, and my own children and grandchildren, but for all others fighting cell-based genetic diseases that might be fixable. And besides, for every embryo that could be used for stem cell research, hundreds of children die in hospitals around the world from *preventable* childhood cell-based diseases.

Abortion limitations, gay marriage restrictions and stem-cell blockades have clearly been sold as "values issues" by the Republican Party to its Conservative Christian base, through the use of referendums that found their way onto the 2004 election ballots. But these "values" merely emphasize the condemnation of their perception of other people's sins. Rather than using values to build up other people and our country, these values are being used to char a rift through the middle of the American people, and self-righteousness is the proverbial blowtorch.

In Isaiah 58, God says, "Do away with the yoke of oppression, with the pointing finger and malicious talk."

The old phrase says nobody's perfect. It is my experience that this phrase also applies to Christians, but they usually choose to prioritize their own sins well below their perception of the sins of others. The disciple Paul often talks about greed, in fact he equates it with idolatry. "Thou shalt have no other Gods (*money, power, money, power*) before me," the First Commandment says. Yet how many church goers vote for Republicans in election after election to save a few hundred dollars on taxes, regardless of the other immoral policies of a given administration. Heterosexual immorality is a much more rampant morality problem among church members than homosexual immorality, yet there are no state referendums about marital infidelity.

There is also an interesting distinction to be made between individual morality and political morality. While individual morality is something to be personally discussed, debated, and measured extensively by religious organizations and families, political morality should be at the heart of every vote that is cast in America.

Here are some things that I have identified as potentially politically immoral. I would venture to guess that most Bush voters never considered any of these things when they cast their vote in November. For example, I have a Red friend who is a vehement supporter of the War in Iraq. I asked him if he would be willing to send his own son, and he laughed. He actually laughed.

I believe it is immoral to support the War on Terror, but not be willing to send your own children to participate. If you are not willing to have your own children or your neighbors children die for the cause, then the cause may not be worth endorsing. If you are not willing to send your own children, then you are implicitly saying that the lives of poor minorities are worth less than your own children's lives. If you want to rationalize this, you may say that the "War on Terror" needs funding, and an economically viable individual on the home front is worth more than a soldier who may have produced less at home. Moral relativism is, of course, alive and thriving in the suburbs.

Unless we have a budget surplus, I would suggest that it is immoral to support the War on Terror and still support lower taxes. It is immoral to support the use of government funds to buy "advertising" in the form of propaganda from political commentators like Armstrong Williams, and still support lower taxes. Future generations will pay tenfold for today's budget imbalances, and it is morally reprehensible to hand them extreme levels of national debt which will burden their livelihood.

I would further suggest that it is immoral to witness the under funding of "No Child Left Behind" and our education system in budget after budget, and still support the War on Terror. Education of our children must come before pre-emptive warfare. If we have an uneducated public, then what are we really defending?

Finally, it is immoral to support a tax code which gives massive tax cuts to the upper one percent of economic society, when there are over thirty-six million people in poverty here in the United States. If everyone is fed and housed, and we have a tax surplus, as we had under Bill Clinton, then and only then should we discuss tax cuts for the wealthy, and only on an equal percentage basis as every other tax bracket.

REAL AMERICAN VALUES

I have considered the issue of values at great length, and I will be teaching my children a slightly different set of values which will serve them well in their daily lives. These are not values which infringe on someone else's rights or freedoms. Rather, these are national values, with the potential for universal application across many specific situations. These values are all driven by the "Golden Rule," which is usually expressed with the phrase, "Do unto others as you would have them do unto you."

For some reason, values based on the Golden Rule were overlooked by voters on November 2, 2004. But you can be sure that my kids will grow to understand these values better than our current leadership. On second thought, I believe my six year old son *already* understands most of these American values better than the President of the United States.

1) Don't kill innocent people. Even if you think they are going to hurt you, don't kill them. If you think they looked at you funny, don't kill them. If they are different from you or have a different God, still don't kill them. If you are really, really afraid of them, then you may talk to them, but you may still not kill them. Killing innocent people is a strict violation of the Golden Rule. When I am sitting with my family eating dinner in our suburban dining room, I would really prefer not to have someone drop a bomb on our dinner table. Therefore, I am not willing to support or mandate actions which do the same to other innocents.

2) Don't rip people off. If someday you are very successful and you run a large corporation, don't stick it to your workers. Don't ship their jobs overseas to take advantage of a tax loophole, and lift your stock options and your bonus. Nobody wants their job shipped overseas. Yet if it means a bigger bonus, most corporate decision-makers today will not hesitate to outsource the jobs of others. Don't cut employee benefits when the company is rolling in profits every quarter. Don't commit accounting fraud. Be honest. If you happen to make it into a political office, don't cut special deals with the elite. Instead, cut special deals with the poor. If you ever get a call from a guy named Kenneth Lay, just hang up. He is an evildoer.

3) Don't lie or mislead. If you say that another country has weapons of mass destruction, and by chance they don't have

weapons of mass destruction, then just admit that you screwed up. If you happen to mistakenly imply that Iraqis were on board the planes that hit the World Trade Center, and it turns out that no Iraqis were on the hijacked planes at all, then apologize profusely. We all make mistakes, and real men admit their own. Don't compound errors through stubborn consistency. Most people don't want to be misled persistently by others, therefore they should not mislead people persistently.

4) Don't be greedy. If you make a lot of money through hard work or you inherit a lump sum, do not vote based on this income or ownership. Put yourself in someone else's shoes, and vote as though you are a single parent of three kids, working sixty hour weeks at two jobs earning minimum wage. If this vote means that you pay $1,000 per year more in taxes, then you have voted correctly. Money is fleeting, and someone else needs it more than you do. Not every poor person is lazy and undereducated, as the Republican "hard working values" myth perpetuates.

5) Be a good person. Be fair and accommodating to all people. Don't prejudge any group of people—even those who you have been pre-warned about. If you think someone might potentially be an evildoer, first picture them in their underwear. Seeing an evildoer in their underwear quickly washes away some of the Osama stigma. After you stop laughing, go talk to the evildoer. They are probably just like you, with the same real hopes and real fears. Again the Golden Rule applies. Someday, will you be part of the minority? And how will you want to be treated when that day comes?

6) Think about current events. Come to your own conclusions based on the facts. Independently verify everything you see and hear. Try not to watch too much TV, since it puts your brain to

sleep and makes you apathetic. And most importantly, hold your government accountable. It is your government. They work for you and they answer to you; not the other way around. That is the great thing about Democracy.

THE NEW MORALITY

In conclusion, there is an absolute paradox that is expressed through the very careful framing of morality and values in today's Christian church. Somehow, morality has taken on only one specific meaning—that of personal, mostly sexual morality. In the meantime, questionable national morality in the context of war and the record-high national deficit has been mostly absent from public discussion. While Red Americans perceive homosexuality as incredibly immoral, the deaths of at least fifty thousand innocent people in the name of an inadequately justified "War on Terror" are not even on their morality radar.

The resulting strange paradox is simple to demonstrate. President Bill Clinton is perceived as having an immoral presidency because he lied about sex in the Oval Office. Yet, most of his actual policies were moral, from his tax cuts for the lower class to the budget surplus, and its positive fiscal effect on future generations. On the other hand, Bush is widely perceived by his base as one of our most religious and moral presidents ever. But his policies justify or at least don't forbid abuse or torture, he misled the American people on the issue of invading Iraq, and he consistently plays on the fears of average Americans to gain and preserve power for the Executive Branch and his neo-Conservative friends. These are immoral policies.

Pro-Life is an incredibly strong line item from the personal morality agenda of the Conservative Christian voter drives. But that same Pro-Life line item was conveniently left off the global morality agenda. If you are an unborn-American still in the womb just three weeks beyond conception, you are worthy of full Compassionate

Conservatism. But if you are a two-year-old Muslim evildoer playing on the floor of your house when a missile or a cluster bomb submunition comes through the ceiling, then we have no particular Pro-Life agenda for you.

A group called The Center for Moral Clarity keeps an updated list of moral issues facing America today, called "Pray for America." In November 2004, this list consisted of the following items:

- Pray for the nearly two million men, women, and children who have been driven from their homes by Sudan's radical Muslim regime to die of starvation and exposure.

- Pray for the following states that passed constitutional marriage amendments on November 2nd defining marriage as the union of one man and one woman.

- Pray for the passage of a Federal Marriage Amendment to the Constitution.

- Pray that President Bush's judicial nominations will get a vote on the senate floor.

- Pray for passage of Kansas Senator Sam Brownback's "Unborn Child Pain Awareness Act".

The main categories to pray for are protection from Muslim evildoers, passage of gay marriage bans, and revision of abortion law. But there is no mention of Iraq on their moral compass at all. There is no prayer for the morality of our troops and their leaders, that they would receive guidance to follow the rules of the Geneva Convention and avoid temptations of abuse or torture in the Iraqi prisons. There is also no prayer for the Iraqi people, many of whom have also been "driven from their homes" by a radical regime called the "Coalition of the Willing."

The Center for Moral Clarity group visited churches around the country handing out Bush campaign materials, and yet they clearly demonstrate the moral hypocrisy of the religious right by denying the mere existence of multiple clear moral problems related to the War on Terror, which far outweigh the significance of the last four items on their list.

In the context of morality and war, Jesus was also carefully removed from the discussion. Jesus' clear statements about violence and revenge, peacemaking and forgiveness, have been cleverly left out of the public debate. Many of our country's Christian pastors and religious leaders, straight up the ladder to the Vatican, have done a great disservice by perpetuating this misrepresentation.

With a more complete idea of the scope of Red America's morality conflict, I come back around to my mom and my dilemma. On one hand you have an elitist President who misled the American people, put his own questionable priorities ahead of the lives of tens of thousands of innocent non-Americans, and began the process of picking apart the Bill of Rights. On the other hand you have my mom, who made the best peanut butter and jelly sandwiches, mostly apathetic toward the bloodshed and abuse in Iraq. That is an eerily disturbing partnership, and it is enough to make a brain explode. Considering everything that happened during Bush's first term, my mother still voted Republican, as she always does. If Bush was not the exception to the rule for Christian voters, then is an exception even possible? What are the limits of immoral actions that would be required to breach the unholy trinity of God, Country, and Republicans?

Unfortunately, there may be no limits. For Red-tinted Americans, God, Country, and Republicans will always and forever more remain, one in the same. It is one thing to understand exactly what is causing the selective perceptions, and another thing to change those perceptions and influence public debate. It is fun sometimes to dance around in the ignorance of Red America, and wonder what it must be like to be so politically satisfied in such a whirlwind of global hell, and yet it is impossible to join them.

Talking to a Red believer is like a bartender telling a drunk they have had too much. "I'sh am shober," he will repeatedly say, even in the face of increasing evidence to the contrary. If you clearly remove one piece of this wall of bullshit, he's got a head full of identical blocks of drunken empty language fresh out of Rush Limbaugh's mouth to replace each one that is torn down. Even if every single block in his wall is miraculously removed, greed immediately builds a brand new wall of rationalization. The drunk displays greed for a few more drinks, while the Red believer engages in the more traditional kind of greed. Five hundred dollars saved in taxes can easily trump the lives of millions of evildoers.

In the meantime, I cannot sleep at night with images of Iraqi children haunting me, while many unconvertible Reds snooze away on a fuzzy blanket of mental bliss. While I count sheep, they fall into dreamland on the basis of platitudes like "Freedom" and "Democracy".

Meanwhile, I and those like me are described as un-American for our failure to "support the troops". I support the troops, because I want all of them home tomorrow—I never wanted them there in the first place. I support the troops by attempting to hold their Commander in Chief accountable for inadequate protections on the battleground and sorely lacking physical and mental support structures at home. I support the troops because I want them to return to a country that is better than the country they left. None of these things will be accomplished through blind faith.

My wife and I recently spoke up quite vigorously against the steady stream of emails that come from both of our families. One day it was, "A parable about the hard working rich and the lazy poor." Another day it was, "A prayer for the troops who are protecting our country from the Muslim fascists." And the next day came, "The truth about Iraq that you don't hear from the Liberal media."

After a time, we both simply got fed up with the barrage, so we started to respond with facts to contradict the jingoism. If the sender copied us on a distribution list of twenty people, then twenty people got our response. Based on these exchanges, some members of our families have concluded that we both need psychological counseling. "Why do you care so much," they say. "Just let it go."

To them, the election is over, and discussions of morally indefensible foreign policy can finally take a back seat to Survivor and American Idol again. To me, the election is over, and now the real defense of America begins. Just because the election is over, does not mean that we are no longer individually responsible for the daily actions of our government, pre-emptive or otherwise. Just because life in a Red house has returned to its usual distant carefully-defended artificial reality, doesn't mean that I have to live there as well.

Such is life for a converted Red House kid. They say you can never really go home again, and this is one time when "they" are absolutely right.

4

War and Country and The American Media

> *"The process of creating new democratic organs of government power is beginning, and, as never before, the greatest responsibility rests with the broadcast media."*
> —Eduard Sagalaev

> *"No matter how much spin, effort, lunch or dinner you give the media, they will not fail to notice whether you have won or lost."*
> —Robin Renwick

MEDIA COMPLICITY

To be fair, there are a number of good reasons why my family and friends are able to be so apathetic about the many disturbing facts of war. The national and local news media have been apathetic as well. As of early 2005, there was still no consistent discussion of the tragic human cost for Iraqi families, except in the carefully-worded context of dead "insurgents" or dead "terrorists." Even when a story does reach the news, it is almost always led by other "critical" news about tainted drinking water on airplanes, exploding cell phones, or a human interest piece on finding a competent babysitter. In fact, on the issue of Iraqi civilians, mum is usually the only word on the "Liberal" nightly news. Almost two thousand American soldiers are dead, and these are brave men and women who should be with their families right now. The loss of each individual soldier impacts hundreds of people. When you take the number of people impacted by these American deaths and multiply it by twenty-five, you get some feel for what everyday life was like for Iraqis during the past two years.

Saddam was a brutal dictator and it was a pleasure to see his tyranny come to an end. Just how brutal was he? Before the war, the U.S. State Department released a report, called has a report *Life Under Saddam Hussein: Past Repression and Atrocities by Saddam Hussein's Regime.* This report documented the killing of 300,000 innocents during Saddam's thirty year reign. According to the report, about 10,000 prisoners were executed at Abu Ghraib from 1984 to 2001, and the 1987-88 campaign against the Kurds took somewhere in the neighborhood of 50,000 lives. Beyond these two numbers, the State Department document contains questionable data. The document cites the Human Rights Watch organization when it says that 250,000 Iraqi's were killed during the Shi'a uprisings following the first Gulf War in 1991. But the actual Human Rights Watch text reads as follows.

> "No reliable figures are available concerning the number of persons killed or wounded by either side during the uprising. Iraqi authorities have not released such statistics. One journalist reported from Iraq that the government 'has forbidden Shi'as from displaying traditional signs of mourning—black flags and paper streamers printed with the names of the dead—because it would enable visitors to count the numbers of Shi'a 'martyrs.'" But senior Arab diplomats told the London-based Arabic daily

newspaper *al-Hayat* in October that Iraqi leaders were privately acknowledging that 250,000 people were killed during the uprisings, with most of the casualties in the south. Independent investigation to verify this figure has not been possible, nor has it yet been possible to determine how many of these casualties were non-combatants."

Giving the State Department the benefit of the doubt, the results are a total of 10,000 prisoners, plus 50,000 Kurds, plus 250,000 Shi'a and others who took up arms in the uprising in 1991. The sum of the lives lost nets to a total of 310,000 Iraqi civilians killed in thirty years of Saddam Hussein's reign in Iraq. 10,000 civilian deaths per year are a tragedy, and they prove that Saddam was indeed, not a good guy. This is no surprise. Despite all of the difficulties, certainly the U.S. occupation of Iraq is still a better option for the Iraqi people than Saddam's regime. Or is it?

The Center for International Emergency, Disaster and Refugee Studies at the Johns Hopkins Bloomberg School of Public Health in Baltimore released a study in October 2004, which claimed the Iraqi civilian death count topped 100,000 since early 2003. This conclusion was estimated based on interviews with 7,868 Iraqis in thirty-three neighborhoods, where civilian deaths were documented with death certificates in most cases. The number of deaths discovered through the door-to-door study was then extrapolated to the larger population. For the sake of argument, let's divide the high number in half to account for estimation or bias problems with the studies. There are other studies which show between 20,000 and 60,000 civilians dead. Keep in mind also that all of these studies were finalized *before* the battle of Fallujah, one of the bloodiest confrontations of the war from a civilian casualty perspective.

That leaves *at least* 50,000 dead Iraqi civilians in less than two years of American occupation, compared to 310,000 dead civilians in thirty years of tyranny under Saddam. Adding up the numbers, the "Coalition of the Willing" are killing civilians, through our early-war bombing campaigns and more recent use of cluster bombs in heavily populated areas, at a rate that is two to three times the murder rate of a tyrannical dictator. Iraqis cannot be liberated from tyranny if they are dead, and Iraqis cannot vote if they are dead.

Mark Belling, a Conservative radio talk show host in Milwaukee, praised the President for his overwhelming success in "breezing through" the war to get to the Iraqi elections in January 2005. He said, "The only way this war could not be considered a huge success is the body count.... But I just don't think 2,000 soldiers is unacceptable for what we have accomplished." He used this same statement five or six times in one show, and never did he qualify his remark with, "United States casualties." Apparently, Iraqi civilians are not even part of the "body count" when a right-wing talk show host adds up the tragic losses.

A major cause of civilian deaths in Iraq is the United States use of ground-based cluster bombs in heavily populated areas. Dr. Sa`ad al-Falluji said that ninety percent of the injuries that he treated during the war, in the city of al-Hilla, were from cluster bomb sub-munitions. When a ground-based cluster bomb hits, it releases bomblets and grenades, which are dispersed over a wide area. In October 2003 alone, Central Command (CentCom) reported the use of 10,782 cluster munitions, which contained between 1.7 and 2 million sub-munitions. In just one attack, cluster bombs fired at Iraqi troops dispersed their sub-munitions over the surrounding civilian area of al-Hilla, killing thirty-eight civilians and injuring one hundred and fifty-six.

A further complicating matter is the difficulty in distinguishing civilian from enemy. The longer the conflict wages, the more the people we went there to "set free from Saddam's brutal rule" become the ones we fight against. One marine had this to say after the battle of Fallujah.

"Hah. The enemy, who is the enemy? The enemy is just other people. Mostly is people who are seeing their way of life destroyed and have no one left to live for, no job left to work at, no family to protect. They are always young men and when captured talk as if all hope has left them, as if life itself was so meaningless that they choose to play the Russian Roulette that fighting against the Marines really is."

The most troubling aspect of recent strategic developments is a very discouraging, unethical similarity to Vietnam, in which large areas of combat zones, such as Fallujah, are classified very liberally as "Weapons-Free" areas. "Weapons-Free" means the Marines can shoot whatever they see—anybody present in that area is considered hostile.

I guess that is what Secretary of Defense Donald Rumsfeld meant when he was asked about efforts to minimize civilian casualties in Fallujah. He said tritely to the reporter, "They have rules of engagement that are appropriate to an urban environment." This policy was further documented by an Associated Press photographer, who witnessed a civilian family of five being gunned down by snipers as they tried to cross the Euphrates River to escape the carnage. Let me be perfectly clear about this. I do not blame the troops on the ground for this policy. It is the direct responsibility of those making "Weapons-Free" classification decisions to act humanely. To remain consistent with the current stated strategy, the people of Iraq cannot be liberated if they are dead.

In my opinion, the turning point in public war sentiment toward Vietnam was that the media began to talk about and show pictures from the "Free Fire Zones", where virtually anything that moved was defined by U.S. policy as a fair target. In this regard, the American media has been a huge failure in its coverage of the war in Iraq. The necessary comparison must be made between documented policy in parts of Vietnam and apparent policy in urban Fallujah.

In the Dellums Committee Hearings on War Crimes in Vietnam, Captain Robert Johnson gave the following testimony.

> "While our operation was going on, which is about two to five miles south of Danang, ninety percent of the surrounding countryside was a free-fire zone. It was understood by me, by all of us in Tactical Operations Center and elsewhere, that we were allowed to shoot anything that moves in that area. It became clear to me that harassment and interdiction of was not designed to interdict the enemy, but rather to terrorize and intimidate the surrounding villagers in an effort to get them to move into detention camps along Route One."

In November 2004, Jules Lobel, Vice President of the Center for Constitutional Rights, commented about the Vietnam similarities following the now infamous shooting of an injured Iraqi "insurgent" in a Fallujah mosque.

> "Kevin Sites, the NBC cameraman…He says the Marines say they were operating under rules of engagement, which said this was a weapons-free zone. And what they meant by weapons-free was that they could shoot at anything. They didn't have to determine whether it was hostile. Anything that they saw was deemed to be hostile in Fallujah. It reminds you of the free-fire zones in Vietnam. Under the Geneva Conventions, commanders have a responsibility to ensure that civilians are not indiscriminately harmed and that prisoners are not executed. The real problem here is coming from the top, not from the individual soldiers."

Another example of selective media coverage is evidenced within the documented abuses at Abu Ghraib prison. The atrocities of abuse committed at the prison were somewhat well-documented by the American media, but the worst of the pictures were never shown publicly. After all, pictures and video are the silver bullets into the average American's werewolf psyche. If I cannot give my Red family and friends a picture or a video of an event, then it just did not happen. Even if I do have a picture, it better not be electronic. To them, if that picture does not appear on the front page of the Wall Street Journal or the New York Times, then it is not legitimate news.

Rescuing Jessica

One carefully-selected war story received significant and detailed attention in the mainstream American media, at the expense of other news stories, during one of the bloodiest weeks of the war. Following disproportionately strong encouragement from military public relations personnel at CentCom in Qatar, the story of captured nineteen year old Army clerk Jessica Lynch was front page news in every American newspaper. As you know, the original story, as released without video or eye-witness testimony, claimed that Lynch's supply convoy was ambushed by Iraqi soldiers. The Army released almost immediately that Lynch heroically emptied two revolvers at her attackers, before she was shot, stabbed, and taken prisoner. Of thirty soldiers traveling in the convoy, eleven were killed and six were captured. Eight days later, Lynch was rescued from an Iraqi hospital, where she was recovering from a broken arm, a dislocated ankle, and a broken hip. The rescue was displayed through dramatic video footage of the hospital raid, including gunfire and a lot of yelling and screaming. Reports cited heavy enemy fire, both inside and outside the building.

The Lynch story was pushed as the "lead story" by United States military public relations professionals, even while heavy fighting reached the outskirts of Baghdad. When reporters at the daily press conference at CentCom tried to obtain information about the circumstances around Baghdad, they were redirected to focus on Lynch.

CNN's veteran reporter Tom Mintier noticed that there was a clear attempt at news management underway at CentCom. "Seems like there's an effort to manage the news in an unmanageable situation," Mintier said. "They tried it in the first Gulf War. This time it was supposed to be different. They buried the lead [story], and they're pretty good at it."

Looking back with full knowledge of Lynch's first-hand account of the events and comments from her Iraqi doctors and nurses, there was almost nothing from the original story of her capture and rescue that turned out to be true.

Iraqi doctors in Nasiriya disputed the official story almost immediately after Lynch's rescue. Dr Harith a-Houssona, who took care of Lynch, said, "I examined her, I saw she had a broken arm, a broken thigh and a dislocated ankle. There was no [sign of] shooting, no bullet inside her body, no stab wound—only road traffic accident. They want to distort the picture. I don't know why they think there is some benefit in saying she has a bullet injury." The official Army report of the incident released in July 2003, based on an extensive commander's investigation, officially debunked the original accounts of gunshot and stab wounds. An army source said of the report, "Lynch survived principally because of the medical attention she received from the Iraqis."

In a November 2003 interview with Diane Sawyer, Lynch said, "I did not shoot, not a round, nothing. When we were told to lock and load, that's when my weapon jammed…I did not shoot a single round…I went down praying to my knees. And that's the last I remember."

Lynch also said that she was treated well during her eight days at the hospital, "No one beat me, no one slapped me, no one, nothing…I mean, I actually had one nurse, that she would sing to me."

In the movie *Wag the Dog*, current events are staged for news broadcast, in order to influence public opinion in desired directions. At Lynch's hospital in Nasiriya, truth appears to be stranger than fiction. Two days before the rescue operation, Iraqi doctors attempted to drive Lynch to drop her off with U.S. troops, but when they came to a checkpoint the ambulance came under fire, and they had to return to the hospital. Iraqi special-forces fled the hospital the day before the raid, and the doctors say the U.S. knew that the hospital was free of enemy forces when they came to retrieve Lynch.

Dr. Anmar Uday said, "It was like a Hollywood film. They cried 'go, go, go', with guns and blanks without bullets, blanks and the sound of explosions. They made a show for the American attack on the hospital—action movies like Sylvester Stallone or Jackie Chan."

In the Diane Sawyer interview, Lynch said that one soldier ripped an American flag off his suit and handed it to her. "I would not let go of his hand. I clenched to his hand because I was not going to let him leave me here. He was going to take me out."

Footage of Lynch's rescue was shot by the military, and released by the military after editing. And sure enough, draping over Lynch's body is what appears to be a full-size American flag. The flag combined with the Iraqi doctor's statement is all the proof I need that her capture was nothing more than a made-for-television war movie. A soldier undergoing a rescue operation, with full night vision goggles and firing rounds left and right, is unlikely to have the means or mindset to drape Jessica Lynch in a United States flag at the moment of rescue.

In the documentary film *Control Room*, Donald Rumsfeld said the following of Al-Jazeera war coverage:

> "It seems to me that it's up to all of us to try to tell the truth, to say what we know, to say what we don't know, and recognize that we're dealing with people that are perfectly willing to lie to the world to attempt to further their case. And to the extent that people lie, ultimately, they are caught lying, and they lose

their credibility. One would think that wouldn't take very long for that to happen dealing with people like this."

I think you will find, as I do, that this quote applies to war coverage on both sides, regarding issues of propaganda or government-sponsored favorable opinion. During a time of war, the Secretary of Defense cannot be counted on to be an unbiased objective source of news, and nor can the public relations branch of the United States military. The U.S. media outlets who take the military-directed news stories verbatim with little or no follow-up investigation of their own are simply not doing their jobs.

Deducing a Draft

Given the American media's lack of adequate journalism during wartime, it is natural for an informed American to search for alternative news sources. For me, this means using the Internet for raw news whenever possible.

"You can't believe everything you read on the Internet, Tim." I cannot tell you how many times I have heard that. While it is true as a general statement, most rationally thinking human beings have the ability to discern fact from fiction and rumor from truth, based on supporting or circumstantial evidence. Deduction-based results are achieved in court rooms across America every day, even in most murder trials. Jurors are asked to take various pieces of seemingly unrelated evidence, and come to a conclusion of believability beyond a reasonable doubt.

For example, in the months prior to the November elections, there was a lot of discussion between my extended family and I about the eventual need for a military draft. At one point, a few Democrats presented bills in both the House and the Senate proposing a military draft to support our "Imperialistic goals." In both cases, these bills were clearly intended to be baiting, in order to raise the issues of our dwindling military enlistment rates and our perpetual war national defense strategy. The basic context of the bills was the following: With continuing problems in Iraq and plans for Iran and Syria on the near horizon, it would only be fair to make sure that all parts of society are equally represented in our armed forces overseas.

Plenty of circumstantial evidence reinforced this claim. First of all, a backdoor draft had been in place for nearly a year, preventing many enlisted soldiers from returning home to America through the use of a "stop-loss program". This is a form of a draft, since the soldiers, in most cases, want and need to return home, but they are not allowed to. In many of these cases, their military service time is expired, and they are still not allowed to come home. In addition, others who had been out of the military for as long as seven years were called back, under a rarely used loophole called the Individual Ready Reserve (IRR).

Numerous news stories also circulated (in mainstream media outlets) about the problems military recruiters are having reaching their enlistment goals. As a matter of fact, they were not even *close* to reaching their numbers. Finally, the Iraqi quagmire continues and Iran talk has already begun in much the same vein that Iraq did two years prior. We have a President who has said hundreds if not thousands of times that we are in a never-ending war against an elusive enemy. Unfortunately, never-ending wars require never-ending troops to replace those who are seriously wounded (physically or mentally) or die.

According to their own quarterly newsletter, the Selective Service System (SSS) hired a consulting company to investigate the best way to market and implement a targeted skills-based draft for health care and technology professionals. Also, the SSS was asked to initiate the reactivation of local draft boards, with a readiness target of the second quarter of 2005.

"Talking to the manpower folks at the Department of Defense and others, what came up was that nobody foresees a need for a large conventional draft such as we had in Vietnam," said Richard Flahavan, a spokesman for the Selective Service System. "But they thought that if we have any kind of a draft, it will probably be a special skills draft."

Using the facts listed above, the need and the preparation for a draft are fairly obvious conclusions. If Bush were on trial on the question of whether the War on Terror requires some sort military draft to continue, forty-nine percent of juries in America would convict him.

As I debated my family on this issue, nearly all of them independently came to the conclusion that my points were invalid, because I must not understand that these bills were proposed by Democrats. Finally, I told a family member that these were clearly "Protest Bills."

A few minutes later she responded to me, saying "There is no such thing as a Protest Bill. I looked it up and it doesn't exist."

I responded, "I made up the term. Do you understand the word *Protest*? Do you understand the word *Bill*? Put the two together. These bills are meant to be sarcastic in order to raise a relevant issue prior to the election. They have all said they won't even vote for their own bill! How much more evidence do you need?"

In a lifetime of growing up Red, I have learned one thing very clearly; if it did not appear on TV or on the front page of a conservative newspaper, it literally does not exist. It did not happen. It is not possible that, as a rationally thinking individual, a person can conclude things without prompting from a third party. The thing that separates human beings from animals, our ability to *reason*, is now frowned upon.

If I can take a number of disparate facts and put them together to come up with a new fact, that makes me a normal human being with the ability to think and reason and conclude. But the Red portion of our society has been conditioned to look down on those who think for themselves, instead of regurgitating opinions heard on Rush Limbaugh or Fox News. Whether they be professors in a University (Liberal wacko anti-American Socialists), stem cell researchers (Baby Killers), Vietnam-veteran Democrats (Lying Flip Floppers) or just a regular guy like me (Tin Foil Hat Wearer), their opinions or even facts are not to be trusted.

Even Bush got in on the medium-bashing during the second Presidential debate, when he said, "I heard there's rumors on the Internets that we're going to have a draft."

If a pastor and three different teachers tell me that God created the world to look like it evolved, then that is "good Christian logic" that ultimately gets me a D grade in Freshman English class at a Christian University. But if I rationally conclude that there definitely might need to be a draft to support the War on Terror, given a number of specific reasonable facts, then that makes me a "conspiracy theorist." I just cannot win!

If I think independently, I become a tin foil hat wearer, alienated by friends and family. "Just drink the kool-aid Tim; Fox News will tell you if something important comes up. By the way, did you happen to see Desperate Housewives last week? That was hot."

SAVING PRIVATE FACE

While I was deducing the need for a draft with little or no help from the "Liberal" media, many ABC affiliates were engaging in efforts to keep fictional war violence away from their schedules. In November 2004, during the peak of the major U.S. offensive on Fallujah, ABC decided to air the full unedited version of "Saving Private Ryan" on all of their national affiliates on Veterans Day. Nineteen local ABC affiliates decided not to air the movie in favor of alternate programming. The reason given by most stations was that they did not want to receive a fine from the Federal Communications Commission for violating indecency rules. These same stations showed toned down footage of American soldiers conducting actual warfare in Fallujah just hours before the movie's broadcast.

The important difference between these two broadcasts? The movie shows American soldiers wounded and dying on D-Day, while the news displays American soldiers peeking around corners and through blown out windows, sleeping in a foxhole, or smoking cigarettes. The narrow gap between a movie's reenactment of blood and death and the news video of the not quite real warfare in Iraq was probably a little too narrow for some local network execs to stomach.

Augmenting my complete confusion is the statement on the airing of the movie by the American Family Association, a group that describes their purpose as follows, through their web site, OneMillionMoms.com:

> "OneMillionMoms.com was begun to give moms an impact with the decision-makers and let them know we are upset with the messages they are sending our children and the values (or lack of them) they are pushing. We are searching for one million moms who are willing to join the fight for our children. We want our children to have the best chance possible of living in a moral society."

The goal of the American Family Association is to push morality and values through the use of pressure on our national television networks and other media outlets. However, their position on the national television airing of "Saving Private Ryan" is absolutely baffling.

> "We believe *Saving Private Ryan* accurately depicted what happens during fierce battles between two armies. The graphic depictions of atrocious injuries, mental stress, profane language, and brutality are likely common occurrences in war. But ABC

crossed the line by airing at least twenty "F" words and twelve "S" words during prime time viewing hours!"

Isn't that an interesting little paradox? A group whose sole purpose is to push Christian morals and values has no issue with airing a graphic, gruesome realistic depiction of war. The brutality? No problem. The atrocious injuries? No problem. Mental stress to the point of complete breakdown? All okay. Just don't use the "F" word or the "S" word, or there will be hell to pay from at least One Million angry Moms.

Apparently, the moral conflicts of war do not count anymore. They have no place in our national discourse or even in letter writing campaigns from people who call themselves Christians. How I would love to be able to dance around in their version of reality, even if just for a few days!

In the minds of a Red household, there is a fundamental desire to believe in our American leadership. With the core trust of leadership in place, and with little or no contrary coverage on the TV news at night, most Americans do not seek out stories of our troops being killed or wounded, or stories of Iraqi civilians suffering and dying. For a Red household, selective ignorance about war is family tradition. Even when one of these stories finally finds its way to their email Inbox or elsewhere, you will find most of them strangely unable to properly frame the real events in front of them.

ARMSTRONG WILLIAMS AND PAY FOR PLAY

In recent years, the core trust of Conservative media outlets was abused repeatedly by the Bush Administration. In early 2005, Conservative newspaper columnist Armstrong Williams admitted to receiving $240,000 from the Department of Education in exchange for promotions related to Bush's No Child Left Behind Act. Williams also hosts a nationally syndicated radio show, "The Right

Side," and owns a public relations firm. This firm contracted through Ketchum Communications in 2003 and 2004, to produce a "minority outreach campaign" on behalf of the Department of Education. Yet, Williams also frequently touted No Child Left Behind on his radio program and in his newspaper commentary, and he hosted former Education Secretary Rod Paige on his radio show several times.

Williams admitted that he should have disclosed that he received the money for endorsing the Act, but he said that he did not plan to return the money that he received, since the Department of Education paid for advertising and they received advertising. Williams said that the whole situation was a "gray area," as he was caught between his commentator job and his public relations job. Yes, that is indeed a tough distinction to make.

During informal follow-up questioning by David Corn, the Washington editor of *The Nation* magazine, Williams desperately defended himself, saying "This happens all the time. There are others." Of course, he refused to name any names. "I'm not going to defend myself that way," he said.

Ralph Neas is president of People for the American Way, a government watchdog group. Neas said:

> "There is no defense for using taxpayer dollars to pay journalists for fake news and favorable coverage of a federal program. It's a scandalous waste. It's unethical, and it's wrong. It reminds me of the old payola scandals in radio. Armstrong Williams received $240,000 of our tax money, yours and mine, to create propaganda for a government program. If that's not illegal, it ought to be."

The Williams situation is not the first time that tax-payer sponsored programming has appeared as legitimate news. Sinclair broadcasting was caught doing this, when its stations occasionally aired prepackaged "news stories," some of which were written and prepared by the Bush Administration, using tax dollars. Other "news stories" were actually purchased by corporations with a product to sell.

In these broadcasts, a "reporter" named Karen Ryan often lauded the policies of the President. The Department of Health and Human Services hired Ryan's public relations firm to coherently explain the benefits of Bush's Medicare prescription drug law. In May 2004, the Government Accountability Office ruled that the broadcast distribution was "covert propaganda." In the decision, the GAO ruled that, "The Centers for Medicare & Medicaid Services' (CMS) use of appropriated funds to pay for the production and distribution of story packages that were not attributed to CMS violated the restriction on using appropriated funds for publicity or propaganda purposes in the Consolidated Appropriations Resolution of 2003."

Despite the reprimand, the Bush Administration was at it again a few months later. Ryan was paid again in October, 2004 to promote the Bush Administration's Education policies, including No Child Left Behind, in "news stories" which also appeared to be legitimate.

Ryan also did news stories on behalf of laser eye surgery, Excedrin, FluMist and the merits of frequent flier programs. There was never any attempt to disclose that these reports were not actually objective. In fact, each report ended with the comment, "In Washington, this is Karen Ryan reporting."

SINCLAIR BROADCASTING: A LIBERAL MEDIA CASE STUDY

One of the networks that regularly aired Karen Ryan's "news stories" was Sinclair Broadcasting Group. Sinclair started out in 1971 with a single UHF television station in Baltimore, Maryland. Through a series of acquisitions and clever circumventing of FCC rules placing limitations on the number of stations owned in the same market,

Sinclair grew to sixty-two stations by 2004, constituting twenty-four percent of the national television market.

Prior to October 2004, most television viewers never heard of Sinclair, since their stations display the flags of other networks—ABC, CBS, NBC, FOX and the WB. Sinclair is the "filter" between the network programming and the public, and they take full advantage of their unsuspecting widespread national viewer base.

A public company started by founder Julian Sinclair Smith owns ninety-five percent of Sinclair, and Smith's four sons constitute the board of directors of the company. Politically, Sinclair management is admittedly far right-wing, and there is nothing inherently wrong with this, placed in the right context. It is certainly no surprise that a family with ninety-five percent ownership of sixty-two television stations might be interested in supporting Republican causes. They are simply supporting their own elite interests. However, numerous examples exist of Sinclair far overstepping appropriate journalistic boundaries in emphasizing certain network content while pre-empting other broadcasts. Additionally, Sinclair has inappropriately blurred the line between news broadcasts and political opinion, far outdoing even the most "Liberal" network news broadcast in lack of any attempt at objectivity.

For example, none of Sinclair's six ABC affiliates were allowed to air *Saving Private Ryan*. In a press release, Sinclair cited "ambiguities in the Federal Communications Commission indecency rules" as the reason for not showing the movie, specifically mentioning the use of the "F" word. Strangely, the movie aired in many other ABC markets without FCC incident or fine. It is certainly possible that Sinclair did not feel it was appropriate to air a movie about the harsh reality of war, during a major U.S. offensive in Fallujah, Iraq.

After the terrorist attack in 2001, Sinclair required their on air personalities to express statements of full support for President Bush. No personalities were exempted. From news anchors to sports broadcasters to weathermen, all had to go on the air and read a statement to the effect of "We want you to know that we stand one hundred percent behind our President." Several staff members at the Baltimore affiliate, WBFF, objected to the requirement, because it made them appear to be endorsing government actions and overstepping their bounds as objective journalists. No kidding.

When ABC's *Nightline* planned to devote an entire episode to displaying pictures of all the dead American soldiers from the war in Iraq, Sinclair refused to air the broadcast. In a statement, Sinclair said that the episode "appears to be motivated by a political agenda." Republican John McCain tore into Sinclair in a public letter, in which he said:

> "There is no valid reason for Sinclair to shirk its responsibility in what I assume is a very misguided attempt to prevent your viewers from completely appreciating the extraordinary sacrifices made on their behalf by Americans serving in Iraq. War is an awful, but sometimes necessary business. Your decision to deny your viewers an opportunity to be reminded of war's terrible costs, in all their heartbreaking detail, is a gross disservice to the public, and to the men and women of the United States Armed Forces. It is, in short, sir, unpatriotic. I hope it meets with the public opprobrium it most certainly deserves."

In July 2003, Sinclair refused to allow its FOX affiliate in Madison, Wisconsin, to air an ad critical of President Bush. The ad contained the now famous inaccuracy from Bush's State of the Union address, "Saddam Hussein recently sought significant quantities of uranium from Africa". Three other stations in Madison aired the ad without objection.

Perhaps Sinclair's most objectionable practice is their recent decision to centralize "local" news broadcasts from a location near Baltimore. This practice is done without knowledge of the local viewers, who see a mixture of local and national news stories, and can easily assume that the entire news broadcast is locally produced.

Sinclair also packages an overtly biased opinion segment in each nightly news broadcast. In this segment, called The Point, the host is Sinclair Vice President and commentator Mark Hyman, a self proclaimed twenty year military veteran and former intelligence officer. Hyman's *The Point* broadcasts are some of the most incomplete, misleading, biased tripe I have ever seen on my television set.

On *The Point*, members of Congress who voted against a resolution affirming the righteousness of the Iraq War are labeled "Unpatriotic politicians who hate our military." The French are referred to as "Cheese eating surrender monkeys". The rest of the mainstream media is called the "Hate America crowd," and peace activists earn the sparklingly intelligent moniker, "Wack jobs".

Hyman referred to Bush's 2004 election victory margin as "equivalent to the populations of Delaware, Montana, Wyoming, Alaska, and both Dakotas, combined!" I would like to point out to Mr. Hyman's selective perception that Bush's margin of victory is *also* equivalent to about ten percent of the population of California. It is funny how perception can be abused to prove a point drastically in either direction.

Of course, Hyman also had something to say about Bush's election "mandate," stating that "Bill Clinton never once broke the 50 percent barrier in his two elections...Yet in their eyes, Bubba had a mandate." Hyman also repeatedly stated that "No Presidential Candidate in history received as many votes as did George Bush."

The reality is heavy turnout and lack of a well-funded third-party candidate combined to cause the high raw number of votes. Bush did receive the most votes ever, with sixty million. In fact, John Kerry received the second most votes ever, with over fifty-seven million. As for Clinton's mandate, everybody knows he crushed his opponents in both elections, winning the Electoral College 370 to 168 over incumbent George H.W. Bush in 1992, and 379 to 159 against Bob Dole in 1996. However, Clinton faced both the Republican candidate and a credible third party contender, Ross

Perot, in both campaigns, resulting in more of a distributed result of raw vote counts. Again, Hyman tells only part of the story to reach the desired conclusion—"Bush has a strong mandate." In addition, only about sixty percent of eligible voters turned out on Election day. If the vote counts are broken down as a percentage of all eligible voters, Bush beat Kerry about thirty-one percent to twenty-nine percent. This is not exactly an overwhelming majority of America, but I don't expect to ever see these numbers parsed out on Mark Hyman's *The Point*.

SEEKING OUT VARIED OPINIONS

The lesson to be learned from the Sinclair example is this. Don't rely on any single source of news to provide information. For that matter, don't rely on one medium to provide information. The only way to come to any logical interpretation of current events is to watch multiple television broadcasts, and listen to multiple radio shows with different political views. Use the Internet for raw news as much as possible, and specifically include some international media outlets in your information gathering experience.

Unfortunately, nobody has the time or desire to do this research. I usually spend at least three hours gathering information after my kids go to bed, using multiple news outlets. On the other hand, my father's news gathering consists of a handful of highly Conservative radio hosts on a local AM radio station, a local television news broadcast full of fear and consumption, and an occasional dose of Rush Limbaugh. For one of my Conservative coworkers, news gathering consists primarily of reading the Wall Street Journal. For both of these individuals, they are only getting one side of the story, and it is certainly not the "Liberal" side.

Even with the desire to collect news from multiple sources, the actual collection of diverse opinions is easier said than done. Media mergers have reduced diversity of ownership. The Telecommunication

Act of 1996, which eased ownership limitations by medium and by market, was the primary cause of this change. Senator Russ Feingold is an outspoken critic of these types of rules, because of the squelching impact on diversity of opinion that results from a shrinking media ownership base. Feingold said, "Further concentration in these industries will guarantee that the range of voices that Americans have come to expect—whether we open the newspaper, turn on the television or tune into the radio—will continue to fade away."

The first step to becoming an independent media participant is to denounce the myth of the "Liberal mainstream media". Immediately discarding information from a primary source is cutting off any chance to possibly balance the barrage of right-filtered news from a variety of media. Even if this is balanced with thirty minutes of "Liberal" network news it still does not add up to a zero-sum game. For example, Rush Limbaugh has over twenty million listeners per week, which rivals his television national network news competition.

Since at least World War II, the "Liberal" media consisted primarily of newspapers like the New York Times and the Washington Post, television networks like ABC, NBC, CBS, and more recently, CNN. I will concede that through the mid-1990s, there was a decided "Liberal" bias to these media outlets. If one concedes to the common consensus that the nightly news shows *still* slant left (a concession I will not personally make), then one still needs to consider the balancing effect of Rush, Fox News, the National Review, Bill O'Reilly, Ann Coulter, the Free Republic, Sean Hannity, The Wall Street Journal, and most local newscasters and radio talk show hosts in the country's heartland. For most of the day at work, I have a hard if not impossible task trying to find one radio station or web site to give me raw news without Conservative opinion cleverly thrown into the mix. On any radio station in the Milwaukee market, for example, a news story about tragedy and death in Iraq quickly turns into a reminder of the ever-changing laundry list of reasons why Bush says we are there. It is very difficult to find raw unbiased news.

Email can also be defined as another form of news and information gathering. How many times do I open my email to find patriotic or pro-war emails, bashing Democrats, war protestors and Muslims, usually all lumped into one email? Compare that to the very few times I get emails reminding me about the human cost of war, on either side. Studies have shown that if people hear a piece of information ten times, then it will begin to be perceived as true in their minds, even if they did not initially find it credible. Because of this, email is a critical form of information gathering, and yet another over-balancing factor against the so-called "Liberal" media.

The news media in America, including local and national television, radio, newspapers and Internet sites are largely pro-status quo, pro-war, pro-consumerism, pro-fear, anti-intellectual and strongly anti-reality. None of these are "Liberal" principles.

5

America On a Bumper

"That's just the nature of Democracy. Sometimes pure politics enters into the rhetoric."
—President George W. Bush

"Too often we enjoy the comfort of opinion without the discomfort of thought."
—President John F. Kennedy

BUMPER STICKER POLITICS

When I was growing up in suburban Wisconsin, I was often warned by friends and family about the lack of depth in the politics of the Democratic Party. On issues from environmentalism to education to war, I was warned about any political view that consists of only enough words that can be fit onto a bumper sticker.

"Tim, you might have become a Liberal when you were off at college," said a coworker in the mid-1990s. "But you have to understand, the policies of the Democratic party have no depth. You can fit the whole policy on a bumper sticker. There's nothing more to it than that."

"No Blood for Oil"

"Make Love not War"

"Save the Planet: Plant a Tree"

At its surface, this argument is nice and tidy for a Red house. It implies that Republicans are consistently well educated, intelligent people who are perfectly willing to debate an issue for hours on end without ever resorting to theme words, emotionalism or knee-jerk reactions. In contrast, they believe that all of the Democrats' issues are founded on nicely packaged politically correct statements that roll off the tongue with ease. And of course, they say Democrats have to use this approach because most of the people that are willing to listen to them are frankly just not very smart. Ahem…

Don't forget, I am a converted Red kid. I still find myself looking at a "No Blood for Oil" bumper sticker, and shaking my head. After all, it is a bit disappointing that after all these years, Democrats cannot find some new phrases. Besides, if someone wants to use bumper stickers to express a brief political statement, how about "THINK." Or better yet, "WAKE UP", or "TURN OFF THE TV." If everyone did those three things, this country would never again have another Republican President.

I actually tend to agree with my Red acquaintances on the issue of using catch phrases in a political context. Most political issues are extremely complex, with many different angles playing into the ultimate answer. It is dishonest to attempt to summarize an issue with just one sentence, or only a few words.

Politicians in the first two hundred years of our country's history realized that serious issues deserve appropriate treatment. Throughout the first half of the twentieth century, politicians spoke about complex issues in the language of adults. Audiences expected their political leaders to *elevate* public discussion, and challenge the listeners to follow sophisticated thoughts and concepts. They actually used big words during their public speeches. They encouraged debate by fully presenting both sides of an argument. They frequently referenced philosophers and scientists. They referenced specific phrases from the Constitution, and provided logical interpretation of those snippets, applying them to current events. Their use of abstract interpretation was a sign of respect for their audience, and assumed that the speaker and his listeners were on equal intellectual ground.

Sometime in the last twenty-five years, we have become a nation that targets its political discourse to third graders. Much of what is called politics today is focused around symbols instead of words, and I find that when I debate family or friends on current issues, I am regularly encountering that same level of symbolic Bumper Sticker mentality. Only now, over the last few years (since September 11th, really) a very strange and unexpected thing has occurred. Instead of the Democrats, it is now the Republican platform which has precious little depth or factual basis on which to stand. So, in our flip-flopped post-September 11th world, the Republicans have become what they always disliked most about their Democrat counterparts—Bumper Sticker Politicians.

John Kerry did not appear to be targeting third graders on the campaign trail. He quoted Ralph Waldo Emerson's *Essays: First Series* in one of the Presidential debates. He used many conceptual analogies to make relevant points. In contrast to the President, it was more challenging to listen to Kerry because his responses were complex and thought provoking. For most Americans, this came across as "overly intellectual" or "flip-flopping." Kerry talked about complex issues in complex ways, instead of trying to "dumb down" his language to try to appeal to the critical thinking and language skills of the lowest common listener.

"A foolish consistency is the hobgoblin of little minds, adored by little statesmen and philosophers and divines," wrote Emerson in 1841. "With consistency a great soul has simply nothing to do. He may as well concern himself with his shadow on the wall. Speak what you think now in hard words, and to-morrow speak what tomorrow thinks in hard words again, though it contradict every thing you said to-day."

SAFE FROM THE EVILDOERS

For example, in a discussion on the topic of terrorism, no simple answer exists. This is a debate that constantly changes, and the root causes demand adequate dissection and exploration. However, I usually get one of two possible answers from my Red family and friends that prematurely ends the conversation.

"We have to get them before they get our families."

"Those people are all evildoers."

"Saddam was a terrorist."

"Everything changed on 9/11."

These are bumper stickers! These phrases are the "No Blood for Oil" equivalents of this decade. They are stock-phrases which are specifically designed to avoid critical examination and therefore defeat debate before it can start. The same theme words were repeated over and over again since September 11th, to the point that these empty catch phrases became part of the daily vernacular of many Red families. They are used interchangeably without any thought or context, right alongside other tried and true roadside mind billboards like "Clinton was immoral" or "Bush is a Christian."

Take just the simple word "terrorist", for example. These days, it is used to describe virtually everybody who takes up arms against Americans. The angry Iraqi dad, whose family was lost when their house was bombed during dinner, is now a terrorist. He has dark skin, he has taken up arms against those who killed his family, and those people are Americans, so he must be a "terrorist." An Iraqi college kid who wanted to have political meetings with his friends is held at Abu Ghraib prison and abused, all because he is a "terrorist." The guy blowing up a roadside bomb because he came from Syria to kill Americans is a terrorist also. Only one of these three people is actually a terrorist, but they are all portrayed using the same language.

Another term for the use of this technique is "Empty Language." This term describes sweeping generalizations that are so abstract and meaningless that they are virtually impossible to debate. Empty language is the emotional equivalent of junk food. It might taste good to eat, but it has little or no nutritional value. Just like pigging out on a bag of popcorn, empty language quickly fills up a listener, and leaves little room for argument or opposing viewpoints, but the listener believes he or she is full of good quality ideas.

This language is also referred to as phatic communication, that is meant to "establish or maintain social relationships rather than to impart information." Phatic language is also used "for establishing an atmosphere rather than for exchanging information or ideas."

I have always been terrible at phatic communication in the context of a serious discussion. This is the language of "How's it going?" and "Have a good one." If I have an important question to ask a coworker, I don't really toil with niceties. I get right to the issue. If that person answers my question with, "Hey how's it going anyway?" or "How are the kids?" I never really know how to properly respond. With that single phatic phrase, the conversation transitions from a legitimate targeted discussion to one that suddenly becomes unfocused and rambling.

When phatic communication creeps into a political discussion, the appropriate response usually stumps me also. How can any intelligent person respond to any of these statements, without resorting to empty language themselves? The statements are so watered down from the real complexity of the issues, that they discourage further discussion by instantly invalidating all previous and future debate.

Empty language may be common on the campaign trail, and is used by both sides to some extent. But, as the stated reasons for invading Iraq evaporated into the bloody desert sand, all that remained was empty language to justify the massive loss of life. There were no Weapons of Mass Destruction. There was no connection between Saddam Hussein and Al Qaeda. The President of the United States took our country and its' kids to war against a sovereign nation without the support of the United Nations. Americans should demand that he produce a more concrete justification than the phatic phrases "Axis of Evil" or "War on Terror."

There are many other examples from the 2004 campaign season. On Iraq:

> "We will answer every danger and every enemy that threatens the American people."

> "Saddam Hussein now sits in a prison cell. America and the world are safer for it."

On Health Care:

> "No one has ever been healed by a frivolous lawsuit."

On Taxes,

> "The best and fairest way to make sure Americans have that money is not to tax it away in the first place."

On Defense:

> "September the 11th changed how America must look at the world."

"This nation of ours has got a solemn duty to defeat this ideology of hate."

"We have a duty to our country and to future generations of America to rid the world of weapons of mass destruction."

All of these examples narrow down to a single common theme. Republicans are using the language of the American people, and unfortunately that language is an empty one, barely one step removed from baby talk. And the sad thing is, it actually *works* to win votes.

Who's Your Daddy?

The gradual decrease in intelligent political discussion directly relates to a change in the priorities and habits of many Americans. As a whole, the motivations of the average American in 2004 are a mystery to me. Most people I know seem content to go home at night and lose themselves in hours of reality television, as though living vicariously through someone else is somehow comforting. It is clear that large portions of America do not want to engage in any serious thought or challenge themselves in any way.

One sign of maturity in a person is the realization that significant challenges in life are often complex and long lasting. They are difficult to solve, they rarely just go away by themselves, and they cannot be described in just a few words or catch phrases. But most people that I know appear to be stuck in some sort of never-ending childhood, especially when it comes to their denial of current events. They want to repair any conflict as quickly as possible, preferably in a disconnected manner, without really experiencing the situation. A quick update on the nightly news is more than enough information for them. Unfortunately, if they are not willing to even experience the reality of the conflict or engage in an individually-formed opinion, there is also no chance that they will actually learn anything from it.

I frequently get the feeling that many people I know could be drafted, shipped to basic training for eight weeks, flown to Baghdad, and put in a bunker on the edge of the Green Zone, before they even realized they were not on the couch anymore. They would wake up one morning and wonder where they are and whether they missed *The Apprentice*.

Given this general apathy, is it any surprise that we look for a strong, decisive father figure in our political leadership? Americans seem to be searching for a Daddy who keeps them safe from their fears and keeps things simple. To them, this is certainly preferable to a politician who uses big words and analogies, and presents both sides of an issue including contrary arguments. For example, to many Americans, talk of raw vengeance is preferable to a nuanced argument about lack of appropriate justification for a war. This is a childish mentality.

We are less interested in what a President actually does, and more interested in how he makes us feel about ourselves and our safety. We are less concerned with coming to our own conclusions about our nation's policies, and more concerned with letting Daddy make the important choices. Daddy will reward our lavish successes, punish us for our unmotivated failures, and protect us from those who would take our successes away, whether they be external (Evildoer Terrorists) or internal (Anti-American Liberals).

Could the Republican think tanks be deliberately driving this decisive change in the tone of political language? We already know that significant effort was put into selecting just the right imagery to use for the "War on Terror" and the careful phrasing of things like "evildoers" and "with us or against us." History also shows us that Hitler put into place a similar pattern of simplifying his rhetoric to the German people in the 1930s, in order to discourage their intellectual ability to prepare themselves mentally for what he planned to do.

A conservative think tank called the "Manhattan Institute" is responsible for the origination of the phrase "Axis of Evil." This empty language played a prominent role in the Bush Administration's framing of Iraq, Iran and North Korea during Bush's 2002 State of the Union speech. Later, it became representative of Bush's war on terrorism.

The Manhattan Institute was founded in 1978, by former CIA director William Casey. Casey is probably best known for his involvement in the Iran Contra affair, but he was also responsible for funding future terrorists in Afghanistan with billions of dollars in arms, training, and cash. According to Fred Kaplan in an MSN *Slate* article, Casey viewed the struggle between Afghan mujaheddin and the Soviet Union as a "titanic struggle in the war between Eastern tyranny and Western freedom." At the recommendation of Casey, in March 1985, President Reagan signed National Security Decision Directive 166. Among other things, this directive authorized the significant increase of covert military aid to the mujaheddin, which included many future members of al Qaeda. In fact, it was on the heels of this increased funding that al Qaeda was born.

President Bush can also thank the Manhattan Institute for guiding him down the path of "Compassionate Conservativism." Bush states that, besides the Bible, the book "The Dream and the Nightmare: The Sixties Legacy to the Underclass" is the most important work he has ever read. This book was written by Myron Magnet, a Manhattan Institute research analyst. Among other things, this book encourages America to "stop the current welfare system, stop quota-based affirmative action…stop letting bums expropriate public spaces…stop Afrocentric education in the schools."

Another think tank contributing various empty language phrases to the Bush speechwriters is the Project for a New American Century. Credit this group of insightful gentlemen with coming up with the phrase, "Pre-emptive War." Reading this organization's public policy agenda is like reading a cross between the Old Testament of the Bible, Hitler's Mein Kampf, and George Orwell's

1984. The goals of the PNAC are stated right on the front page of their public web site:

> "The Project for the New American Century is a non-profit educational organization dedicated to a few fundamental propositions: that American leadership is good both for America and for the world; that such leadership requires military strength, diplomatic energy and commitment to moral principle; and that too few political leaders today are making the case for global leadership."

American leadership is good both for America and for the world. Right there on the front page of the PNAC web site, American imperialism is defined in very clear terms. Even more interesting is the laundry list of signatures on the PNAC Statement of Principles. Among the signatures are Dick Cheney, Donald Rumsfeld, Paul Wolfowitz, Lewis Libby, Frank Gaffney, and finally Florida Governor and Presidential Brother Jeb Bush.

DOOMED TO REPEAT

Think tank analysts are notorious for "borrowing" themes and catch phrases from other historically successful marketing campaigns. Here are some quotes that I found, compared with their modern day equivalents.

> Anonymous said: "I believe today that my conduct is in accordance with the will of the Almighty Creator."

> Bush says: "I trust God speaks through me. Without that, I couldn't do my job."

> Anonymous said: "Those who want to live, let them fight, and those who do not want to fight in this world of eternal struggle do not deserve to live."

Bush says: "Either you are with us, or you are with the terrorists."

Anonymous said: "Strength lies not in defense but in attack."

Bush says: "But the truth of the matter is, in order to fully defend America, we must defeat the evildoers where they hide. We must round them up, and we must bring them to justice."

The anonymous speaker in all of the above examples was really Adolph Hitler, another leader with imperialistic goals who liked to play the role of Daddy, while scaring his citizens right out of their common sense to unite against a common enemy with a different ethnicity. Hitler was also strong on "moral values" and called the Christian community his "base." Other than those few things and a few dozen quotes that are sort of eerily similar, there's really no comparison between the two men. Seriously, there is nothing more to see here. Move along.

By a contrast in level of complexity, the change in the quality of public discourse over the past few generations is well demonstrated by the depth of this quote from President Teddy Roosevelt from 1899:

> "Patriotism means to stand by the country. It does NOT mean to stand by the President or any other public official save exactly to the degree in which he himself stands by the country. It is patriotic to support him insofar as he efficiently serves the country. It is unpatriotic not to oppose him to the exact extent that by inefficiency or otherwise he fails in his duty to stand by the country."

Thoughtfulness and honesty in political discourse can also be seen in the magnificence of this quote from Dwight Eisenhower:

> "In the councils of government, we must guard against the acquisition of unwarranted influence, whether sought or

unsought, by the military-industrial complex. The potential for the disastrous rise of misplaced power exists and will persist."

These quotes, unlike quotes based in empty language, are designed to encourage independent or additional thought about a complex topic. Today, many people would call Roosevelt a flip-flopper for his patriotism quote, and Eisenhower would likely be labeled a conspiracy theorist for his very pertinent warning. "You can't believe everything you read on the Internet, Dwight."

Ultimately, the blame for tolerating this clear degradation of the quality of public discourse has to land squarely on our education system. After multiple generations of having one of the worst public school systems in the entire world, this chronic problem has finally caught up with America.

Educating to Comply

In 1943, a man named Albert Jay Nock published a book called "Memoirs of a Superfluous Man." Nock was a Conservative, but by today's standards he would probably be a Libertarian. Nock's school of thought centers on freedom and civility, and was thought to be the start of a new conservative movement in America. But it was pushed aside by the start of the Cold War, which led conservativism down a much more nationalistic and militaristic path. In his book, Nock explored the problems with the American education system of sixty years ago. Nock wrote:

> "Our system of education had succeeded in making our citizenry much more easily gullible. It tended powerfully to focus the credulousness of Homo sapiens upon the printed word, and to confirm him in the crude authoritarian or fetishistic spirit which one sees most highly developed, perhaps, in the habitual reader of newspapers. By being inured to taking as true whatever he read in his schoolbooks and whatever his teachers told

him, he is bred to a habit of unthinking acquiescence, rather than to an exercise of such intelligence as he may have."

Reading this text in 2005, one could easily come to the conclusion that it was written yesterday. This observation, made in 1943, served as an amazingly relevant warning to America. Nock foretold that America needed to change its method of educating, or face a society of adults with no ability to use their own intelligence—generations of unthinking followers prone to believe whatever they see (or disbelieve what they don't see) on television. Nock also wrote:

> "I suppose that in the whole country today one would have to go a good long way to find a boy or girl of twenty who does not automatically take for granted that the citizen exists for the State, not the State for the citizen; that the individual has no rights which the State is bound to respect; that all rights are State-created; that the State is morally irresponsible...Such is the power of conditioning inherent in a State-controlled system of compulsory popular instruction."

With this observation, Nock gets to the heart of the problem with education in America, and it is even worse now than it was sixty years ago. Our schools today spend so much time on the minute details of proper curvatures in handwriting and rote memorization of mundane historical references, and far too little time on critical thinking and philosophy.

A friend told me once that at least Americans can claim to be smarter than third-world nations, despite our poor performance in comparisons to industrialized nations. I was surprised to find that I could actually debate him on this statement with reasonable success. Our nation, and other "industrialized" nations, may be well informed. Or at least we think we are well-informed because we are smothered with information, on the radio in our cars, on our computers, and on TV. But I cannot equate being informed with being intelligent or smart. I would venture to say that a tribe in a third world country has more critical thinking capability, better ability to reason, and better ability to frame events in the proper perspective. I would mark all of these things as core components of "intelligence."

Our textbooks and teachers speak of abstract concepts like freedom and patriotism. But these things are taught *concretely* in the form of events, dates and people. In doing so, our schools do not adequately prepare students to be good practitioners of either freedom or patriotism. American kids learn the structure of government ad nauseam, memorizing and reciting and repeating fact after fact, without ever truly understanding that the real power in a Democracy is held by the governed, not by their elected representatives.

Our kids go to school and learn that Benjamin Franklin flew a kite with a key on it to discover properties of electricity. Then they spend an hour drawing a picture of Ben, flying the kite in a thunderstorm. They are not told that he said the following in 1759: "They that can give up essential liberty to obtain a little temporary safety deserve neither liberty nor safety."

We teach our kids all about Thomas Jefferson as the author of the Declaration of Independence. We make them memorize the first paragraphs, the signatures, the date and time that it was signed, but we do not teach enough of the representative *meaning* that it has to our lives today. We also do not teach this Jefferson statement: "When the government fears the people, you have liberty. When the people fear the government, you have tyranny."

We teach our kids that the few rights that they are granted by society are nebulous within the walls of the school building. Metal detectors and locker searches teach our kids that they are not trusted, and that privacy is a fallacy. Student newspaper censorship and excessively enforced dress codes teach our kids from an early age that free speech is encouraged, but only if authority figures agree with the content. In summary, we teach our kids that any rights they are actually allowed to keep are a generous gift from the school administration. These are not teaching methods that lead to independent, critical thinkers later in life.

In fact, courts have repeatedly given schools much flexibility in their ability to implement 'in loco parentis', a Latin phrase meaning that the school can act as the parent in absence of the parent. However, there are limitations and exceptions to this general precedent. In the 1969 case of Tinker vs. Des Moines, the Supreme Court ruled that students could wear black arm bands to protest the Vietnam War, and these armbands could not be removed by school administrators. In the Tinker ruling, the Court wrote, "It can hardly be argued that either students or teachers shed their constitutional rights to freedom of speech or expression at the schoolhouse gate." But the Court also warned against free speech, at the threshold where it becomes a disruption to learning. "[If] conduct by the student, in class or out of it, which for any reason—whether it stems from time, place, or type of behavior—materially disrupts classwork or involves substantial disorder or invasion of the rights of others is, of course, not immunized by the constitutional guarantee of freedom of speech."

As per usual, when it comes to balancing the rights of students to ask tough questions of teachers, and creating an atmosphere of "education", it is a fine line. Every situation is mostly a matter of interpretation, but it really should not be. It is tough to make the case that the squelching of free speech in public school hallways and classrooms can result in a student body full of critical thinkers. And private schools may set limits to students rights arbitrarily, almost without any legal restriction.

Given this information, the results of a 2005 First Amendment study should be no surprise. According to the study, more than one in three high school students said that the First Amendment "goes too far" in its guarantees of free speech. Half of students also said that newspapers should be censored by the government, and should not be allowed to publish information freely.

"These results are not only disturbing; they are dangerous," said Hodding Carter III, president of the John S. and James L. Knight Foundation, which sponsored the study. "Ignorance about the basics of this free society is a danger to our nation's future."

YOU HAVE THE RIGHT TO GO BACK TO CLASS

When I was a senior at my incredibly Red, Lutheran High School in Greendale, Wisconsin, I had a bit of a run-in with the administrators. Toward the start of the school year, an announcement came over the hallway speakers. The nominations for Student Council were being taken through the end of the week. For quite some time, I had been speaking with friends about running for the Council in order to shake things up a bit. Another friend named Dave, would run with me, and we would have the start of a nice voting block in any poorly-attended meetings.

We went to the school office and turned in our nomination forms. A few days later the ballots came out, and my name was on them, but Dave's name was missing. A visit to the school office eventually led me to the principal's office. He was happy to speak with me. "Tim, we have come to the conclusion as a faculty that Dave's nomination was not submitted in a serious manner. As you know, Dave is not the type of student who would normally run for Student Council, and we don't want to make a mockery of the process." I asked if there was any formal document describing Student Council eligibility rules, and I was told that there were no guidelines. It was purely a judgment call on the part of the faculty.

In the words of President Bush, "That's just the nature of Democracy. Sometimes, pure politics enters into the rhetoric."

That day at lunch, I went from table to table in the lunchroom and explained my conversation with the principal. I proposed a sit-in following the lunch hour on the front steps of the school. After lunch, about fifty students gathered on the steps and milled around.

Eventually the principal came around and said "What's this all about?" A few of us stepped forward and said, "Put Dave back on the Student Council ballot." What was their response? "We will not do that. Everyone get back to class." About twenty-five students cowered away immediately, and twenty-five remained. Even with a truly good cause, the default Red mentality says that individual rights are not worth fighting for.

A minute passed, and the principal spoke again, "I repeat, we will not put Dave on the ballot. Get to your next class or we will call your parents." Another fifteen students cowered back to class. There is little or no persistence to fight against injustice in society for a Red house kid who has never experienced injustice.

At this point, only ten of us remained. We looked at each other, gathered our collective will, and said once again, "Put Dave on the ballot." The principal simply turned around and said, "Follow me, let's go call your parents." As he walked down the hall, we all took off running back to class. There is strength in numbers, and in a community of mostly Red individuals, there will never be strength in opposition because there will never be numbers to back it up.

The next day the Student Council winners were announced, and I made it onto the Council. Much to my surprise, it was announced in our first meeting that guests were allowed to attend the weekly meetings, as long as they were accompanied by a Student Council member. You might guess what came next.

Starting in week two, my buddy Dave was my permanent guest in Student Council. I thought they would make him leave, but either they did not notice him or they just let it slide. As it turned out, he was never disruptive. He was patient and followed the rules of order. He attended most meetings, and he seemed to take the whole experience rather seriously. When it came time to allocate funds for the coming academic semester, Dave and I cast the deciding votes on funding significant student library improvements instead of new equipment for the athletic teams.

Teaching Directly to the Tests

In early 2002, President Bush signed the No Child Left Behind Act. By definition, this Act is designed to "change the culture of America's schools by closing the achievement gap, offering more flexibility, giving parents more options, and teaching students based on what works."

Under the Act's accountability provisions, states and school districts must produce annual report cards that inform parents and communities about state and school progress. This progress is measured through the use of standardized tests, which are to measure the success or failure of a school system. By the 2005-2006 school year, states must implement their system of student academic achievement standards for grades three through eight, in reading, language arts, and math.

But in January of 2004, the National Education Association released a study that showed No Child Left Behind was severely under funded and poorly executed. The NEA report indicated a $9.4 billion shortfall in Bush's 2004 budget proposal compared to the amount originally written into the law. This information was made public right around the time that an additional $87 billion was allocated to continue war efforts in Iraq and Afghanistan, raising a very pertinent question. Do we have our national priorities correct?

This question becomes even more relevant when considering the main purpose of the law—standardized testing as a measurement tool which is meant to be representative of "good education." If tests are to be used as the only measurement of good education, then won't teachers be encouraged to teach the answers to the test questions first? Educators and more importantly, school administrators, would seem to have some incentive to define curriculum which will appear on the tests and emphasize this content over other important content. My parents were both teachers, and I have heard many stories from my father about how he was required to "teach to the test" during standardized testing periods.

In 2003, only forty percent of school time was actually spent in the classroom, and starting in 2005, most of this time will now be spent "teaching to the test." This leaves precious little time for teaching kids how to think critically about the world around them, or how to properly relate historical events to present day.

- Educating to specific test questions with inadequate funding results in an undereducated public.

- An undereducated public results in more ability to push empty language onto a public that does not demand more complexity.

- Empty language results in more poorly justified wars against poorly defined enemies.

- Never-ending war results in more hyper-patriotism-driven safety-induced Republican election victories.

I would like to see someone try to fit that logic sequence on a bumper sticker.

If you do not want to believe me on the issue of education and its impact on our Democracy, then listen to Walter Cronkite. President Lyndon B. Johnson once said, "When you've lost Cronkite, you've lost America." Based on this statement, Bush has lost America.

In an interview from November 2004, Cronkite absolutely slaughtered the Bush Administration, accusing them of destroying America's education system to the point that Democracy itself is in danger.

"You want to get down to the nub of how this Democracy is going to defend itself," Cronkite said. "We've got to have an intelligent electorate and we're not going to have it because our education system is in a shambles right now."

As history limped along through the last fifty years, somehow "intellectual" and "well-educated" came to be portrayed as "elitist" or "Liberal" and used as a term of ridicule. This is a success of the Republican think tanks and it is right up there with "War on Terror" in terms of effectiveness on the general public.

When a political party has to start talking about dumbing down their language and terminology in order to win a Presidential election, so as not to be perceived as overly-intellectual or elitist, I think we have a serious education problem in the United States of America.

DON'T CHALLENGE ME, PLEASE!

According to many religion-based Reds, the higher education teachings of philosophy, history and literature are "taking education too far." A philosophy class wakes up the brain and teaches it how to think and how to approach complex situations. A history class, with adequate perspective, also teaches lessons that can be applied to modern scenarios, instead of simply memorizing facts and figures. Reading a wide variety of literature gives perspective on diversity and fairness, which may provide a nice conflict with the racist undertones coming from many Red families, including my own upbringing. None of these things are explicitly intended to lean toward one set of political beliefs; rather, new beliefs are the logical consequence of the constant repetition of diversity, perspective, logic, and common sense.

But many students are not interested in challenging their own predetermined belief systems. Three students at the University of North Carolina sued the school in 2004, over a reading assignment that they said offended their Christian beliefs. They were simply asked to read a book about the Muslim Quran in their summer required reading list. Someone needs to talk to these kids. College is not about acquiring a trade. Only a small percentage of specific "trade skills" learned in college are ever used in actual practice beyond college. The whole point of education beyond high school is to learn how to think and how to apply logic to situations. Why would anyone be opposed to challenging their own belief system in an effort to prove that it is the right belief system? After all, self-validation is the only way to achieve firm and irrefutable confidence in ones beliefs.

The Students for Academic Freedom is a group created by right-wing talk show host David Horowitz. According to their web site, this organization is "dedicated to restoring academic freedom and educational values to America's institutions of higher learning." On the group's "Academic Complaint Form," they raise a number of ways that students' "academic freedom" can be violated. I have listed some of the criteria below.

> *-Required readings or texts that cover only one side of an issue.* In classes for my Journalism major, I was repeatedly required to read books about how Dan Rather was the downfall of CBS. Is this a fact, based on the ratings trends? Or, is this an opinion with two sides? If it was considered an opinion, then I think I have a complaint to file. Who is going to police every statement in every book used as material for a class in a college setting?
>
> *-Introducing controversial material that is unrelated to the subject.* Analogies are these great conversational and instructional tools that can be used to emphasize an important point by making a comparison to a similar situation. For example, in a course on ethics, one of the topics might be the ethical consequences of using excessive vacation or sick time to con one's employer. An analogy might be made to the ethics of President Bush's use of

over ninety-six days of vacation, or forty percent of his presidency, prior to the September 11th terrorist attack. I think this is a good analogy, which is supported by numerous facts (Fifty-four days at the Texas ranch, thirty-eight days at Camp David, and four days in Kennebunkport). The Students for Academic Freedom would undoubtedly view this as off-topic belief-bashing.

-Forcing students to express a certain point of view in assignments. Ever heard of the High School debate club? The whole point of debate matches is to take one side or the other of a particular issue, and back it up in the best way possible. Of course, it is more of a challenge to take up the side that you are less comfortable with or maybe the side that you don't agree with. But in the end, it all evens out. About half the time, you get a paper assignment that you feel very strongly about, and you nail it with ease. The other half of the time, you are challenged. And this is a good thing. Challenging yourself to argue contrary to your own opinions, whether or not you actually believe your own argument, is an absolutely essential part of the learning process. Don't believe me? Aristotle and Socrates can confirm the effectiveness of this approach.

I had a strongly Republican political science professor at Valparaiso University. I disagreed with nearly everything he said. I asked questions after class, and challenged some of his assumptions. I also challenged those around me in class who agreed with his positions. This is called education. Education is defined as "the knowledge or skill obtained or developed by a learning process" or "an instructive or enlightening experience." This class was certainly enlightening for me. Many times I was convinced my test grades were marked down due to the content of my test answers, instead of the logic and historical reference I used to achieve those responses. Yet, I did not run to an academic fairness club and scream bias.

The Supreme Court agreed in the 1967 case of *Keyishian v Board of Regents*, where the ruling defended the free exchange of ideas within the bounds of the learning process. In the case, teachers from State University of New York claimed that the New York State "teacher loyalty" laws were unconstitutional, since they required each University employee to state that they were not a Communist. "The classroom is peculiarly the 'marketplace of ideas,'" read the Court's ruling. "The Nation's future depends upon leaders trained through wide exposure to that robust exchange of ideas."

Ohio Legislators attempted in 2005 to bypass the 1967 precedent, by drafting a bill to form an "Academic Bill of Rights for Higher Education." So much for the "free exchange of ideas" guaranteed by the *Keyishian* case. Among other things, the bill includes language similar to the Students for Academic Freedom:

> "Faculty and instructors shall not infringe the academic freedom and quality of education of their students by persistently introducing controversial matter into the classroom or coursework that has no relation to their subject of study and that serves no legitimate pedagogical purpose."

Our education system in America is under attack. The basic principles that constitute higher education are now considered biased and Liberal. Bumper sticker politics have returned with a strong vengeance, and yet most people don't realize they are regurgitating empty language phrases. And many Conservatives do not have enough confidence in their own beliefs to back up those opinions with some good-natured verification against knowledge and the Golden Rule.

6

The Reality-Based Chapter

> "There are some people who live in a dream world, and there are some who face reality; and then there are those who turn one into the other."
>
> —Douglas Everett

MARKETING AMERICA'S ARMY

Recently I was in a Blockbuster Video store with my son, and as usual we found ourselves in a long line to checkout. Right in front of us were two teenage boys, probably about sixteen years old. They had chosen a few video games with a realistic war theme and "Mature" ratings. While waiting, they were playing out scenarios of how to work together to draw the fire of the enemy and then flank them. They debated which weapons were the best, and whether it was worth it to upgrade their body armor.

When they got to the front of the line, the woman behind the counter took their games, and asked them if they had their parents' permission to rent games for mature audiences. Their quiet reluctant answer was somewhere between "I don't know" and "No probably not." There would be no excessive Xbox violence on that day.

They trudged out of the store with their heads down, mumbling about stupid policies.

Blockbuster has a corporate policy to not allow kids under the age of seventeen to rent rated "M" video games. But the United States military also has a minimum recruitment age of seventeen, with parental permission. So the age at which kids are deemed old enough to play a realistic violent video game is the exact same age at which they can participate in the real thing.

It is ironic that the kids in Blockbuster are probably already bombarded by calls from military recruiters at home, since they are less than one year away from military eligibility with parental approval. One year after being denied access to an "M" rated video game, these kids could be just a basic training session away from battling real Iraqis or Iranians.

This appears to be a blurry distinction that even our own armed forces organizations are happy to encourage. In 2002, the United States Army released a downloadable video game called "Americas Army." Paid for with ten million tax dollars, the game is one of the U.S. Army's most popular and effective recruiting tools. It is conceived, designed and distributed free to reach the thirteen to twenty-one-year-old age group, and it has been a marketing juggernaut. When the Army missed its recruiting goals in 1999, officials got together with the directors of a Navy think tank to discuss how to lure computer "combat gamers" into the armed forces. After all, it is the perfect target audience, because kids who play these games well can think quickly under fire, they are the right age, and they have learned to work well as a team.

Released on the first Fourth of July after September 11th, the game has been downloaded more than sixteen million times in two years. It is given away at state fairs, and it comes bundled for free in gaming magazines. Since the game's release, players have logged over sixty million playing hours. It is the number one on-line action game, with over four million registered players. The army estimates that over one-third of all prime recruiting age kids have been exposed to the game.

The colonel who supervised the game's production says that only forty-one percent of the game is simulated combat. He says more than half the game relates to "adventure training" such as parachuting, medic training, weapons training, and team-building. The game, he said, depicts the Army's values of respect, discipline, and camaraderie. "Kids aren't stupid," he said. "They know the Army is not a game. What the game does is allow them to try it on for size and get more information about the many job opportunities." There is a problem with this logic. That is, I have met plenty of suburban thirteen year olds. They may not be stupid, but they are just starting to be driven by hormones, they are certainly not world-savvy, and they are especially susceptible to carefully concocted marketing ploys.

Under normal circumstances, most people would take issue with an expense of ten million dollars on a questionable recruiting tactic that targets thirteen to fourteen year old kids. With a backdrop of September 11th, no one seems to notice that this is even going on, or they have no problem with the technique.

Michael Zyda, the director of the Navy think tank involved in the game's development, was surprised at the lack of concern from the American public. "We thought we'd have a lot more problems," Zyda said. "But the country is in this mood where anything the military does is great....9/11 sort of assured the success of this game. I'm not sure what kind of reception it would have received otherwise."

It gets even better. The Army is so desperate to recover from their recent significant shortfall of recruiting goals that the latest recruiting tactic is to host "LAN Parties." At these parties, they provide free food, free game play of America's Army on a group of computers, and of course free access to recruiters. In fact, the kids—and they are just kids—get all the recruiter marketing magic that their impressionable minds can handle. The age requirement to get into one of these LAN parties is only thirteen years old. A full four years before they can walk into Blockbuster and rent a similar game, a kid can march right into a government sponsored party and play rated "M" video games for as long as they want to slaughter "insurgents." What is worse, these same thirteen and fourteen-year-old kids are essentially being recruited, far before legal recruitment age, through the loophole that is the America's Army video game.

What are the ethics of force feeding this type of propaganda to thirteen and fourteen-year-olds? After all, the army is not selling SpongeBob Squarepants trading cards. They are selling complex life-or-death situations and ethical dilemmas. No game can begin to capture what it feels like to kill another human being or to see your buddy blown apart by a grenade. The game sells the army as nonstop excitement with unlimited lives, no ethical consequences, no Geneva Convention, no innocent civilians, and really kick-ass weapons. Strangely, the game does not cover stop loss programs, Individual Ready Reserve fine print, bed pans, night sweats, impotence, and high rates of suicide from Post Traumatic Stress Disorder.

The usage of the data collected in the game is even more difficult to believe. One of the games' developers confirmed in a fan site interview that development is underway for an integrated stats tracker, which would allow the game to be used as the equivalent of a military aptitude test. This would, of course, lead to personalized emails directly from recruiters congratulating them on their success in the game, and inviting them to come in to discuss a military career. In fact, player information has been captured in a large database called "Andromeda", which can be utilized when an Americas Army player shows up in a recruiter's office. This is confirmed on the Americas Army web site, where they state that players who request information on a career in the Army may have their gaming records matched to their real-world identities. Their personal gaming data would be used to suggest personally popular areas of the game as a desired career path to that individual.

Ironically, recruiters do not tell the story of Andres Raya, a kid from Modesto, California. Raya was just nineteen years old, and he was always cracking jokes. Somehow the class clown ended up in Iraq for two tours of duty. Upon returning home for Christmas, his family said he was acting different. George Alvarez, a longtime friend and neighbor said that Raya was having trouble with nightmares, "Lots of problems sleeping, a lot of mental things going on inside." When his family tried to talk to him, he would not talk about what was bothering him. He only said he did not want to go back to Iraq.

On Sunday, January 9, 2005, Andres guaranteed that he would not be going back to Iraq. He lay in wait for police outside a liquor store, with an assault rifle in hand, and committed "suicide by cop." In the process, he took police officer Howard Stevenson along with him. A mother of one of Raya's high school classmates said, "He was very, very polite and so proud of himself for being in the military. I can't believe it. People need to know that he was a good kid. Now he's going to be known as a cop killer."

War was certainly not a video game for Andres Raya, and it is not a video game for the 5,500 American soldiers who have opted for Canada and eventual prosecution instead of returning to Iraq for a second or third tour of duty. The lighthearted artificial-reality video game recruitment phase is officially over for these soldiers.

Lt Col Joe Richard, a Pentagon spokesman, said "The men in Canada have an obligation to fulfill their military contracts and do their duty. If and when they return to this country, they will be prosecuted."

In January 2005, more than three hundred gaming and military leaders met in Orlando for a GAMES (Government, Academic, Military, Entertainment and Simulation) summit. Doug Whatley, founder and chief executive officer of BreakAway Ltd., attended the summit.

"There's an awareness among military leaders and video-game developers on the value of working together," said Whatley, whose company has developed training games for the military. "This conference is symbolic. There's been an awakening by the military to the technology revolution. The military can't practice war without tools that put troops in a virtual environment, so the video game is real and it's here to stay."

If a news story aired on CNN about al Qaeda agents creating a reality-based game to use as a recruiting or training tool to kids as young as thirteen, what do you think the reaction would be in Red America? The technique would be quickly condemned as immoral and a typical example of how al Qaeda devalues human life. How do you think Iraqis view this practice? What will we tell the Iraqi moms whose children are dead from a misplaced cluster bomb? It is not our fault, there was a bug in the simulator code!

American society has apparently decided that the right to engage in fake killing is roughly on par with the right to participate in real killing. Therein exists the greatest problem facing America in 2004, the quickly emerging confusion between actual-reality and pseudo-reality. From news organizations to campaign speeches to military-sponsored video games, my friends and neighbors seem to have lost their ability to separate reality from fantasy. In the suburbs, this phenomenon takes on an additional aspect. Not only have suburbanites lost their ability to make these distinctions up front, but they have also lost their ability to reassess the original question even when the truth is finally evident. Instead, time after time they choose instead the comfort and safety of the original much-desired reality.

Long Term Avoidance

The most profound national impact of the September 11th terrorist attacks was not the civilian deaths; it was also not the increased airport security or the terror alert system or the War on Terror. Easily the farthest reaching impact of the planes hitting the towers was the psychological impact on suburban and rural middle America. The whole country was obsessed with the television news for weeks, and repeatedly saw the flash of the explosion from the impact of the planes, the buildings collapsing, and people jumping from the towers. In the days following the attacks, reports from around the country estimated that ninety percent of the country experienced some form of Post Traumatic Stress Disorder associated with the attacks. Even I can still hear the screams of the onlookers and see the crumpled metal as the plane goes through the outer walls like crepe paper.

According to the National Center for PTSD, fear and anxiety is the number one symptom of the disorder. Anxiety is the brain's natural response to a dangerous situation. For many people anxiety and fear lasts long after the end of the actual event that caused the trauma. The symptoms of PTSD can also be triggered if the person's views of the world and sense of safety have significantly changed. From day one, public statements seemed to encourage people to experience prolonged PTSD as a result of the attacks. Our President has approached the podium thousands of times since that day to say, "The World will never be the same." Or "That is a pre-September 11th mentality." These are all friendly reminders to the nations psyche. Do not forget to be anxious, and do not forget to be afraid. Do not forget that you are not safe anymore, and everything has changed. The exact nature of these phrases was not accidental.

Another defense mechanism for managing trauma-related anxiety is avoidance. The most common method is to avoid situations that remind the individual of the traumatic event. Another way for a victim to increase their comfort level is to avoid or reject painful thoughts. Through the numbness defense mechanism of the brain, people with PTSD have an especially difficult time paying attention to or properly interpreting any events that trigger memories of the trauma.

Finally, the disorder causes a significant shift in the way the individual views the world. Most suburbanites, for example, used to view the world as a very safe place. But the experience of the trauma and the subsequent reminders suddenly made them feel vulnerable. After all, the Muslim guy down the street might have a suitcase bomb in the back of his kid's Power Wheels Jeep. These extreme upfront fears (in contrast to the everyday underlying ones) are unusual even for a typical suburbanite. They give people the misleading feeling that they, and the world, have been completely changed forever by the trauma.

With these symptoms in mind, it is my belief that the vast majority of the United States is still suffering from a mild form of PTSD, even more than three years after the terrorist attack. Furthermore, I believe it is impacting our collective ability to rationally process news and events. The world of a Manhattan resident is very different than it was before the attack. Each time the security level is raised, just getting to work becomes a chore of checkpoints and pat downs. Bomb-sniffing dogs patrol office buildings all over the city. Many New Yorkers knew someone who was involved in the rescue efforts, or even someone who was killed when the buildings fell. In Manhattan, where real justifiable fear is front and center every day, brave American voters overwhelmingly chose John Kerry, with eighty-two percent of the vote.

The daily life of a suburbanite in America has not materially changed. Before you string me up by an American flag, let me explain. Three thousand Americans died in the September 11th attacks, and for their immediate families, the world will never be the same. I feel immense sorrow and pain along with these families, and I would give anything to go back and undo what happened to them. But, as a country, let's retain some semblance of perspective here. In the period of time since 2001, over 100,000 people have died from adverse reactions to prescription drugs. Why are we not waging a War on Pharmaceutical Manufacturers by pursuing stronger safety and testing regulations? Suburban Americans still take their kids to the doctor over the slightest sniffle, despite the fact that the drugs they get from the doctor are one of our country's biggest killers. Over ten thousand Americans died from accidental drowning since September 11th. Are suburban security moms keeping their kids out of swimming pools out of their intense fear of drowning? No, it's too damn hot in the summer to worry about a routine thing like swimming. And finally, suicide took the lives of over 90,000 Americans since 2001, and homicides took another 60,000 lives. We are thirty times more likely to kill ourselves than to be killed by a terrorist, and twenty times more likely to be killed by one of our own neighbors.

When the terror alert is raised, bomb-sniffing dogs do not wait at the entrance to a suburban office in Nebraska or a daycare in Minnesota. When the terror alert is raised, barricades do not go up in front of "targeted" buildings in Appleton, Wisconsin. Ask yourself again, what are you afraid of? Has everything changed, really? Will life in the suburbs really *never* be the same again? Is life in the suburbs *really* not the same *now*?

HARD-CODING SADDAM TO THE PTSD

To remain loyal to Bush means to enter into the false reality that surrounds him. There is reality, there is perceived reality, there are straight lies, and then there is this strange new area in the middle, somewhere between perceived reality and ambiguously worded lies. This hazy, murky neck of the woods is where you will find Bush himself, and the majority of Bush supporters. If you ever make it to that area of the forest, you will see unicorns and heffalumps, and trolls with suitcase nukes. You will see weapons of mass destruction behind every tree and terrorists in the highest branches. Most of all, you will see thousands of GMC pickup trucks with gun racks in the rear window, and Support the Troops ribbons on the back of their extended cabs, right next to their brand new "W The President" bumper stickers.

Right from the start of the justification of the invasion of Iraq, Bush and others in his Administration linked Saddam to Al Qaeda, and Osama bin Laden to Iraq. This was done in a very "flexible" manner, carefully worded to allow for liberal interpretation by each listener.

On Sept 12, 2002, Bush said, "Al Qaeda terrorists escaped from Afghanistan and are known to be in Iraq."

On March 17, 2003, Bush said, "The (Saddam Hussein) regime has a history of reckless aggression in the Middle East. It has a deep hatred of America and our friends and it has aided, trained and harbored terrorists, including operatives of al Qaeda."

Through the non-specific nature of these statements, the listener is forced to come to their own conclusion about Iraq's exact involvement with Al Qaeda. It is not much of a leap for my Red acquaintances to say, "Bush said Saddam knew that Al Qaeda was in Iraq, and Saddam did not try to forcibly remove them." Or, "Bush said Saddam aided, trained and harbored the September 11th terrorists."

Finally, in May 2003, the lid was blown off the ambiguity. On May 1, Bush said, "The liberation of Iraq is a crucial advance in the campaign against terror. We have removed an ally of al Qaeda and cut off a source of terrorist funding."

There is a significant problem with these statements. They are not exactly true. Al Qaeda is an extremist religious organization, and Saddam was a secular leader. In fact, the two entities were subsequently proven to be incapable of working together on anything. Saddam Hussein was not an "ally" of al Qaeda. Al Qaeda terrorists were not in Iraq until well after we "liberated" the country. Iraq did not train al Qaeda terrorists (That was actually our job, when we backed the mujaheddin in Afghanistan with training, weapons and cash). Saddam and Osama were not even on speaking terms at the time of our invasion.

Conservatives love to hang their answer to this question on a report from October 2003, called the "Feith Memo." This memo was sent from Douglas Feith, the Undersecretary of Defense for Policy, to Senators Pat Roberts and Jay Rockefeller. In summary, the memo states that Osama and Saddam worked together from the end of the first Gulf War until 2003. Their involvement, according to the memo, included logistical support for terrorist attacks, safe haven for al Qaeda training camps, financial support, and training in WMDs and explosives.

However, the truth about the Feith Memo may be stranger than fiction. In August 2002, Feith's team went to brief the CIA, at the suggestion of Donald Rumsfeld. In these meetings, they shared their "new" information about Iraqi/al Qaeda connections with the professional analysts at the CIA and eventually with other branches of the intelligence community. The CIA response? Well, there were crickets chirping, legs kicked under the table to keep from laughing, and the painful clearing of throats that goes with an embarrassing situation.

Pouring over piles and piles of raw data to find only the specific bits and pieces that confirm a predetermined conclusion has a name in the intelligence community. This practice is called "Cherry picking", and the findings in the Feith memo are a classic example. Since Feith also claimed to have conclusive pre-war evidence about WMDs in Iraq, it might be safe to assume that Feith and his staff have a history of cherry picking just the right set of "facts" out of a crowd. In February 2005, after the search for weapons was finally called off, Feith resigned his position at the Pentagon to "spend more time with his family."

"If anybody doubted that there was such a thing as intelligence with a [predetermined] purpose, this is a case study," says retired CIA intelligence analyst Larry Johnson. "Just because someone says something and it gets 'classified' stamped on it, doesn't necessarily mean it's true."

The *9/11 Commission Report* clearly agrees with Johnson. The report, issued on June 16, 2004, clearly states that there was no link between al Qaeda or Osama bin Laden and Iraq. "We have no credible evidence that Iraq and al Qaeda cooperated on the attacks against the United States," the report says. "Bin Laden is said to have requested space to establish training camps, as well as assistance in procuring weapons, but Iraq apparently never responded." The report said that despite evidence of repeated contacts between Iraq and Al Qaeda in the 90's, "they do not appear to have resulted in a collaborative relationship."

Therefore, with the Feith memo largely discredited, and the September 11th Commission's report clearly demonstrating no decisive connection between the two entities, certainly Americans now understand that there is no connection between Iraq and the War on Terror. Or maybe not. The haze of assumed or desired reality wins again.

A poll by the Program on International Policy Attitudes (PIPA), conducted just days before the election, showed that seventy-five percent of Bush supporters believed Iraq was directly involved in the attacks or at least gave Al-Qaeda financial support. The same seventy-five percent of Bush supporters believed that Bush was still *saying* that Iraq was directly involved, despite evidence to the contrary in the official *9/11 Commission Report*. And the most damning survey result of all, a full fifty-six percent of Bush supporters actually said that the *9/11 Commission Report* claimed there **was** a connection between Saddam Hussein and the September 11th attacks.

So the original facts were clearly misleading to many Americans, yet they were repeated over and over again by the mainstream media and by Cheney and Bush themselves. Substantial time passed, and no connection was found, but the original statements were never corrected or improved. The *9/11 Commission Report* states otherwise, but the media downplays this fact, and not enough people actually read the full report. The end result is a large portion of

America who still believes we are in Iraq because Saddam directly participated in or aided al Qaeda in the September 11th attacks. With the media's help, misleading statements have gradually become perceived reality. Like Nayirah, the cute little Kuwaiti girl who told the story about the babies taken from the incubators during the build up to the 1992 Gulf War, untruths can quickly take on a life of their own for those who hear only what makes them feel confident about their existing opinions.

If seventy-five percent of his supporters still believe that Iraqis were on the planes on September 11th, or the terrorists were funded by Saddam or Iraq, the moral thing for Bush to do would be to take a public position that he was given bad intelligence. Instead, he chooses to let the misleading or abstract information fester, just beneath the surface of reality, instead of admitting a mistake.

Through late 2004, Bush held only fifteen solo press conferences, less than any President in recent history. By comparison, his father held eighty-three and Bill Clinton held forty-two press conferences during the same period of time. Press conferences are a great opportunity to express a clear message. Mistakes can be clarified and confusion can be eliminated. But with only three or four press conferences per year, misinformation can fester and take on a life of its own.

In one of the few press conferences during his first term (April, 2004), Bush was asked if he thought he made any mistakes. He said he was sure he made mistakes but he could not think of any on the spot. "I wish you'd have given me this written question ahead of time so I could plan for it…I hope—I don't want to sound like I have made no mistakes. I'm confident I have. I just haven't—you just put me under the spot here, and maybe I'm not as quick on my feet as I should be in coming up with one."

Here is a mistake for Bush's future reference. A January 2003 Knight Ridder newspaper poll asked the following question: "As far as you know, how many of the September 11th terrorist hijackers were Iraqi citizens: most of them, some of them, just one, or none?"

Twenty-one percent of Americans answered "Most of Them." Twenty-three percent answered "Some of Them." Six percent answered "Just One." Thirty-three percent said "Don't Know." And just seventeen percent of respondents got the answer right. "None." None of the hijackers were Iraqis. Sixteen months after September 11th, eighty-three percent of Americans still did not know that none of the September 11th hijackers were Iraqis. Is this any surprise, when even the President of the United States has still not clarified this deception?

Bush Administration officials must give up the falsity that Iraq and al Qaeda were connected in any way. They must apologize for misleading the public. But, of course, this will never happen. They needed to connect Saddam into the nation's collective post-trauma condition. They needed Joe Six-Pack in his GMC truck to assume that Saddam equals Osama, and Osama equals Saddam. They clearly got the end result they were looking to achieve—Support the Troops and "W the President."

HOMERS AND PILLS AND SHOTS IN THE ASS

Further evidence of the preference for a falsely shiny world of glory over actual messy, tainted reality is visible in the National Pastime. During September of 1998, I attended a sold out baseball game at Milwaukee's County Stadium to watch the Milwaukee Brewers take on the St. Louis Cardinals. September baseball games in Milwaukee do not sell out unless there is some secondary reason to go, like a bobble-head doll giveaway or a player from another team chasing a record. In this case, it was the Cardinals' Mark McGwire, who was competing with Sammy Sosa to break Roger Maris' single season home run record.

The sold out stadium went absolutely bonkers every time he stepped to the plate to hit. Dads were there with their sons, and the kids were hoisted on dad's shoulders for every pitch. If the home team pitcher was a little wild or if he was intentionally pitching around McGwire, boos would cascade down toward the mound. Fans were there for one reason only—to see a Mark McGwire home run. And he did hit a towering home run to left field on that night. It was a real spectacle to see, since McGwire was built like an ox. When McGwire really got into a ball, it would soar over the outfield wall like I have rarely seen.

In the middle of McGwire's 1998 season, a reporter discovered Androstenedione (or "Andro") in McGwire's locker. Andro is a muscle-enhancing supplement which is similar to Creatine. Although not banned by Major League Baseball in 1998, Andro was banned by the NFL, NHL, NBA, MLS (soccer), NCAA, and the International Olympic Committee. The Olympics banned the substance because it is a precursor to anabolic steroids, which are also banned in the Olympics.

Immediately, testosterone enraged fans rushed to McGwire's defense. "There is nothing wrong with Andro," they said. "He takes Andro to help his bad back," they said. "Andro doesn't give him any advantage over anyone else," they said. But years later, when McGwire was retired from the game, and most people had forgotten, the Commissioner of Major League Baseball banned Androstenedione from the sport. He banned it on April 12, 2004. On that same day, the Food and Drug Administration banned the sale of Andro.

On September 7th, 1998, McGwire hit his 62nd home run of the season, and broke Roger Maris' single season record. After the game, McGwire said, "I tell you what, I was so shocked because I didn't think the ball hard enough to get out. It's an absolutely incredible feeling. I can honestly say I did it."

McGwire can honestly say he did it, but can he say he did it honestly? It certainly seems that McGwire does not believe his success had anything to do with the use of performance enhancing supplements. "I study pitchers. I visualize pitches. That gives me a better chance every time I step into the box. That doesn't mean I'm going to get a hit every game, but that's one of the reasons I've come a long way as a hitter."

Not only did McGwire cheat to break one of baseball's most treasured records, but he clearly does not even think he cheated. In 1999, McGwire quietly confessed that he stopped taking Andro, and said that he didn't want kids taking Andro because of its possible negative long-term side effects. But Major League Baseball will never put an asterisk by his name. McGwire sees no evil, the baseball community hears no evil, and the fans speak no evil.

It was somehow fitting that McGwire's record was smashed just three years later when Barry Bonds, another enhanced cheater, hit eighty home runs in the 2001 season. There are others, both admitted and obvious—Sammy Sosa, Ken Caminiti, Jason Giambi, Jose Canseco. The list of steroid or enhancement users is long, and the list of abused enhancements is long as well: Human Growth Hormone (HGH), Andro, Creatine, and Steroids.

Let's face it, Sammy Sosa's head is about three times the size that it was when he came to the majors as a scrawny kid with a quick bat. His helmet barely even fits on his head anymore, yet he was still cheered with incredible passion and ambivalence by the Wrigley Field faithful until he was traded in 2005. Sammy's following is even more of a paradox, since he was also caught using a corked bat during a game in 2003. Again, most fans rushed to his defense. "It was a mistake. He usually only used it for batting practice," they said.

Finally, in January 2005, baseball players and owners reached an agreement on a tougher policy on performance enhancing substances, including steroids. But the push for this change did not come from the fans. Rather, it was threats from members of

Congress in the wake of the trial of Bonds' trainer and other executives from a San Francisco-area nutritional supplements lab that finally forced baseball to take appropriate action.

Instead of condemning McGwire for his Andro use, fans searched for loopholes in baseball's rule book. Instead of condemning Bonds when his own personal trainer was arrested for distribution of steroids, fans rallied to his defense and came to see him in record numbers in stadiums all over the country. In a suburban Red community, things like cheating apparently do not matter. By taking suburban kids to sit in the front row and idolize a cheater, we are teaching them that only the results matter, and the ends almost always justify the means. There is no more accountability, only a very comfortable artificial reality. When these kids grow up and the next version of Bush is in the White House "padding the stats" for starting the next war, they will remember what they saw in that baseball stadium in 1998. Namely, they will remember the awe and respect in their father's eyes. They will not question the method, since they have already learned that only the achievement matters.

That is the great thing about pseudo-reality. Each person invents his or her own version, and everything stays straight and tidy, comfortable and safe in the minds of Red America, which is nothing if not consistent in their denial of anything real.

HAVE FAITH YOUNG MAN

Throughout history, men have debated whether the earth was flat, or round. The ancient Greeks actually understood meridians and parallels, and identified the concepts of the poles and the equator. But the Greek's theories did not prevail. By the 14th century, there were very few people remaining who believed in the concept of a spherical Earth. As time and scientific understanding advanced, more facts began to support the round-Earth conclusion. Ships would disappear as they passed over the horizon. The shape of the

Earth could be observed on the moon during a lunar eclipse. In 1530, Polish astronomer Nicholas Copernicus proved that the Earth and other celestial bodies were actually round, and that the sun was the center of the solar system. His research and theory was outlined in his book, *De Revolutionibus*. However, even today, with pictures from satellites and enough physics-based proof to fill hundreds of textbooks, there are still people, in America, who believe that the Earth is flat. They believe this purely because the Bible makes reference to the "four corners" of the Earth a few different times. For these thousands of International Flat Earth Research Society members, faith is able to trump thousands of years of knowledge passed from generation to generation.

Growing up in a strongly Christian family, I learned a great deal about the concept of faith. Faith is used almost weekly in Bible studies and sermons as a badge of honor for those involved. Remember Jonah? He had faith that God would rescue him from the belly of the whale. Noah had faith that if he built an ark, the rains would come and he and his family would be saved. In Bible stories, faith is often rewarded by eventual fact which fully justifies the originally irrational faith. There are very few cases in the Bible where an individual's faith in God is not eventually rewarded. Faith in Christianity is even given a personification, in the form of the "Holy Spirit." According to my childhood pastors, it is the Holy Spirit's job to eliminate belief-based doubts from a Christian mind, and to fill an individual with truth ("He will guide you into all truth"-John 16:13) and counsel ("The Counselor"-John 14:26). So the Holy Spirit magically turns faith into truth, without any supporting facts, *when there are none available.* I have no problem with faith from the perspective of religion. Faith provides comfort and grounding for those who need such things. It would be virtually impossible to believe in any religion without some level of faith in things that cannot be seen or comprehended.

Even in a non-religious setting, there are plenty of appropriate applications of faith. For example, I have faith that the guy I pass on the street late at night will not take out a knife and stab me. I have faith in the basic goodness of the average man. I have faith that people can be trusted. When my son tells me he has no homework, I usually have faith that he is telling the truth. I have faith that my bank will process my paycheck deposit correctly. Non-religious faith is used every day, in normal life situations, without thought or even question.

However, there are plenty of examples of inappropriate non-religious faith. Should Americans have faith in politicians? The correct answer is no, clearly not. There is no role for faith in the political process, mostly because there does not need to be. Faith is only necessary when there is insufficient knowledge, or fact, on which to base an opinion. When we are told by the President that there is a connection between Saddam Hussein and al Qaeda, most trusting Americans are inclined to believe the initial claims. Imagine a pitcher completely filled with the water of faith. However, as time passes, it becomes sufficiently clear that there was no traceable connection between Saddam and al Qaeda. Fact rocks are gradually dropped into the pitcher, forcing out the faith water. Eventually, with enough facts in the pitcher, there is very little room remaining for faith water. Even when the pitcher is now almost entirely filled with rocks, most Bush supporters continue to cling to the two remaining drops of water, so thirsty are they for faith to become truth. They so irrationally want their original faith to be rewarded, just like Jonah, Abraham, or Noah.

The inclination to cling to faith on political issues is a side effect of the deeply religious upbringing of most Republicans. From the day I was baptized, I was taught to have faith. Have faith in God. Have faith in your parents. Have faith in your neighbors. Have faith in yourself. Have faith in the President. He is a good Christian man and he is guided by the Holy Spirit. Remember the Holy Spirit? The guy who magically converts faith to truth? In a Red house, perception is everything I suppose.

A little knowledge is a good thing in any faith-based relationship, as some of the faith water is removed in favor of more believable rocks. But too much knowledge appears to be frowned upon in highly religious circles. In fact, there is even a genuine distaste for higher education in Red households. There is a fear that a little education is good, but only in Christian schools and only to a point where the content of the curriculum cannot be "corrupted" with false teachings.

Is this any surprise? My entire upbringing was about faith, not logic or reason. For example, since my first Christmas, I was told that Santa Claus was real. No matter how many times my dad left us in the car in the driveway on the way to church on Christmas Eve, while I saw his head bobbing under the window as he attempted to crawl back and forth, putting the presents under the tree. "Oh yes, Santa Claus is real," mom would say as my sister snickered in the back seat. "But mom, I now have knowledge that he is not! I know that you and dad buy the presents! My friends told me, and besides, I just saw dad crawling under the window." No, Tim, you must have faith. Santa is real. Iraq was a legitimate threat. WMDs are out there somewhere.

FINDING TRUTH ON A TURKEY FARM

There were no Weapons of Mass Destruction found in Iraq. The story is well documented by now, and it sounds very similar to the al Qaeda connections and home run records. There was ultimately proven to be little or no factual basis for the WMD statements, but nobody admitted a mistake, and nobody in suburban or rural America cared much either way. Bush, Cheney and Rumsfeld repeatedly told the same story over and over about WMDs in Iraq, and when the whole country was bombed and searched, they were not there. Did they receive bad evidence from the CIA, or did they fabricate? Once again it doesn't really matter.

There are a number of good quotes documenting these distortions, but Donald Rumsfeld's was my personal favorite: "We know where they are. They're in the area around Tikrit and Baghdad and East, West, South and North somewhat."

Rumsfeld was not alone in his non-specific confidence. Cheney mentioned nuclear weapons on Meet the Press on March 16, 2003: "We know he's been absolutely devoted to trying to acquire nuclear weapons, and we believe he has, in fact, reconstituted nuclear weapons."

And of course, President Bush himself said all of the following statements in his now notorious State of the Union Address on January 28, 2003.

- "We have also discovered through intelligence that Iraq has a growing fleet of manned and unmanned aerial vehicles that could be used to disperse chemical or biological weapons across broad areas."

- "U.S. intelligence indicates that Saddam Hussein had upwards of 30,000 munitions capable of delivering chemical agents."

- "Our intelligence officials estimate that Saddam Hussein had the materials to produce as much as 500 tons of sarin, mustard and VX nerve agent."

- "Our intelligence sources tell us that he (Saddam) has attempted to purchase high-strength aluminum tubes suitable for nuclear weapons production."

On November 3, 2002, Bush said, "Saddam Hussein is a man who told the world he wouldn't have weapons of mass destruction, but he's got them." In reality, the inspections prior to war worked. This time, Saddam Hussein was telling the world the truth.

When former UN Weapons Inspector Scott Ritter said that the inspections worked, he came under criticism for treasonous actions and exhibiting biased opinions. In late 2002, Ritter said, "These concerns are almost exclusively technical in nature and do not overcome the reality that Iraq, during nearly seven years of continuous inspection activity by the United Nations, had been certified as being disarmed to a 90 [percent] to 95 percent level." In retrospect, Ritter was absolutely right.

In February 2003, the United States was only able to conjure up four potential votes in the United Nations Security Council for a resolution authorizing the use of military force against Iraq. The US, Britain and Spain submitted the resolution, and only managed to garner Bulgaria's support in addition to the submitting members. The remaining members did not find the United States' evidence of WMDs credible, and who can blame them. In retrospect, the inspections worked, France was correct, and Colin Powell's famous mobile weapons labs were actually weather campers with nothing but helium balloons inside their metal walls. Yet, in June 2003, a national Harris Poll showed that thirty-five percent of Americans believed that WMDs had already been found in Iraq.

As months passed, and no weapons were found, there came a time where a courageous leader needed to be able to admit that he made a mistake. This admission never came. Instead, all we got were more commissions, more investigations and search parties, and more stubborn consistency that the weapons must be out there somewhere.

As John Kerry pointed out in one of the Presidential debates, Ralph Waldo Emerson once wrote that "Foolish consistency is the hobgoblin of little minds." Bush wears his consistency on his sleeve as a tattoo of strength. Throughout the Presidential campaign we learned that "flip-flopping" is bad and consistency is good. But some kinds of consistency, like consistency in perpetuating mistakes and never admitting errors, are *not* ideal qualities for the President of the United States.

Anonymous may have said it best when they said, "Life is change. Growth is optional. Choose wisely." Or perhaps Benjamin Franklin outdid anonymous when he said, "When you're finished changing, you're finished."

Yet even into 2004, Bush refused to change his position on this topic. "See, I'm of the belief that we'll find out the truth on the weapons. That's why we sent up the independent commission. I look forward to hearing the truth as to exactly where they are. They could still be there. They could be hidden, like the 50 tons of mustard gas in a turkey farm." These reassuring words were used in April 2004, more than a year after our troops were on the ground in Iraq.

This was also a full three months *after* Bush withdrew a four hundred member military team from Iraq, that was on the ground exclusively to scour the countryside for WMDs and military equipment. The team found no biological weapons. The team found no chemical or nuclear weapons. The team found no gasses or mobile weapons trailers. This was clearly no surprise to anyone who was paying attention. Most of the United Nations pre-warned the United States that the inspections were working, and there was no need for a pre-emptive invasion. But, in the name of foolish consistency, we persisted. Bush said he would be consistent, and he certainly has been.

Over six months later, in January 2004, former Chief Weapons Inspector David Kay testified before the Senate Armed Services Committee. In this testimony he said, "We were almost all wrong." The following day during an interview on PBS, Kay said, "Going in we expected to find large stocks of chemical and biological agents, weaponized, ready for use on the battlefield, as well as a fairly substantial nuclear program. We did not find that. We have found it a lot. We have found program activities in those areas. We found a resurgent missile program. But, the large stockpile of actual weapons, chemical and biological weapons simply have not yet been found."

In March 2004, U.N. weapons inspectors released a report stating that there were no weapons of mass destruction of any significance in Iraq after 1994.

And finally, Kay's replacement, Charles Duelfer reported to Congress in October, 2004. Duelfer's report showed that Iraq's nuclear capability was "decaying rather than being preserved." He said it would have taken years to rebuild the program, and it was far from being reconstituted, as claimed by Cheney and others before the war.

After the Duelfer report, Bush and Cheney finally reluctantly admitted that they received "bad intelligence" about the existence of WMDs in Iraq. By December 2004, the search by the Iraq Survey Group (ISG) was called off. It was official, the weapons inspections did not find anything. In retrospect, the United Nations inspection teams worked, and Saddam Hussein was telling the truth.

Despite all of the clear evidence to the contrary, a large majority of Bush supporters still believe the *original* statements about WMDs. As of October 2004, seventy-two percent of Bush supporters still believed that Saddam had WMDs or a major program to create WMDs before the war. Eighty-two percent perceived that the Bush Administration was *still* saying that Iraq had WMD or a major program.

Again, the strange disconnect surfaces between reality and carefully chosen pseudo-reality among Red households. Facts which fit with a certain perception of reality are accepted, and any facts which are not in synch are simply bounced out of hand, with no consideration whatsoever. They are never even received for processing. "Bush said there are WMDs, so there are WMDs," say the Reds. "If the media is saying that there are no weapons, that is because the media is controlled by the Liberal elite, and they will say anything to make

Bush look bad. If the world media is saying there are no WMDs, that is because the world hates us and they will also lie to make America look bad."

In dealing with Soviet Russia and Mikhail Gorbachev, Ronald Reagan once said "Trust, but verify." This is true not only when dealing with national rivals, but also with our own government. When it comes to Bush's statements about Iraq, some of Reagan's biggest supporters are having a serious problem remembering the verification part.

THE FALLBACK REALITY

When asked in early 2003, the majority of Bush supporters stated that the United States should not have gone to war with Iraq if there were no connections to Al Qaeda and no Weapons of Mass Destruction. As it turned out, bygones became bygones and there were no connections and no weapons. With the original primary reasons already gone or going quickly, we immediately started hearing the fallback excuse for attacking Iraq. Repeat it with me, you have heard it hundreds of times by now:

"Saddam tortures his own people, and the world is a safer place without him. And the Iraqi people are also better off now that they have freedom."

Let us now take these claims one by one and see if they hold up to scrutiny. First, Saddam was a ruthless leader. There is no debating this fact. But were there human rights violations taking place of a magnitude which would justify humanitarian intervention?

The Human Rights Watch is an organization which is dedicated to protecting human rights and political freedom for people around the world, and they supported the 1992 Gulf War for purely humanitarian reasons. Surely an organization like the Human Rights Watch would support a humanitarian effort like the liberation of Iraq. However, in January 2004, the Human Rights Watch said "No" to purely humanitarian-based intervention in Iraq, issuing the following statement:

> "Because the Iraq war was not mainly about saving the Iraqi people from mass slaughter, and because no such slaughter was then ongoing or imminent, Human Rights Watch at the time took no position for or against the war. A humanitarian rationale was occasionally offered for the war, but it was so plainly subsidiary to other reasons that we felt no need to address it. Indeed, if Saddam Hussein had been overthrown and the issue of weapons of mass destruction reliably dealt with, there clearly would have been no war, even if the successor government were just as repressive. Some argued that Human Rights Watch should support a war launched on other grounds if it would arguably lead to significant human rights improvements. But the substantial risk that wars guided by non-humanitarian goals will endanger human rights keeps us from adopting that position.
>
> In examining whether the invasion of Iraq could properly be understood as a humanitarian intervention, our purpose is not to say whether the U.S.-led coalition should have gone to war for other reasons. That, as noted, involves judgments beyond our mandate. Rather, now that the war's proponents are relying so significantly on a humanitarian rationale for the war, the need to assess this claim has grown in importance. We conclude that, despite the horrors of Saddam Hussein's rule, the invasion of Iraq cannot be justified as a humanitarian intervention."

Even without adequate humanitarian justification, at least the world is a safer place without Saddam Hussein. Children can play safely on the streets, puppy dogs can be taken for walks, and all is right and good again in suburban America. National Security Advisor Condoleezza Rice agrees. In a newspaper column in July 2004, Rice said, "Saddam's removal has advanced peace and

Democracy throughout the broader Middle East. America and the world are clearly safer with this tyrant in the jail cell he has earned."

But world leaders tend to disagree—especially those leaders who would know given their proximity to terrorist breeding grounds. In December 2004, Pakistan President Gen. Pervez Musharraf said on CNN that the invasion of Iraq has made the world less safe. "With hindsight, yes. We have landed ourselves in more trouble, yes."

A May 2004 poll conducted by the University of Maryland and Zogby International showed that ninety percent of Saudis, ninety-four percent of Egyptians, and seventy-one percent of Jordanians thought that the war in Iraq will direct *more* terrorism toward the United States. Only two percent, one percent, and eight percent, respectively, said that the war would lead to less terrorism.

Regardless of how safe or dangerous the world is with Saddam gone, Red Americans are convinced that Iraqis owe us a debt of gratitude. According to the Harris Poll from October 2004, seventy-six percent of Americans believe that the Iraqis are better off now than they were under Saddam Hussein. As previously mentioned, two to three times as many Iraqi civilians have died under our watch than Saddam's. Outside of the Green Zone in Baghdad, there are scare few areas of the country with any consistent ability to safely engage in daily life. But as long as Americans *believe* that Iraqis are better off, the mission is accomplished.

The misperceptions do not end with Iraq. Fifty-one percent of Bush supporters believe that he was in favor of participation in the Kyoto agreement on global warming. Sixty-nine percent of Bush supporters think he supports a treaty that bans the testing of nuclear weapons. And seventy-four percent of Bush supporters believe he supports labor and environmental standards in trade agreements. In reality, Bush opposes all of these things.

Blame the Trial Lawyers

Misleading the American public seems to be a pattern for Bush, who has repeatedly claimed that health care costs are out of control due to "frivolous lawsuits." This is a statement that he made dozens of times, at campaign stops and in debates, and he continues this tirade about tort reform even into 2005. Nationalized health care is not the answer, he says. Let's address the problem, he says. The problem, according to Bush, is the trial lawyers. "Frivolous and junk lawsuits are threatening medicine across the country."

I am not yet sure if some form of nationalized health care is the answer to this complex situation, but there is once thing I am sure about. The problem is *not* trial lawyers and frivolous lawsuits. Despite the incessant drilling of this fact into Americans heads for more than two years, the claim is simply untrue. Constant repetition may be able to make a statement sound more credible, but it does not change the basic underlying factual problems.

The Department of Health and Human Services reported that in 2002 the cost of health care was $1.533 trillion. While the National Association of Insurance Commissioners reported that malpractice insurance premiums totaled $9.6 billion for 2002. If you do the division, you will find that less than ONE percent (0.62%) of total health care expenditures went towards doctor's malpractice insurance premiums. Reduction or elimination of these premiums might reduce my monthly health insurance paycheck draft from $240.00 to $238.51, but I do not think that will quite take care of my family budget. In short, the problem with health care is certainly not medical malpractice suits.

Executive pay is one contributor for high health care costs, and the high profitability of the sector is another. For example, the CEO of Tenet Healthcare, Jeffrey Barbakow, made over $143 million in 2002. The chairman of Bristol-Myers Squibb, Charles A. Heimbold, Jr., made almost $75 million dollars in one year. In

2002, Pfizer made $9.12 **billion** dollars in profit, an amount which is nearly equal to the entire cost of malpractice insurance premiums paid by all healthcare professionals. That is an example of one company, for one year. Imagine the total profitability of the entire health care sector for the past ten years.

Making extreme profit from people's sickness is highly immoral, and almost impossible to rationalize. I understand that companies that conduct research need to be rewarded when they achieve results that improve people's lives. But there are forty-four million Americans who lack health insurance coverage. There are millions of people in America every year who have to forego critical medical procedures because they cannot afford them, in part because companies in the health care industry are simply making too much money. At the very least, the industry needs to be regulated to protect the consumer.

Why would Bush repeatedly attack trial lawyers and law suits by harmed patients of malpractice and negligence? Transference is a wonderful thing. Attacking trial lawyers in the health care and pharmaceutical industry also serves to invalidate lawyers who defend victims of corporate fraud. Attacking trial lawyers makes it easier to mercilessly bash the ACLU and attempt to cut off their public funding of the protection of civil rights. After all, trial lawyers defend those accused under the broadly defined boundaries of the Patriot Act. Attacking trial lawyers is wonderful for the Bush Administration. How fortunate for our leaders that voters do not "Trust, but Verify."

But these days are not about reality, as evidenced by the results of the 2004 Presidential election. Instead, these days are about fear and perception. Claiming there are weapons of mass destruction is more important than actually finding them. Keeping images of military deaths off the public airwaves is more important than providing adequate body and vehicle armor. Denouncing Saddam Hussein as the world's largest human rights violator is much easier than finding a legitimate reason to secure foreign oil fields. Yes, these days are definitely about perception more than facts, and the American people have clearly been swindled. Let's hope that this spell can be broken before it is too late for our children. This hope is part of my reality, and I'm sticking to it.

7

The Dawn of Fear

"And Moses said to the people, 'Do not fear; for God has come to test you, and that His fear may be before you, so that you may not sin.'"

—Holy Bible, *Exodus 20:20*

"Fear is the path to the dark side. Fear leads to anger. Anger leads to hate. Hate leads to suffering."

—Yoda

PILFERING PLAYBOYS

When I was about twelve-years-old, I found myself in league with a bit of a bad crowd. By suburban Red neighborhood standards, this was a gang of thugs. I was friends with a really decent kid, and he knew these other guys from school, who knew some other guys from the neighborhood, so I started to hang out by association. It's funny how that works in the 'burbs. You know a few kids, and they know a few kids who can get you into all kinds of bad situations. It was Six Degrees from Kevin Bacon, Red neighborhood style.

My friend's name was Derrick, his friend was Paul, and the thug's name was Dax. I am totally serious. The kid's real name was Dax. I'm afraid his name might invalidate the whole story since it is so stereotypical. But the facts are the facts, what can I say?

Dax always had some kind of scheme in the works, but none of them could match the quality of the scheme he had mapped out on the first day I met him. On this particular day, Dax knew of a guy who knew a guy who had a stash of Playboy magazines in his backyard tree house. Derrick, Paul and I listened intently. Dax detailed the plan in the dirt for us, describing where the house and the tree house were in relation to the street, and where we should position the neighborhood kids so they could not see the area of the tree house. Derrick, Dax and I were to decoy, while Paul went up into the tree house and hooked the porn. Off on the bikes we would go, with porn in tow in Paul's bike basket. We would reconvene back at Paul's house, where we would put on Michael Jackson's *Thriller* album and grow up five years in about fifteen minutes. For twelve-year olds, it was quite a scheme.

The four of us rode our bikes a few miles to the crime scene. Sure enough, it started off exactly according to plan. Derrick, Dax and I kept the area kids busy with tales of our neighborhood travels, while Paul disappeared into the backyard. He was gone a really long time, and finally one of the kids we were talking to became suspicious: "Hey, where'd that other kid go?" Ummm…

Suddenly, Paul came bolting out from behind the house, porn in tow. Only there was a problem. The kid who owned the tree house was tailing Paul by about twenty feet. "Go! Go! Go!" Paul yelled. I still remember clearly the look of fear on Paul's face. So great is the fear of a parent's wrath engrained in a Red house kid that he probably really thought he was running for his life.

He tossed the Playboys into his bike basket, jumped on his bike and started to pedal. The other three of us took off pedaling too, and for a moment it looked like a clean get away. But then tragedy struck. Paul's bike basket crumbled under the weight of fifteen Playboy magazines, and the basket and the magazines fell in a heap on to the street.

"Don't ever come back here, you kids!" yelled the tree-house kid as he gathered up his pile of Playboys. We laughed the whole way home, and yelled at Paul for dropping the magazines. Paul was visibly shaken, and certainly not laughing along with us. But for me, it was still high times in Redville.

LEARNING TO FEAR

A few weeks later, the four of us discovered the pit. The pit was a short tunnel that went under the main road through Hales Corners. The speed limit on that road was about forty miles per hour, and every time a car would approach we could hear it coming. When it hit the area above the tunnel, there would be a whirr from the car tires over the hollow surface below. This was followed by a *thunk* as the car passed over a bump and back onto the portion of the road beyond the tunnel.

We spent a lot of time in the pit, doing things that twelve-year olds do. To be honest, we mostly just talked about girls and punched each other a lot. One day Derrick and I arrived to find Paul and Dax already there, each with a handful of rocks. As each car would start to pass over the tunnel (*whirr*), both of them would heave a rock up onto the overpass. With each rock they threw, my stomach turned. I wanted to leave, but I could not make my legs move. Luckily, they didn't have very good reflexes or timing. A second later, the rock would miss the car, and we heard the *thunk* as the car drove on.

After awhile, we all got bored, so we started to head back up toward the street. Derrick and I were relieved that nothing had happened. Just as we started leaving, we heard a car coming (*whirr*), but no *thunk* ever came. The car had stopped right above us. Doors opened, and a voice called down from the road.

"You, kids. Come up here!" It was an elderly man, with his wife behind him. His car was a brand new 1984 Buick.

"Are you kids throwing rocks?" We were all looking down at our feet. Derrick looked like he was about to throw up.

"Are you throwing rocks? Huh?" This guy was really fired up. He grabbed Paul, who was closest, by the arm. Paul was shocked. When Paul was grabbed, Derrick immediately took off into the nearby forest. When Dax saw Derrick take off, he high tailed it right after him. Paul used the distraction to wriggle free from his captor's grasp, causing the old man to fall roughly onto the street. Then Paul bolted into the woods as well.

I stood there frozen, like a terrorist with a lit match in my shoe. I was shaking. Fight or flight. Everything in my upbringing was telling me to go over and help the man get up, apologize, make things better. He was right, after all, and I was a good kid, so I would do the right thing.

The man's wife helped him up, and he was brushing himself off when he noticed with some surprise that I was still standing there. "Hey, you. Get over here," he roared. I instantly flashed forward through our miserable trip to the police station, my breakdown as I ratted out my friends, and the look on my parents' faces as they picked me up, shaking their heads at me in disgust.

Now *that* was fear. That was also enough to uproot my legs. Finally, my flight instinct took over and I ran off into the woods after my friends.

A few minutes later, the four of us sat in Paul's bedroom with the shades drawn and the door locked. We checked every few minutes for any sign of the Buick, or worse, the police. After about an hour, the four of us put on hats, bandanas, and other disguises, and frantically headed back to the safety of our Red homes.

The next few weeks were miserable. I stayed inside for most of those days, and I refused to wear the clothes that I wore on that fateful day. My mom could not understand why I would not wear my favorite shirt anymore. I was terrified to put it on. I was sure the police were still looking for me, with a detailed description of my clothes. Fear of being caught consumed me. Gradually (very gradually) my fear dissipated, my life returned to normal, and I ventured outside again.

But I never threw rocks or went near the pit again. I steered clear of Dax. I learned at a young age how fear is a very effective method of changing bad behaviors. Give a clockwise turn to that screw of real fear just a few times, and you will never have to worry about compliance. Trust me, the victim of fear will be perfectly willing to comply.

SUNDAY DRIVERS ON A BEAUTIFUL TUESDAY MORNING

Like most people, I will always remember where I was when the planes hit the towers on September 11th. I was commuting to work when it happened, and I was listening to music. I had the Counting Crows on the car stereo, *August and Everything After*. It was a clear, sunny day, typical of early fall, and I was trying to make it to a distant office building in time for a 9:00 a.m. meeting.

People were driving so slowly that morning, and it took me well over an hour to get to work. That long commute should have been longer. It should have taken weeks for me to get to work that day. Or months. Years. Remember those *Twilight Zone* episodes where the guy would get in his car and drive for hours and never get anywhere, driving through a mysterious fog? I would do anything to be back in my car that morning complaining about slow drivers on the freeway. I would freeze time at 8:00 a.m. on the 11th day of September, never to move it forward again.

When I arrived at work and went to my meeting, I learned about the four planes and the World Trade Center towers. And I sat in my car in the parking lot and cried, while I listened to the reporters in

New York, with their voices cracking and breaking as they watched in horror.

Like every other American that day, I swore I would never forget. I swore vengeance on the terrorists. Less than a week later, I attended the Green Bay Packers Monday night football game at Lambeau Field. The energy and the *synergy* in the crowd that night was something to remember. Flags flew everywhere, and patriotic songs played over the stadium speakers during every commercial break. Jets and helicopters patrolled the sky overhead, and the Packers won.

No Really, You Will Never Forget

George W. Bush encouraged Americans to express two immediate reactions to the September 11th terrorist attacks, vengeance and fear. The focus on vengeance came immediately, with his first public comments from Booker Elementary school:

"Today we've had a national tragedy. Two airplanes have crashed into the World Trade Center, in an apparent terrorist attack on our country. I have spoken to the Vice President, to the Governor of New York, to the Director of the FBI, and have ordered that the full resources of the federal government go to help the victims and their families, and to conduct a full scale investigation to hunt down and to find those folks who committed this act. Terrorism against our nation will not stand."

These were the first four sentences out of our President's mouth at 9:29 a.m. EST on September 11th, twenty-six minutes after United Flight 175 crashed into the South tower at the World Trade Center. There was no action plan for protecting my family, and there was no description of safety measures already in the works to end the attack. Two hijacked planes were still in the air! American Flight 77 crashed into the Pentagon at 9:45 a.m., seventeen minutes later. United Flight 93 crashed in Pennsylvania at 10:10 a.m., forty-one minutes later. Neither tower had yet collapsed. Instead of leading our country through the ongoing terrorist attack, the President of the United States was already preparing us for the eventual response.

"Terrorism against our nation WILL NOT STAND." Over the next few days, our nation was constantly reminded of that fact.

On September 13, Bush framed the conflict as the first war of the 21st century, and vowed that America would "lead the world to victory" over terrorism. We learned from Colin Powell that Osama bin Laden would be our primary target. We learned from Deputy Defense Secretary Paul Wolfowitz that we would respond with a sustained military campaign, not a single strike.

On September 15, Bush says that the American people have a desire to end "barbaric behavior" and a need for revenge. At the same time, the State Department warns foreign nations that they will be isolated if they tolerate or assist terrorist groups.

The next day, Bush first uses the terms "crusade" and "evil-doers", pledging to rid the world of the latter by using the former. Meanwhile, Vice President Dick Cheney warns that any country that protects terrorists will face "the full wrath of the United States."

Finally, on September 20th, Bush states: "Either you are with us, or you are against us. From this day forward, any nation that continues to harbor or support terrorism will be regarded by the United States as a hostile regime."

Historian Howard Zinn found this distinction very interesting: "Immediately President Bush declared a War on Terrorism, which in itself is absurd, because you can't make war on terrorism. Terrorism is not that sort of thing. It's not a country. It's not a place. It's not something finite, identifiable. It's an ideology."

DON'T MESS WITH TEXAS

Workers at Ground Zero were not even finished searching for bodies in the rubble of the towers, when Operation Enduring Freedom began. Just twenty-six days after September 11th, we were at war against the Taliban in Afghanistan, going after Osama bin Laden. The first strikes started on October 7, in the form of fifty Tomahawk missiles. According to CNN, the first strikes began about 8:45 p.m. on a Sunday and "targeted the Taliban's air defense installations, defense ministry, airport-based command centers, airfields, electrical grids and other energy production facilities."

Unfortunately, some of our missile targeting technology did not work properly, and some of our intelligence was not the greatest. There was a close proximity of densely populated civilian areas to military targets. Some of the Tomahawks missed their intended marks, but somehow they still hit targets—like houses, hospitals, and mosques. Many of the intended military targets that were actually hit were already abandoned, or left in a state of disrepair by the Taliban. Most news articles from the first weeks of bombing contain the same line toward the end of the story. Exact phrasing varies, but they all say the same thing—"Targeting effectiveness has not yet been confirmed."

On October 11, a farming village of four hundred and fifty people was bombed repeatedly, killing at least one hundred and sixty civilians. The village of Karam, located west of Jalalabad, had forty-five of sixty mud houses destroyed by the bombing. The people of the village had this to say: "Bin Laden is not here. Why are we being bombed?"

A woman named Tur Bakai survived the attack, but all of her children were killed. "I was asleep. I heard the prayers and suddenly it started. I didn't know what it was. I was so scared…"

Ten days later, U.S. bombs were aimed at a Taliban military base in Kabul. The target was missed, and instead the payload landed on an Afghan house in Khair Khana, a residential neighborhood in Kabul. Just sitting down to breakfast, eight family members were killed.

On November 29, village elders from the village of Kama Ado came down the mountains to Jalalabad to meet with the Governor of Nangarhar. American night time attacks around their village had depleted their water supply and killed their livestock. They came to plead with the governor to try to stop the attacks. Two days later, as part of the intense hunt for Osama bin Laden around the area of Tora Bora, two B-52 bombers made two passes over Kama Ado, dropping twenty-five one thousand pound bombs. Kama Ado is a ten hour hike away from Tora Bora. One woman who was wounded in the attack said that she lost thirty-eight of her forty relatives. Others reported that the following day, only forty of the village's 250-300 residents remained alive.

When journalists visited Kama Ado the following day they reported huge bomb craters and debris of houses spread over two hillsides, along with children's shoes, dead cows and sheep, and the tail fin of a U.S. MK-83 bomb.

The people in those houses and villages never even saw photographs of the twin towers, much less hijacked planes and knocked them down. But they paid the full price of our vengeance.

They were certainly not with us, so they must have been against us.

THE WAR ON MUD HUTS CONTINUES, NEWS AT 11

Twenty-six days after September 11th, moral relativism was already thriving in Red-tinted America. In a Red house, bombs that missed their mark are either the "human cost of war", or obvious Taliban propaganda. How many times have my Red acquaintances used those two terms? For that matter, how many times have they used the phrase "towel head"? After all, "they" killed three thousand American civilians—innocent Americans who were just going to work, supporting their families. According to many of my Red acquaintances, nobody in Afghanistan is really a civilian, they are terrorists. They support the Taliban, and the Taliban support terrorists.

And thus the "War on Terror" began, not with a bang, but with both whimpers and cheers. For those are the sounds of more than three thousand dead Afghanistan civilians between October 2001 and January 2002. In contrast, at least fifty million angry, writhing American suburbanites cheered every bomb that hit. Our metal packages shall carry out our national vengeance, regardless of precisely where they shall land. Lest we forget, terrorism against our nation *will not stand*.

So much for an end to "barbaric behavior."

I originally supported the invasion of Afghanistan to go after bin Laden. I found it to be a prudent course of action, assuming that we would be sending in special ops teams for a few months in an effort to isolate and eventually capture the September 11th mastermind.

I also recognize that a war against terrorism is different from a traditional war. A target is usually a very specific individual or individuals, not an entire nation or an entire army. So, Red-tinted or not, I could logically conclude the following: The use of missiles from hundreds or thousands of miles away, without guarantee of accurate technology or infallible intelligence, is probably not the most efficient way to go after terrorists.

Rather, it is a carefully planned tactic designed to avoid excessive U.S. casualties and expedite the timeline of war. With the public reaction to Vietnam still somehow fresh in military planners' minds, the tactic of distant bombing clearly results in higher civilian casualties, as a trade off for future ground-based U.S. military casualties. In a war of public relations, this is a very important trade off.

But the obvious price of this tactic is the routine underreported "Oops." When dealing with two thousand pound cluster bombs, which have a damage range of at least a mile, a single "Oops" can be pretty emotionally significant for an entire Afghan village or neighborhood.

A few weeks after September 11th, and before the bombing of Afghanistan, late night talk show host Bill Maher said that it was cowardly for the United States to launch cruise missiles on targets thousands of miles away. Maher was criticized widely for this comment, and many sponsors dropped advertising on "*Politically Incorrect.*" ABC canceled the show at the end of the season due to the controversy.

The White House press secretary, Ari Fleischer, denounced Maher, warning news organizations and all Americans that, in times like these, "people have to watch what they say and watch what they do."

Despite Fleischer's warning, I found myself wondering about our secondary or conjoined goals in our Afghanistan efforts. Sure, we were trying to isolate and kill Osama, at least at first. But we were also clearly trying to wipe out the Taliban. Why were the two goals seemingly intertwined? Osama had already been blamed for September 11th, and we were after Osama, right? Shouldn't Taliban targets have taken second priority to presumed Osama and Al Qaeda targets?

I believe I learned the answer to this question years later when I finally read the personal profile of new Afghan Prime Minister, Hamid Karzai.

PUPPETS AND THEIR PIPELINES

In 1996, Karzai was supposedly an advisor for the U.S. oil company Unocal, one of two companies that were bidding for a contract to build a two billion dollar pipeline from Uzbekistan through Afghanistan to seaports in Pakistan. Five of Karzai's brothers and a sister now reside in the United States and run a successful chain of Afghan restaurants. The restaurants are named Helmand, after the Afghan province west of Kandahar. Based on this information, it becomes clear that though Karzai is a native of Afghanistan, he may have core interests that lie elsewhere.

Karzai was sworn in as interim Prime Minister of Afghanistan just before Christmas 2001. Just two months later, Karzai met with Pakistani President Gen. Pervez Musharraf. Soon after that meeting, the two leaders announced their endorsement of the construction of a trans-Afghanistan oil and gas pipeline from Turkmenistan to processing centers in Pakistan.

Unocal had lobbied the Taliban for this pipeline for years, but the Taliban was not willing to cooperate. In 1995, Unocal vice-president, Marty F. Miller told the *Washington Post* that the company had plans for "two mammoth pipelines across Afghanistan to carry oil and gas from Turkmenistan to Pakistan."

By 1998, Unocal was changing its official story, stating in a press release, "As a result of sharply deteriorating political conditions in the region, Unocal, which serves as the development manager for the Central Asia Gas (CentGas) pipeline consortium, has suspended all activities involving the proposed pipeline project in Afghanistan."

In May of 2002, Afghanistan, Turkmenistan and Pakistan signed a trilateral agreement to develop a natural gas and oil pipeline from Turkmenistan through Afghanistan into Pakistan. By December, Karzai delivered a more detailed framework agreement between the same three countries to deliver a three billion dollar gas pipeline.

As part of the 2002 meetings, there was an interesting twist, again involving Unocal. Afghanistan's minister for Mines and Industries, Mohammad Alim Razim, told Reuters that U.S. energy company Unocal was the "lead company" among those that would eventually build the pipeline.

In 2003, under enormous public relations pressure resulting from Michael Moore's *Fahrenheit 9/11*, Unocal *again* renounced their pipeline plans, and issued the following statement:

> "Unocal has absolutely no intention of participating in an Afghanistan pipeline project nor are we in discussions with any parties about doing so."

Therefore, I would like to issue a challenge to the executives at Unocal. Can the American people quote you on that press release? Do you solemnly swear that you will not be involved in any way with this three billion dollar pipeline? You will not only abstain from participating in building the pipeline, but you will also consciously avoid any gas which comes over this pipeline, no matter how attractive the price? My bottom line for Unocal? Please define "no intention of participating." Please put it in writing for all of us to see.

Many meeting notes and summaries on the subject of the pipeline consistently cited stability concerns and security in Afghanistan as major roadblocks. However, they also repeatedly mentioned the October 2004, Afghan elections as a chance to give legitimacy to the Afghan government and stabilize the country. And in fact, just weeks after the election, the feasibility study of the pipeline was ready, and the next meeting of the steering committee was set to be held in Islamabad in early 2005. Just three months after the elections in Afghanistan, Turkmenistan went public to say that the pipeline construction would begin in 2006.

In summary, I believe that the pipeline played a role in our decision to topple the Taliban government in Afghanistan. Building and planning a three billion dollar pipeline does not happen in a month or a year, but here are the facts that we know. Karzai took extremely quick action to include the Trans-Afghanistan Pipeline into rebuilding plans, and the planning process continues to progress.

Additionally, I believe the pipeline goal directly impacted the method of invasion. The facts prove that we did not engage in a focused attack targeted against Osama bin Laden, who was likely in the mountains during the entire bombing campaign. Instead, it was a general attack against the Taliban, in a clear effort to install new leadership. This method of attack resulted in thousands of additional Afghan civilian casualties. Unfortunately, someone had to pay the price for our collective fear.

In Hamid Karzai, the United States has a valuable new friend, and Afghanistan needs to rebuild its economy with something lucrative, so why not a pipeline? If this newly-forged friendly relationship results in pipeline-based benefits to fill the energy needs of Americans, won't the ends ultimately justify the means? For me, the answer is "no." Cheap energy will never compare to the value of human life, even if there is a terrorist attached to the back end of the pipeline path-clearing process.

8

Fear's Agenda Takes Hold

> *"I must not fear. Fear is the mind-killer. Fear is the little-death that brings total obliteration. I will face my fear. I will permit it to pass over me and through me. And when it has gone past I will turn the inner eye to see its path. Where the fear has gone there will be nothing. Only I will remain."*
>
> —Frank Herbert, *Dune*

> *"All of us are born with a set of instinctive fears—of falling, of the dark, of lobsters, of falling on lobsters in the dark, or speaking before a Rotary Club, and of the words 'Some Assembly Required.'"*
>
> —Dave Barry

WAVES OF FEAR

When I was in my early twenties, I spent a lot of time at the Indiana Dunes National Lakeshore. One summer, I kicked off from my summer job a few weeks early, and I hit the beach with my friends every day until school started, and even a few days after classes began. I would haul up to the beach with my friends in one of our beat up old hatchback cars. We would spend the day playing volleyball, doing handsprings in the sand, and body surfing in the perfectly sized waves. That was probably the best time of my life, and it didn't last nearly as long as it should have.

Toward the end of that summer, I went to the Dunes with four friends on a cloudy Saturday morning. There was a storm approaching, and a nasty low pressure system was circulating in the upper part of Lake Michigan, causing a vicious undertow and much larger waves than usual. When we pulled into the parking lot, we immediately saw the signs marking the sand. "High surf. Beach closed. No lifeguard on duty."

High fives were exchanged all around as we prepared ourselves for some wicked body surfing and frolicking in the high surf. There were a handful of other brave souls around on that morning, and a few of them had ventured out to a sand bar, which was about one hundred feet off the shoreline. It was a relatively narrow sand bar, so you had to stagger your departure spot carefully. If you started parallel to the sand bar, the tow would take you to the left of the shallow spot, and by the time you got out there you would be swimming in water that was fifteen feet deep.

After a few minutes of surfing around and body slamming each other into the surf, a friend and I decided to hit the sand bar to join the others who were out there. We were both strong swimmers and neither of us thought twice about the short swim. The waves were coming in so harshly and frequently that it took a few minutes of struggling just to get halfway to our destination. We were just at the point where our toes no longer touched the sandy bottom with the sharp sea shells.

Then we plunged into the waves head first, bobbing up and down at least five feet from trough to peak. For the first few minutes we were laughing, then after a few more, we were gasping. It was hard work staying afloat, and making forward progress at the same time against the steady pounding of surf. Struggling to swim the last few feet to the sand bar, we were both gasping for air. We looked at each other on one of the troughs, and we both simultaneously realized that we needed to make it to a spot where we could stand and catch our breath, or face dire consequences.

We got to within ten feet of the others who were out there, and they began to talk to us. I was so relieved to have made it. I put down my feet, and I was so surprised not to feel the comforting sand below me that I actually went underwater. At that same moment, I realized that I was not between the others and the beach at all. Instead, I was ten feet to their left, and there was no sand bar beneath my feet. We had missed the shallow spot. As the precious seconds passed, I was drifting out and left, farther from the shoreline and away from the safety of the sand bar. My friend was even farther left and farther out. We were both in big trouble.

I had barely enough energy to take a deep breath and hold it, but I did, and that breath brought me close enough to the surface that I could level off horizontally and float. My head was almost completely under, and I was swallowing water by the bucket full. I was coughing and wheezing, all the while thinking only one thing over and over. *Float. Just float. The waves are strong and they will take you back to shore. Breathe and float, and you will live.*

I have no idea how many minutes passed as I lay on my back bobbing in the waves. I had virtually no oxygen left in my lungs. When I finally lifted my head and looked toward shore, I didn't see it anywhere. I was incredibly disoriented and short on oxygen, and I thought for a moment I was done for. But I had actually been turned around in the process of floating and tossing about in the waves, and the shore was behind me, only about five feet away. I put my feet down and felt the tear of a hard broken shell into my toe, and then collapsed onto the rough sand, still in about two feet of water.

I just sat there kneeling and sobbing for a few minutes, and I threw up buckets of sea water. Then I suddenly realized—*I had left*

Mark. My friend had been even farther out than I was, and he was not a strong swimmer. I looked over to my right about three hundred feet down the shoreline, and there I saw him, lying on his back, sobbing. I picked myself up and trudged over to my friend, and I grabbed him by the arm and helped him over to a piece of driftwood. We both sat there for awhile, gasping for air, speechless.

Mark broke the silence first. "What the fuck were we thinking?" Then he just looked at me and started to laugh hysterically. "Yeah," I said, "I was so scared." His laughter stopped as suddenly as it had started. "I wasn't," he said. He was looking right at me. "I wasn't scared at all. It was strange, like I had no fear."

Three years later, I was in graduate school, and I got a call on my answering machine. "Tim, I'm not sure how…" said the voice. Then, after a long pause, "Mark is dead. He killed himself yesterday." He had been married and divorced, started a business that failed, and his severe dyslexia proved to be too challenging without a partner to assist him. As I stood at his funeral next to his sobbing ex-wife, one thought circled through my head over and over. *He had no fear that day in the water. He did not fear death. And he knew it. He wasn't scared of death, but that lack of fear surprised him, and he never forgot it. He did not fear death.*

That was when I realized the power of fear, both too much and too little. A little fear is a very good thing, because it has a regulating effect on daily life. It causes you to *not* enter the water when the surf is high, and it causes you to stay alert and in tune with your instincts (*just float and you will stay alive*) during a critical life or death situation. On the other hand, a lack of any fear is a terrible thing. With no fear of death, there is no reason to live. With no fear of consequences, there are no self-imposed restrictions on otherwise debatable actions.

I once read a news article about a little girl with no sense of pain. She had an extremely rare nerve disorder which prevented any sensations of pain from reaching her brain. When she was going through teething, she would chew her own tongue until it bled, and she would chew her fingers almost to the bone. She touched a hot stove, and did not recoil. In fact, she left her hand on the burner, until her hand was a smoldering mass of charred flesh. When her parents found her, she was looking at her hand with an inquisitive look, not understanding what everyone was so upset about. This girl had no fear of anything, and she would visit the emergency room at least a couple of times per month. A little fear goes a long way.

Too much fear is the opposite extreme, and it is equally as debilitating. Too much fear can reduce life to a perceived struggle of daily survival. It can keep a person locked in their house for fear of the unknown. And after a long enough period of overemphasized fear, people will sacrifice just about anything to get rid of the constant reminders and associated anxiety. Imagine waking up one day and your knee hurts. You don't know why and you don't think you did anything to it, but it just hurts. It is not at the front of your consciousness, but it is always there, nagging at you from just below the surface. For weeks you hobble around on that knee, and you are ready to go to the doctor or a faith healer or anyone who can make that pain go away, through any means necessary. So the doctor rubs on some lotion, and tells you not to ask him what it is. "It will make the pain go away," he says. "What difference does it make what it is or how it works." When you wake up the next morning, the pain is gone, and you never think about that pain again. Once it is gone, you are happy to be rid of it.

SAFE AND WARM IN THE SUBURBS

The War on Terror is this generation's Cold War, and it is my kids' Cold War. Next year or five years from now, we will be at the point where just about every governmental decision, from budget to civil rights to immigration, will ultimately link back to the single overriding fear of the detonation of a dirty bomb in a major city. Some day soon, I will have to explain to my daughter what a dirty bomb is, and try to convince her that she does not need to worry about it—just as my parents assured me that reason would ultimately prevail, and the button would never be pressed to launch the intercontinental ballistic missiles. Eventually, I will have to explain biological weapons to my son. I will have to try to convince him, and myself, that our armies and his childhood friends are going into other countries to try to find the ingredients of these devices before they are used against us. I will have to explain to my kids that tomorrow, they will be safe. Tomorrow, nobody will detonate a dirty bomb on the street outside our house in the suburbs.

At the same time, I will have to listen quietly during meeting breaks at work, as moms and dads talk about new fears, and new ways to protect their children. I will bite my tongue to keep my job, and for the sake of my family. Talking about political topics in politically mixed company is frowned upon at work, for good reason. We live in a country that is deeply divided, and political discussions tend to get heated quickly.

So while I listen intently to poorly-justified tales of suburban fear, I will writhe and twist inside, because I know the truth. American suburbanites are some of the safest people in the civilized world, and yet they are eating themselves from the inside out with fear. The last thing suburban America needed was something else to be afraid of, but like an elephant in the room, along came terrorism. Just in time for the 21st century, we have a whole new level of fear which can be poked and prodded and tweaked and *consumed*. Fear drives absolutely *everything* in suburbia, and the end result is usually some form of consumption.

Suburbanites love the evening news. Everyone I know watches the news religiously. From watching the news, with its dramatic lead-in music and colorful imagery, they have learned that there are actually a lot of things to fear in suburban America. Who knew?

Kids that go to school can be shot by their classmates. The odds may be astronomical but it can happen. Kids can be abducted on their way to school, and kids can be coerced by their friends into taking drugs. Crash tests have shown that sport utility vehicles have a higher bumper height than economy cars and mini SUVs, and this can result in catastrophic damage to the smaller vehicle in a crash. Tap water contains germs and chemicals, and e-coli can live on improperly cleaned kitchen counters. Recently, I actually saw a story on the evening news describing how a cell phone can explode and burn the user's face.

Consumption is the standard response from suburban America to all of these irrational fears. We perceive that the safest way to get the kids to school is to drive them in the car. We buy bigger and bigger vehicles, like a twisted fight-or-flight mechanism to our fear of car accidents. After all, a big SUV exchanges our safety as a trade off for the safety of others, and that is just fine with us. Public schools are filled with troublemakers whose parents probably own lots of loaded guns, so we send our kids to expensive private schools. We will work long hours or an extra job, because we fear our children will not succeed without the finest schools, and those schools are not cheap. Our kids will miss us, but it is for their own good. The water from the tap will make us sick, so we need to buy bottled water, which will keep us safe from contaminants. The bigger the size of our yard, the safer we will be. The higher the fence between our yards, the more privacy we will retain. Basic human connections take a back seat to our privacy. The more blinds on our windows the better. Our doors are always locked at night. We check them two or three times before we turn off the lights. When we are walking upstairs to go to bed, we take one last look out the window just to make sure nobody is milling around outside. If we can afford to live in a gated community, we will do it, and we will ask the guard on our way in to keep an extra careful eye out tonight, because there is a full moon. The loonies come out when there is a full moon, and we need to know that out kids are safe from the loonies. Bush is strong on security so we will put W '04 bumper stickers on the back of our SUVs with the high bumpers and the airbags. Kerry thinks terrorism could get to a point where it is considered just a "nuisance" for America. What an idiot. How could anything this important ever be just a nuisance? Everybody knows there is a lot to be afraid of, and we need to go get them before they get us.

"Terrorism" in Iraq or the threat of terrorism at home is one of the top stories on the news every night, and at least a third of all the other stories have some reference to increased security or September 11th. Terrorism is front and center, every day, on every mainstream media news broadcast. Over forty-three thousand people died in car accidents in 2003, but rarely if ever does a car accident lead the news. If it is even mentioned, it will be toward the end of the broadcast, and there will be more images of the flashing lights of the emergency vehicles than of the mangled cars. We are directly warned of the dangers of getting behind the wheel almost nightly, but we don't think twice about running a few errands. Yet when it comes to terrorism and middle-eastern Muslims sitting in their living rooms half a world away, suburbanites are *terrified*. Even an indirect reference to a dirty bomb is enough to make a Security Mom shudder in fear for her children.

A nationwide poll from December 2004 showed that almost half of all Americans believe that the civil rights of Muslims should be restricted in some way in the name of national security. The Cornell University survey also showed that twenty-seven percent of Americans believed that Muslim Americans should be required to register their address with the government. Respondents who regularly watched network news found themselves much more likely to support such restrictions. This is no surprise, since fear is pounded home night after night in so many ways. Even a news story about the World Series quickly turns to the focus on extra security precautions and pat downs.

During World War II, Hitler bombed London for fifty-seven consecutive days. Day and night the bombs fell in what became known as "The London Blitz." Fear was rampant in London. There were underground shelters across the city that held up to 177,000 people. During the air raids, over twenty-nine thousand civilians were killed in the city. But even in this environment of unrelenting fear, the British Parliament did not convene to pass laws to take away basic freedoms. They did not even draft legislation in the middle of the night due to the emergency conditions surrounding them. How irresponsible of them. Why weren't they thinking about the children?

WINNING OVER THE SECURITY MOMS

On October 11, one month after the terrorist attack in 2001, the FBI warned of imminent terrorist attacks in the United States "in the next several days." On October 29, 2001, the Administration warned of plans to strike the United States "in the next week." On December 3, 2001, Homeland Security Director Tom Ridge warned of terrorist strikes related to the Muslim religious festival of Ramadan. In all three instances, there were obviously no attacks.

On January 17, 2002, we were warned by Attorney General John Ashcroft that suicide attacks may be forthcoming, based on video tapes found in Afghanistan. No specifics were mentioned in the tapes. On February 11, 2002, the FBI warned there was a threat of "imminent attacks on the United States." On May 21, the FBI warned of imminent threat of "attacks against the Brooklyn Bridge and the Statue of Liberty." In March, 2002, Ridge revealed the new color-coded terror warning system. And on September 10, the National Terror Alert Level was raised to Orange on the premise that new attacks were coming on the anniversary of September 11th. In all of these cases, nothing materialized.

On February 8, 2003, the Alert Level was changed to Orange, on the basis of "evidence that terrorists would attack American hotels and apartment buildings." On March 17, 2003, the Alert Level was again raised to Orange, with no specific reason given. On March 18, 2003, we were warned that an attack by al Qaeda agents was imminent, targeted at a nuclear plant in Arizona. And on December 21, 2003, Ridge raised alert levels again and warned of a serious and imminent threat. In all of these cases, there was more fear than action. They were all untrue.

On April 2, 2004, buses and trains were the new targets. On May 26, 2004, a plane attack was again the modus operandi. On August 1, 2004, there was knowledge of plots against U.S. financial institutions, resulting in a near-police state in Manhattan. The knowledge was later determined to be vague in nature and out-dated by four years. Obviously, none of these warnings materialized.

On November 2, 2004, George W. Bush won re-election to his second term as President of the United States, due in large part to the voting patterns of suburban "Security Moms." After all, they would give up anything to be safe—money, time, and even freedom. Even freedom? Yes. And the security moms are not alone in this willing sacrifice.

LEGISLATING PATRIOTISM

According to Floyd Abrams, a First Amendment specialist, issues of free speech and patriotism often become the subject of debate during times of crisis.

> "Hard times for the first amendment tend to come at very hard times for the country. When we feel threatened, when we feel at peril, the First Amendment or First Amendment values are sometimes subordinated to other interests."

The First Amendment did indeed come under fire just weeks after the September 11th terrorist attack. Initially, the attack came in the form of the Anti-Terrorism Act of 2001, a far-reaching piece of legislation designed to "protect" America against "terrorism." A few modifications were hastily made, including sunset provisions on some of the provisions, but the majority of the bill was left intact as written. The final version of the bill was ironically renamed to the USA Patriot Act (Uniting and Strengthening America by Providing Appropriate Tools Required to Intercept and Obstruct Terrorism). The Patriot Act was intended to eliminate checks and balances (i.e. "Red Tape") in favor of increased easy bake surveillance and investigative powers. The majority of the checks and balances that were removed were originally in place not to introduce red tape, but to safeguard civil liberties.

Given the timing of the bill's introduction, Ashcroft gave congress only one week to get the bill passed. In doing so, he warned that additional terrorist attacks were pending, and Congress would be held directly accountable if the legislation was not in place. Predictably, the final version of the bill was printed in the middle of the night, and passed the following day, with a vote of 99-1. Senator Russ Feingold of Wisconsin cast the only dissenting vote. The House passed the bill 357 to 66. President Bush signed it into law on October 26, 2001, just forty-five days after September 11th.

In his *Statement on the Anti-Terrorism Bill* from October 25th, Feingold said the following:

> "We all also had our own initial reactions, and my first and most powerful emotion was a solemn resolve to stop these terrorists. And that remains my principal reaction to these events. But I also quickly realized that two cautions were necessary, and I raised them on the Senate floor the day after the attacks.
>
> The first caution was that we must continue to respect our Constitution and protect our civil liberties in the wake of the

attacks. As the chairman of the Constitution Subcommittee of the Judiciary Committee, I recognize that this is a different world with different technologies, different issues, and different threats. Yet we must examine every item that is proposed in response to these events to be sure we are not rewarding these terrorists and weakening ourselves by giving up the cherished freedoms that they seek to destroy.

The second caution I issued was a warning against the mistreatment of Arab Americans, Muslim Americans, South Asians, or others in this country. Already, one day after the attacks, we were hearing news reports that misguided anger against people of these backgrounds had led to harassment, violence, and even death."

In the group of our one hundred United States Senators, only one of them kept his head in the face of incredible pressure and overriding fear. Only one Senator had the courage to say that if we give up our rights, then the terrorists have won. If we take away that which we hold most dear, our freedoms, then we have nothing left to protect. If we remove checks and balances that have been in place for over two hundred years, and if we give up what makes us so proud to be Americans in the name of some temporary fear, then we do not deserve our own Bill of Rights.

Benjamin Franklin agreed, when he said, "They that can give up essential liberty to obtain a little temporary safety deserve neither liberty nor safety."

But Franklin's quote assumes that the victims of the loss of essential liberty obtain a little temporary safety. In the case of the Patriot Act, the temporary safety part is still open for debate. It seems that the Patriot Act has been more likely to be used to squelch dissent outside Bush's campaign stops and to track down strip club owners, than to actually stop terrorists.

Under Title III of the existing Wiretap Statute, the real-time interception of voice and data communications requires probable cause and a judge's approval. The Patriot Act changes this so that, while a judge's approval is still required, probable cause is not. A government attorney merely needs to certify that "information likely to be obtained by such installation and use is relevant to an ongoing criminal investigation." Interpretation of the actual content of the communication is purely the responsibility of the person or agency requesting the wiretap.

For example, if I write an email to my friends containing certain keywords, and I trigger some kind of FBI email sniffer, I am in big trouble. Previously, under the old legislation, the requesting agency would need to provide evidence to convince a judge that there was probable cause to tap my Internet connection to intercept my emails and other messages. Under the Patriot Act, all they need to do is certify that there is an ongoing criminal investigation of me, based on information triggered from previous emails, and boom—I am tapped. So I can ramble on and on about any random topic containing certain keywords, and every one of my emails will be intercepted and recorded for future reference without my knowledge. In the meantime, if I get a response from friends containing those same keywords, then they could be tapped as well, under the same Patriot Act loophole.

Sections 216 and 220 of the Patriot Act allow for the expansion of jurisdictional authority to authorize search warrants outside of their own district. The net effect of this provision is two-fold. First, it is much easier to find a single court to approve the warrant, regardless of jurisdiction, and it is much harder for the person served by the warrant to object via a court hundreds or thousands of miles away.

The Patriot Act also allows non citizens to be held based on suspicion alone. Suspects charged with no crime can be held indefinitely with only reviews every six months, in the name of preventing terrorism. American citizens suspected of terrorism are also being held without charges, and without access to attorneys. When it comes to law enforcement in the name of fighting terrorism, the Patriot Act clearly denies the guaranteed due process of law.

The most troubling aspect of the Patriot Act is the modified ability to conduct "secret searches" of suspects' property. Section 213 of the Act eliminates the previous requirement to notify the recipient of a search warrant prior to the execution of the search. The official party line on the purpose of this provision is to "speed up" the search process, in cases where the court "finds reasonable cause to believe that providing immediate notification of the execution of the warrant may have an adverse effect." Some of the controversial sections of the Patriot Act, including the "secret search" provision, are limited by a "sunset date" at the end of 2005. But already during the campaign season, Bush began to make the political case for "renewal" of the Patriot Act, which probably means he would like to extend or eliminate the sunset dates. These expiration dates must not be moved.

Evidenced by the dark reality of this provision's actual execution, this feature has been abused nearly every day since the Patriot Act became law. The Justice Department released a report in May 2004, which showed the number of secret searches increasing significantly each year since the arrival of the Patriot Act. The number of approved secret searches in 2001 was nine hundred. In 2002, there were twelve hundred such searches approved. And in 2003, seventeen hundred intelligence cases resulted in secret searches, many of them conducted in the homes of American citizens.

In the 2004 U.S. Senate campaign in Wisconsin, Russ Feingold's competition was a construction executive named Tim Michels. Michels was best known for his "Tough on Terror" campaign platform, which was highlighted by television ads with shadowy middle-eastern looking men stalking around in the woods outside a nuclear power plant. If there was ever a "Fear candidate", it was

Michels. In one of his debates with Feingold, Michels said, "There have been no civil liberty violations via the Patriot Act."

Since the approval of the Patriot Act through the end of 2003, there were 3,800 secret searches approved by courts around the country. 3,800 homes and businesses were ransacked with no knowledge of the individual in question. Were 3,800 terror attacks averted in the last three years? For that matter, did secret searches avert *any* attacks in the last three years? Were 3,800 terrorists captured in these secret searches? No. Therefore, by definition of "emergency", a normal search warrant would have sufficed in 99.9 percent of these cases. If a normal search warrant would have been sufficient, then the use of secret searches is clearly defined as abuse of power. You wanted examples of Patriot Act abuse, Mr. Michels. So there you have them, 3,800 strong.

Feingold firmly stood by his dissenting vote, saying at a commencement ceremony at Beloit College, "There can be little doubt that if we lived in a police state it would be easier to catch terrorists. But that would not be a country in which we would want to live. That would not be a country in which we could, in good conscience, ask our young people to fight and die. In short, that would not be America."

In July 2004, Ashcroft released a report outlining "dozens of cases" of Patriot Act successes. Critics responded by pointing out that the report contained prosecutions on cases involving child pornography and kidnapping, and very little actual terrorism. For example, the Patriot Act was used to prosecute a Madison, Wisconsin man who jammed a police radio with his computer. It was also used to find a kidnapped eighty-eight-year old woman in Wisconsin, by tapping into an Internet Service Provider to find the kidnapper's location. In both of the above examples, there was no terrorist involved. In addition, it is my opinion that these cases would have ended with equal success under existing laws, without the added provisions of the Patriot Act.

THE ANTI-PATRIOTS PROLIFERATE

A strange thing has happened in cities across America since the Patriot Act was passed in 2001. More than three hundred and sixty eight cities and four states have passed resolutions asking congress to change or roll back parts of the Patriot Act that threaten civil rights through unreasonable search and seizure and restrictions on free speech.

From Ground Zero of the "Origin of Fear", even the New York City Council took up a Bill of Rights Resolution in February, 2004. In a written statement, the council said the following:

- ...The protection of civil rights and civil liberties is essential to the well being of a free and democratic society;

- ...There is no inherent conflict between national security and the preservation of liberty—Americans can be both safe and free;

- ...Federal, state and local governments should protect the public from terrorist attacks, such as those that occurred on September 11, 2001, but should do so in a rational and deliberative fashion in order to ensure that security measures enhance the public safety without impairing constitutional rights or infringing on civil liberties;

- ...Certain federal policies adopted since September 11, 2001, including certain provisions in the USA PATRIOT Act and related federal actions unduly infringe upon fundamental rights and liberties;

- ...These new policies include the power to authorize the indefinite incarceration of non-citizens based on mere suspicion of terrorist activity, and the indefinite incarceration of citizens designated as "enemy combatants" without access to counsel or meaningful recourse to the federal courts.

- …The Council of the City of New York opposes requests by federal authorities that, if granted, would cause agencies of the City of New York to exercise powers or cooperate in the exercise of powers in apparent violation of any city ordinance or the laws or Constitution of this State or the United States.

The most compelling opposition to the Patriot Act and its implementation came from the most unlikely of sources, the *9/11 Commission Report*. On page 394, the report states, "The burden of proof for retaining a particular governmental power should be on the executive, to explain (a) that the power actually materially enhances security and (b) that there is adequate supervision of the executive's use of the powers to ensure protection of civil liberties. If the power is granted, there must be adequate guidelines and oversight to properly confine its use." This burden of proof has not been met. There has not been adequate evidence presented to America to prove that our sacrifice of freedom has resulted in temporary safety.

Senator Patrick Leahy agrees that there is insufficient evidence, and he raised this issue in an Oversight Hearing of the Senate Judiciary Committee in June 2004. Speaking directly to Attorney General John Ashcroft, Senator Leahy said, "Mr. Attorney General, I must speak frankly about an issue that has emerged as a basic problem during your tenure. There are two words that succinctly sum up the Justice Department's accountability and its cooperation with congressional oversight on your watch. Those two words are 'sparse,' and 'grudging.' Even those of us who have served through several presidents cannot recall a worse performance record when it comes to responsiveness."

Leahy continued, "Why is oversight important? Beyond the fact that the Constitution prescribes such checks and balances among the three branches of government, proper oversight—with cooperation from Executive agencies—helps make government work better. It also contributes to accountability. How is the Justice Department using all of the tools this Congress has provided in the USA Patriot Act? With the lack of oversight cooperation we have received, and with the secrecy that shrouds several aspects of the law, how would any of us know the real answer to that question, or dozens of other questions on other vital topics?"

Affronting the Real Patriots

Even more offensive than the content of the Patriot Act is the name itself, clearly chosen to play on the overwhelming drenching patriotism that was prevalent throughout America following September 11th. An Act of Patriots. An Act inspired by Patriots, to protect Patriots. A Patriotic Act to support, and an unpatriotic act to oppose. The Patriot Act. Love it or leave it.

The goal of the original Patriots was to free themselves and the American colonies from British oppression. Eventually the persistence and sacrifice of these brave men led to the American Revolution, the Declaration of Independence, the Constitution and the Bill of Rights. But the words "persistence" and "sacrifice" are not sufficient to describe what it took to make the political transition from 1750 to 1800.

A judge's ruling against Irish rebels demonstrated the penalty for treason during the era:

> "You are to be drawn on hurdles to the place of execution, where you are to be hanged by the neck, but not until you are dead; for, while you are still living your bodies are to be taken down, your bowels torn out and burned before your faces, your heads then cut off, and your bodies divided each into four quarters, and your heads and quarters then to be at the King's disposal."

Captain Nathan Hale was hanged as a spy in New York at the age of twenty-one years old. In 1774, Hale spoke to a group gathered in New London, Connecticut, where he was a school teacher and a member of the voluntary militia. "Let us march immediately," he said, "and never lay down our arms until we obtain our independence." It is believed that this was the first time the word independence was used in the modern context. Hale organized the attempted burning of a British frigate, and participated in a number of other revolutionary activities. With his forces in trouble in New York in 1776, General George Washington requested a volunteer to maneuver behind enemy lines and return with valuable information about locations and movements. Hale bravely volunteered. He posed as a Connecticut teacher looking to make a career in New York. But he was captured and falsely blamed for starting a great fire, and he was publicly hanged on an apple tree. Hale's last words were, "I only regret that I have but one life to lose for my country." Nathan Hale was a great American teacher and Patriot, and his name has been smeared and his reputation has been trampled by the Act of October 2001.

Forty-eight year old John Gilbert was killed in the British attack on New Haven, Connecticut on July 5, 1779. He was cultivating his field when the attack began, but he mounted his horse and charged in to fight bravely against his oppressors. During the battle he was overpowered and ordered to dismount from his horse. He refused to leave his mount, so he was shot and stabbed repeatedly with bayonets. John Gilbert was a great American farmer and Patriot. His name has been smeared and his reputation has been trampled by the Act of October 2001.

Thomas Paine came to America from London in 1774, after he was encouraged to move by Benjamin Franklin. Paine became the editor of the *Pennsylvania Magazine* after just a few months, and he became an advocate for the abolition of slavery and the freedom of the colonies. In 1776, Paine wrote what many consider to be the mainstream introduction of the separation movement when he published *Common Sense*. The forty-seven page pamphlet discussed America's independence from England using "nothing more than simple facts, plain arguments, and common sense." Paine served in Washington's army for a short time, and he continued to write. His *Crisis Papers*, written between 1776 and 1783, encouraged the colonists to continue to fight against their oppressors. This was a consistent theme across Paine's writings—freedom from all types of oppression and encouraging expression of one's beliefs. Thomas Paine was a great American writer and Patriot, and his name has been smeared and his reputation has been trampled by the Act of October 2001.

You Don't Need These Anymore Do You?

The Bill of Rights was drafted in the form of ten amendments to the Constitution, which was signed in 1787 in Philadelphia. Many of the original Patriots who signed the Declaration of Independence refused to attend the Constitutional Convention because it failed to contain enough protection of individual liberties. The ten amendments were added by 1789 and ratified in 1791. Many Americans fought and died for these rights between 1791 and 1945, and these rights were once held with high regard by all Americans. But with very little debate, even less appropriate perspective, and a draft printed in the middle of the night, four of the ten amendments from the original Bill of Rights are in limbo, and in serious jeopardy of being phased out altogether. Another amendment is in trouble as well.

The First Amendment used to guarantee freedom of speech, freedom of worship, freedom of the press, freedom of assembly, and freedom to petition the government when citizens are wronged. Not anymore. The Patriot Act takes care of this inconvenience quite thoroughly. Through a redefinition of a term "domestic terrorism" the Patriot Act opens the door for classification of political groups as terrorists. Public speech at a gathering of a political group could also be considered plotting terrorism. The definition of intent is purely at the discretion of the enforcing government body. Once detained, a suspected domestic terrorist can be held indefinitely without charges. Not since the anti-Communist McCarthyism movement in the 1950s has America seen legislation with such a potential for squelching political opposition.

The Fourth Amendment used to protect American citizens against unreasonable search and seizure. Not anymore. The Patriot Act adds exceptions to the Fourth Amendment in the name of pre-empting terrorism on an emergency basis. Unfortunately, the meaning of "emergency" is not well defined, and the number of secret searches requested and conducted has risen substantially each year since the Patriot Act became law.

The Fifth Amendment used to declare that no American citizen shall be held for a crime without indictment, or "be deprived of life, liberty, or property without due process of law." Not anymore. Due process of law is seen as judicial "red tape" in post-September 11th America. Indictments are also no longer required to hold anyone, citizen or non-citizen, in the name of stopping terrorism.

The Sixth Amendment used to guarantee a speedy and public trial with the right to be informed of the facts of the accusation and the right to confront witnesses. Not anymore. Many who are detained under the guidelines of the Patriot Act are never charged with anything. They are held, interrogated, held some more, and released or deported after a variable period of time.

The Fourteenth Amendment used to give all people within the United States (citizens and non-citizens) the right to due process and equal protection. This extends the Fifth Amendment to non-citizens. Not anymore. Thousands of "terrorists" were held for months and even years at Federal detention centers, without being tried for any crimes. The Patriot Act allows this practice, with no recourse for the individual being held. The Seven-Day Rule in the Patriot Act states that an alien can be held and interrogated for up to seven days without any indictment or legal counsel, based on "certification" from the Attorney General. Based on this wording, the Attorney General merely has to point his finger at someone and say "terrorist" or "threat to national security" and the suspect is detained. This action can be taken based on simple hearsay without any proof or evidence.

FREEDOMS LOST—PATRIOT ACT CASE STUDIES

Bio-terrorists in Buffalo

In May 2004, Steve Kurtz awoke to find that his wife was dead from a cardiac arrest. He instinctively called 911. When the police came, they stumbled over some test tubes and Petri dishes that he was using for an art project. That's right, an art project. Kurtz was an art professor at the University of Buffalo, and he was part of an organization called the Critical Art Ensemble. The CAE is a group dedicated to exploring the relationships between art and emerging biotechnologies, and Kurtz was involved in an art experiment using harmless bacteria. Strange? Yes. Terrorism? No!

When the police saw the Petri dishes and the bacteria that was in them, they immediately thought Kurtz was a bio-terrorist, so they called in the Joint Terrorism Task Force. When the agents arrived at his house, all hell broke loose. They closed off his entire block. They impounded the house, his car, his wife's body, his cat, his manuscripts, and his computers. The Buffalo Health Department even condemned the house as a health risk. Weeks later, the Commission for Public Health in New York State tested the bacteria samples from Kurtz's artwork, and announced that there was no public safety threat. Kurtz was allowed to return home and recover his wife's body from the authorities.

The U.S. Biological Weapons Anti-Terrorism Act of 1989 contained a section on bio-terrorism, making it illegal to possess any biological agent, toxin or delivery system with the intent to use as a weapon. Under the Patriot Act, Section 817, proof of intent has been removed. Now, it is simply illegal to possess these things without "prophylactic, protective, bona fide research, or other peaceful purpose."

Apparently art is no longer considered peaceful. A federal grand jury considered bio-terrorism charges against Kurtz and his partners, but eventually issued mail and wire fraud charges. These are charges which are typically used when there are no other charges which can be proven, but the government wants to prosecute to save face. There is a lot of face-saving that needs to occur in the case of Professor Steve Kurtz.

Terrorism in Vegas Flesh Factories?

In October of 2003, the FBI allegedly used provisions of the Patriot Act to investigate strip club owner Michael Galardi and various Las Vegas politicians. The investigation was attempting to find evidence of hidden funds related to bribery from Galardi over his multiple topless clubs in the Vegas area. The FBI issued subpoenas under section 314 of the Patriot Act, that allows investigators to obtain information from financial institutions regarding accounts in their control that are "engaged in or reasonably suspected, based on credible evidence, of engaging in terrorist acts or money laundering activities." Does this section contain a typo? Should it read, "...terrorist acts or (terrorism-related) money laundering activities"? Or was this omission intentional? Regardless, it's clear that the Patriot Act is not just for terrorists anymore.

A Close Match on Fingerprints

On March 11, 2004, bomb blasts rocked train stations across Madrid, Spain. The attack killed one hundred and ninety-one people, and injured another two thousand. Near the scene of the bombing, a blue plastic bag was found and believed to be connected to the attacks. Using fingerprints from the bag, the FBI got involved and found a near match on a thirty-seven year old Muslim lawyer and U.S. citizen from Portland, Oregon.

During the weeks following the attack, Brandon Mayfield knew something was wrong. He and his family would return home to find the front door bolted and locked, when they never used the bolt under normal circumstances. Blinds on the windows were pulled to unusual heights. He also found a large footprint on the carpet in the living room, a print much too large to belong to any member of the Mayfield family. Nothing was missing, but something was not right.

Mayfield was correct in his suspicions. Section 213 of the Patriot Act was used against Brandon Mayfield. His house had been searched repeatedly using "sneak and peek" warrants, which were considered unconstitutional before October 2001. Additionally, Mayfield was detained on May 6th on a Material Witness warrant, another technique added by the Patriot Act. Because he was detained as a material witness, Mayfield was not charged with any crime. He was simply told that he was being investigated for crimes that were "punishable by death", and he was detained for fourteen days. After his arrest, authorities took Mayfield's computers, safe deposit key, assorted documents and some documents in Spanish, which later turned out to be his son's Spanish homework.

On May 24th, Spanish authorities linked the fingerprints from the blue bag found at the Madrid crime scene to an Algerian national, and Mayfield was released. The FBI later issued a formal apology to Mayfield and his family. In later interviews, Spanish authorities said that they had voiced concerns about the Mayfield evidence in discussions with the FBI, but their concerns were dismissed, and the investigation continued.

The New York Times quoted Carlos Corrales, a commissioner of the Spanish National Police's science division. "It seemed as though they had something against him, and they wanted to involve us."

LOYALTY OATHS AND THE REPUBLICAN NATIONAL CONVENTION

At campaign stops around America in 2004, the Bush-Cheney campaign practiced a Republicans-only policy of attendance. People who came to hear Bush or Cheney speak were not allowed to enter until after they completed an endorsement form. The form required the name, address and job title of each attendee, including the statement, "I, _____, do hereby endorse George W. Bush for re-election as President of the United States." Even though these men are elected officials, an American citizen must vow to support them to hear them campaign. The small print underneath the signature line states, "In signing the above endorsement you are consenting to the use and release of your name by Bush-Cheney as an endorser of President Bush."

Numerous attempts were made to bypass the system, but most of them resulted in quick expulsion and usually arrest. A West Virginia woman, who worked for FEMA, was led away in handcuffs from a July 4th Presidential visit to Charleston. The woman, who eventually lost her job over the protest, wore a t-shirt which read "Love America, Hate Bush." Although this was billed as a "presidential visit" and not a campaign stop, she was still arrested. Those wearing pro-Bush t-shirts and buttons were left alone.

A husband, wife and daughter were kicked out of a Bush-Cheney campaign event in Michigan for carrying in a t-shirt with a pro-choice logo on it. A campaign worker confiscated the t-shirt and said that no anti-Republican pro-choice paraphernalia was allowed in Bush campaign stops. Later the worker returned to where the family was sitting, and ripped up their tickets before escorting them from the event. A Bush campaign spokeswoman even defended the campaign worker, stating that those who would disrupt campaign activities should be asked to leave.

Three teachers attended a campaign event in Medford, Oregon with t-shirts that read "Protect our civil liberties." They were admittedly testing to see if they could make a statement that was important, but not offensive, at a rally for the President of the United States. They got their answer when they were escorted from the rally and threatened with arrest, based purely on their t-shirts. "We chose this phrase specifically because we didn't think it would be offensive or degrading or obscene," said one of the women. Apparently these teachers were not aware that any kind of free speech is apparently obscene anywhere within five hundred feet of a public Presidential appearance.

At campaign stops and Presidential visits around America during Bush's first term, designated protest areas were cordoned off, usually far from sight of the President or the media. One such situation occurred in Pittsburgh, in 2002. Some protestors held a sign on the side of the road where Bush's procession would pass, when a local police officer approached them and told them that they would have to move to the "free speech zone", since they were protesting. In this particular case, the designated protest area was a fenced in baseball diamond, barely in sight of the Presidential motorcade. After repeatedly ignoring requests to move, one of the protestors smugly suggested that, actually, all of America is a free speech zone. Needless to say, the sign-holder was promptly cuffed and arrested on a charge of disorderly conduct.

Nearly one thousand and eight hundred people were detained in a "temporary" holding facility in the New York harbor during the Republican National Convention. Some of these people were protestors, and others were walking to work, returning from lunch, or delivering pizzas when they were caught in the roundups. The protestors and innocents were kept in "Little Guantanomo on the Hudson" for up to fifty hours in conditions which included asbestos and chemical spills on the floor. There was no place to sit, and they were packed in shoulder to shoulder, back to back. In November 2004, there was a class action law suit filed by many of the detainees against New York City.

Under the right circumstances, even the most peaceful protest is no longer considered free speech, and protestors are routinely treated like animals. This is no surprise, since the Patriot Act has defined a new category of "Domestic Terrorist." To classify an individual as a Domestic Terrorist, Section 802 of the Patriot Act requires only an act "dangerous to human life" that is a violation of criminal laws and meets one of the following subjective criteria:

- Intended to intimidate or coerce a civilian population;

- Intended to influence the policy of a government by intimidation or coercion;

- Intended to affect the conduct of a government by mass destruction, assassination or kidnapping.

Based on this definition, there is a broad new classification of terrorist. Can protests be considered "dangerous to human life"? In certain circumstances, this standard is certainly met. Can the intent of a protest be construed to "intimidate or coerce civilians" or "influence the policy of a government by coercion"? In certain circumstances, this standard is also met. Has the Patriot Act made previously legal protest nebulously illegal?

THE NEXT GENERATION OF PATRIOTS

When the Espionage and Sedition Acts were passed in 1917 and 1918, the First Amendment was seriously crippled. But it only took two years before most of the fear surrounding World War One had subsided, and common sense prevailed in the Congress. By 1921, the vast majority of the limitations incorporated into both Acts were repealed and the Constitution was back in full effect.

Similarly, there was already an effort to retract a portion of the Patriot Act in July 2004, led by a coalition of Democrats and a few Republicans. The bill would have blocked the part of the Patriot Act that deals with access to library reading records of American citizens. When the fifteen minute time limit for the role call expired, Democrats had enough votes to overturn the law, but Republican leaders in the House of Representatives kept the voting open for twenty-three more minutes, as ten additional Republicans were persuaded to change their original votes. The vote failed, 210 to 210, with a majority needed.

In November 2002, the Homeland Security Act passed the Senate. The bill created the new Department of Homeland Security. But, in doing so, it almost continued where the Patriot Act left off in the strangulation of civil liberties and privacy. The original version of the bill contained language about a program called Operation TIPS. As proposed, this program would have created a citizen reporting program designed to turn neighbors, mailmen truck drivers and meter readers into government spies. Described on the Operation TIPS web site, the program would have worked as follows: "Involving one million workers in the pilot stage, [Operation TIPS] will be a national reporting system that allows these workers, whose routines make them well-positioned to recognize unusual events, to report suspicious activity." Fortunately, there was enough objection to this program to leave it out of the Homeland Security Act.

Senator Patrick Leahy said of Operation TIPS, "We also never received a full understanding of how the Administration planned to train Operation TIPS volunteers. The average citizen has little knowledge of law enforcement methods, or of the sort of information that is useful to those working to prevent terrorism. Such a setup could have allowed unscrupulous participants to abuse their new status to place innocent neighbors under undue scrutiny. The number of people who would have abused this opportunity is undoubtedly small, but the damage these relatively few could do would be very real and potentially devastating. In addition, it was crucial that citizen volunteers receive training about the permissible use of race and ethnicity in their evaluation of whether a particular individual's behavior is suspicious, but the Justice Department seemed not to have considered the issue."

In 2003, various draft legislation surfaced under two different names. First came the Domestic Security Enhancement Act of 2003, dubbed "Patriot Act II." Some of the more Orwellian aspects of this draft are as follows:

- *Enhanced secrecy in government.* The bill would allow Freedom of Information Act officers to deny any information request in the name of national security.

- *Insufficient transparency between the public and the industry surrounding its neighborhoods.* According to the Clean Air Act, private companies that work with dangerous chemicals must produce a "worst case scenario" report and submit it to the EPA. Under this legislation, these documents would be restricted under FOIA requests to only specific individuals, citing that the documents could be used as a "roadmap for terrorists."

- *Creation of a "Terrorist Identification Database."* The bill would create a DNA database for anyone classified by the government as a "suspected terrorist." Based on previous precedent, it is not a reach to assume this would also include many anti-war protestors, Muslim lawyers, and even unsympathetic political opponents.

- *Expatriation of Terrorists.* This text would allow an American citizen to be expatriated by the government, by contributing to or participating in an organization deemed "terrorist-related" by the government. Not surprisingly, it is ambiguous as to exactly what causes a group to be defined as "terrorist-related."

In August of 2003, the Patriot Act II was reincarnated as the "Victory Act." Throughout August, Ashcroft toured America, hitting twenty states in ten days to promote the need for the additional safety measures contained in the Victory Act. The Victory Act was billed to focus on "Narco-terrorism", by attempting to establish a link between drug trafficking and terrorism, both financially and logistically. In fact, the Victory Act provides a partial definition of drug-traffickers as terrorists.

The implementation details of the Victory Act also included a modified treatment of "hawala" transactions, a traditional form of unauthorized banking used in Middle Eastern areas that do not have banks. While such a change may indeed cut back on terrorism-related money laundering, it would also create a situation where an Arab in the United States supporting a large family at home would have no available means to transfer them money.

The Victory Act would also continue where the Patriot Act left off in terms of empowering the FBI and local police officers at the expense of local courts and judges. Specifically, the legislation would allow a wiretap order to be obtained on a wireless device from any district court in the country, similar to what the Patriot Act did for search warrants.

In the coming years, due to September 11th and the events that have followed it, we all have a responsibility to retain perspective on the current situation. We are all responsible to keep a close eye on Congressional debate and proposed legislation. Too many people have worked too hard for over two hundred years to fight for the retention of our freedoms, and we should not give them up without a prolonged and vigilant fight.

SITTING IN THE FAMILY SECTION

Recently I heard a fourteen-year old kid call up the Sean Hannity radio show. Somehow he got past the screeners with a phone mix-up, but Hannity kept him on the air anyway because he sounded like a bright young lad with a promising future.

Kid: "Yeah, I wanted to call you to tell you about something that happened at Boy Scouts yesterday."

Hannity: "OK go ahead."

Kid: "I was at Boy Scouts, and it's in a church, and my friend said to me 'I think Kerry should have won'. And my friend Cameron and I were saying that he shouldn't lie because it's a church and lying is not allowed."

Hannity: "Yeah, that's pretty good."

Kid: "So even though we were in a church, this friend says to us, 'There was no connection between Saddam Hussein and Al Qaeda'. He was lying to us, and lying about George Bush, right there in a church, and that's not allowed."

Hannity: "Great story. Thanks. Throughout your life people are going to disagree with you, and you will learn to stand your ground. Good job!"

While listening to this exchange, I had two thoughts. First, "In just four years this kid can vote. God help us." Second, I realized right away that this kid was me at age fourteen.

When I was that age my parents put me up to calling a local sports talk show to criticize the Milwaukee Brewers for not having an alcohol-free Family section at County Stadium.

> **Me:** "Ummm, yeah, my dad, I mean *I* think there should be a no alcohol section at County Stadium. My neighbor went to a game and had a new coat ruined by a guy who spilled his beer on it."

That phone call to the sports talk show came back to haunt me fifteen years later, when I ended up with tickets in the Family section at the new Miller Park. I had to spend most of the game without a beer in my hand. I quickly learned a basic fact of life—baseball just isn't quite the same without a cold one in tow. Just as debate isn't the same without the equal ability for both sides to express facts as they understand them.

I can only hope that in the next four years somebody gives this kid a serious lesson about distinguishing actual reality versus the Red-tinted version—before he ends up sitting in the heart of America that he desired, unable to enjoy the freedoms that he once had, but didn't want anymore. Just like watching a baseball game without a beer in hand. America just would not be the same without the right to debate and disagree, especially during a period of war and conflict.

9

Most of History's Lessons are Never Learned

"There can be little doubt that if we lived in a police state it would be easier to catch terrorists. But that would not be a country in which we would want to live. That would not be a country in which we could, in good conscience, ask our young people to fight and die. In short, that would not be America."
—Senator Russ Feingold

NAPPING THROUGH HISTORY CLASS

I don't know if it was a problem unique to my teachers in elementary school or if I was the norm. But I absolutely despised history class at Hales Corners Lutheran School in Hales Corners, Wisconsin. This class, above all others, was an exercise in sheer memorization, drilling facts and figures and names into our little heads, only to have them brain dumped onto the page a few days later, after which (in most cases) they would be lost forever. I recall very little practical interpretation of history in these classes.

Now, twenty-five years later, I love history. I enjoy researching history and its practical application to modern situations. In short, I have learned that almost nothing we are experiencing is new. It all has precedence in our almost two hundred and thirty years of shared history. What about the fearful sacrifice of Constitutional rights in the name of an overemphasized and temporary feeling of safety? That is not new. How about the use of government-sponsored propaganda to properly frame a military operation? That is absolutely not new.

Maybe I was sleeping when the Alien and Sedition Act was taught. It was a brazen infringement on the First Amendment, passed for a short period of time in the name of perceived safety from the French. Maybe I was daydreaming about girls when the teacher emphasized McCarthyism, and how it was used to round up thousands of innocent Americans to put them in front of a federal inquisition in the name of fear of Communism. Just on the off chance that you too were sleeping or daydreaming in history class when your teachers emphasized lessons to be learned from the less shining moments of American history, I would like to review a few basic facts.

THE ALIEN AND SEDITION ACTS OF 1798

In the 1790s, some Americans were led to believe that the French were planning to cross the Atlantic to destroy the Constitution. People debated rumors that a French invasion force would team up with Thomas Jefferson and James Madison to overthrow the administration of President John Adams. There was also talk of a French guillotine reserved for patriotic Americans. With this backdrop of overcooked fear, President Adams and the Federalists issued legislation that would protect America from the evildoers, while squelching any political speech that was anti-Federalist party.

In the summer of 1798, the United States Congress passed the Alien and Sedition Acts. The Alien Act gave President Adams the ability to deport any non-citizen that he viewed as a threat, and it allowed aliens to be imprisoned indefinitely without specific charges. The Sedition Act prohibited criticism of the federal government. Americans found guilty of sedition faced prison terms of up to five years. This legislation left the First Amendment in shambles, and unconstitutionally put aliens in a position where they were no longer protected by normal judicial checks and balances.

With their overriding fear of the French revolutionary movement, many Americans initially fell into line behind the Alien and Sedition Acts.

What strange public policy to pass laws to *restrict* freedoms in the name of fear. That is just as true today as it was over two hundred years ago. Thomas Jefferson made some memorable remarks after the passage of the legislation.

> "The people were made for a moment to be willing instruments in forging chains for themselves. A little patience, and we shall see the reign of witches pass over, their spells dissolve, and the people, recovering their true sight, restore their government to its true principles. It is true that in the meantime we are suffering deeply in spirit, and incurring the horrors of a war and long oppressions of enormous public debt......If the game runs sometimes against us at home we must have patience till luck turns, and then we shall have an opportunity of winning back the principles we have lost, for this is a game where principles are at stake."

And sure enough, as time passed and the fear abated, people began to realize that the legislation was not being used to protect them from a French invasion. Instead, it was negatively impacting the civil liberties of Americans. A surge of opposition arose from local meetings and petitions were circulated, and there was even talk of secession. Jefferson and James Madison authored the Kentucky and Virginia resolutions, that claimed Congress had overstepped its powers and declared the Alien and Sedition Acts void.

Jefferson was ultimately elected President in 1800, and his Democratic-Republican party won a twenty-four seat majority in the House of Representatives in what was later termed "The Revolution of 1800." Upon taking office, Jefferson immediately pardoned all those convicted under the Sedition Act. In 1800, the American people spoke, and the people chose freedom over fear-based tyranny. Jefferson himself said in 1800, "I have sworn upon the altar of God eternal hostility against every form of tyranny over the mind of man."

The Alien and Sedition Acts were in place for less than two full years. Ultimately, fear of the French did not outweigh the Bill of Rights.

Espionage and Sedition Acts of WWI

Support for the United States' participation in World War I was not always strong. President Woodrow Wilson was able to keep America out of the first part of the war, and this played a part in winning him a second term in the 1916 election. In fact, Wilson's campaign slogan during the 1916 campaign was, "He kept us out of war."

However, in early 1917, the Germans began to engage in unrestricted submarine warfare. After Wilson broke off relations with Germany, U.S. boats were attacked five times by German U-boats. Finally, in April of 1917, Wilson asked Congress for approval to take the U.S. to war against Germany, and both the House and the Senate strongly approved.

Shortly after the start of the U.S. involvement, the Committee on Public Information (CPI) was formed. CPI was run by former muckraker journalist George Creel. The stated intent of the CPI was to provide an accurate portrayal of wartime events, in order to avoid the rumor and speculation from the newspaper reporting of events. Instead, Creel turned the CPI into a propaganda machine. In the process, the CPI worked hard to discredit any version of information that conflicted with the official CPI version of events.

In his 1920 book, *How We Advertised America*, Creel wrote about the techniques used to win the hearts and minds of American families.

> "The war was not fought in France alone. Back of the firing-line, back of armies and navies, back of the great supply-depots, another struggle waged with the same intensity and with almost equal significance attaching to its victories and defeats. It was the fight for the *minds* of men, for the 'conquest of their convictions,' and the battle-line ran through every home in every country.
>
> There was no part of the great war machinery that we did not touch, no medium of appeal that we did not employ. The printed word, the spoken word, the motion picture, the telegraph, the cable, the wireless, the poster, the sign-board—all these were used in our campaign to make our own people and all other peoples understand the causes that compelled America to take arms. All that was fine and ardent in the civilian population came at our call until more than one hundred and fifty thousand men and women were devoting highly specialized abilities to the work of the Committee, as faithful and devoted in their service as though they wore the khaki."

Under the immense propaganda weight of the CPI marketing juggernaut, Congress passed two laws with free speech implications that make the Patriot Act look tame by comparison. In 1917, the Espionage Act made it illegal for a person to convey false reports or make false statements with the intent to interfere with the success of U.S. army or naval forces, or with the intent to aid the enemy. There are a number of problems with this text. First, the law requires proof of intent, which is difficult to prove beyond individual opinion, especially when it comes to matters of reporting war events in the age before any significant form of mass communication.

The Sedition Act of 1918 amended the Espionage Act in a truly shocking manner. The Sedition Act made it a crime to speak out in any way, no matter how subtle or harmless, against the U.S. government, flag, or armed forces. To add insult to injury, the Sedition Act also empowered local postmasters to deny mail to any war dissenters, with the sole approval of the Postmaster General. President Wilson's Postmaster General did not hesitate to comply, stopping delivery of all sorts of mailings, classifying them as radical or dissenting.

Part of the Sedition Act text reads as follows:

> "Whoever when the United States is at war, shall willfully cause or attempt to cause, or incite or attempt to incite, insubordination, disloyalty, mutiny, or refusal of duty, in the military or naval forces of the United States, or shall willfully obstruct or attempt to obstruct the recruiting or enlistment services of the United States, and whoever, when the United States is at war, shall willfully utter, print, write or publish any disloyal, profane, scurrilous, or abusive language about the form of government of the United States or the Constitution of the United States, or the military or naval forces of the United States, or the flag of the United States, or the uniform of the Army or Navy of the United States into contempt, scorn, contumely, or disrepute, or shall willfully utter, print, write, or publish any language intended to incite, provoke, or encourage resistance to the United States…shall be punished by a fine of not more than $10,000 or the imprisonment for not more than twenty years, or both."

By 1921, the war had been over for three years, and the country began to return to its senses. In 1921, both the Espionage Act and Sedition Act were repealed by Congress. But they were not repealed in time to stop one thousand and five hundred American citizens from being charged with expressing an opinion that the government did not agree with, in clear violation of the First Amendment to the Constitution.

Rose Pastor Stokes was an immigrant who was born in Russia, and moved to London before coming to the United States. She lived in Cleveland, Ohio and worked in a cigar factory. After her marriage to New York millionaire James Phelps Stokes in 1905, she became actively involved in trying to keep the United States out of World War One. Rose was arrested and charged under the Espionage Act in 1917, after writing a letter to the Kansas City Star which read, in part, "no government which is for the [war] profiteers can also be for the people, and I am for the people while the government is for the [war] profiteers." Rose spent ten years in prison for that letter to the editor, and gained the dubious distinction of the longest prison sentence in American history for exercising her First Amendment right to free speech.

Eugene Debs, a prominent Socialist leader in the early 20th Century, defended Stokes in speeches across the country, saying, "If she is guilty for the brave part she has taken in this testing time of human souls I would not be cowardly enough to plead my innocence. And if she ought to be sent to the penitentiary for ten years, so ought I without a doubt." And indeed, Debs was also sentenced to ten years in prison for an academic speech he gave on the economic benefits of war for corporations. He did ask for it, after all. When the law was repealed in 1921, Debs was pardoned by President Warren Harding.

Temporary Insanity for Temporary Safety

In the early 1950s, the book *Robin Hood* was banned from school bookshelves, for its "Communist" principles of robbing from the rich and giving to the poor. This succinctly represents the insanity surrounding the eight years from 1948 to 1956 in America.

Following World War Two, America's focus turned to Communist sympathizers within the United States. The House Committee on Un-American Activities became a permanent committee in 1946. The committee's job was to "investigate suspected threats of subversion or propaganda that attacks the form of government guaranteed in our Constitution." In 1947, under fear of Soviet infiltration of the United States government and society in general, President Truman ordered background checks on every public employee. Wisconsin Republican Senator Joe McCarthy saw his window of opportunity and took it. In a 1950 speech, McCarthy produced a list of two hundred and five suspected Communist party loyalists within the State Department. There was such a media frenzy following McCarthy's speech, that by 1951, the language of proof to dismiss a federal employee was simply "reasonable doubt" as to their loyalty, with any anonymous person as an accuser.

Hollywood, in particular, came under intense fire from the House Committee on Un-American Activities. Included in the indictments were the so-called "Hollywood Ten", a group of ten screenwriters and directors, who had been flagged by another witness as having some connection to the Communist party. All ten of them got together and agreed not to cooperate, citing First Amendment violations in the process. Needless to say, all ten of them were locked up for refusing to answer any questions, and they served between six months and one year in prison for Contempt of Court. In addition, they were "blacklisted" by Hollywood producers, who would not allow them to participate in any movie-making activities until they were cleared of any charges.

In 1950, Maine Republican Margaret Chase Smith spoke out against the witch-hunt practices of McCarthyism, in a speech on the Senate floor. She stated that the basic principles of being an

American were the right to criticize, the right to hold unpopular beliefs, the right to protest, and the right of independent thought.

> "I think that it is high time that we remembered that we have sworn to uphold and defend the Constitution. I think that it is high time that we remembered; that the Constitution, as amended, speaks not only of the freedom of speech but also of trial by jury instead of trial by accusation.
>
> Whether it be a criminal prosecution in court or a character prosecution in the Senate, there is little practical distinction when the life of a person has been ruined."

Finally, in 1954, McCarthy's investigations into the suspected Communists in the United States Army finally took the investigation too far. At one point in the questioning, the chief attorney for the Army, Joseph Welch, issued the famous statement, "Have you no sense of decency, sir, at long last? Have you left no sense of decency?" The media also began to run stories about the frequent lack of evidence behind McCarthy's accusations. These incidents, combined with the media's willingness to put the hearings on television, eventually ended the era of McCarthyism. Americans finally came to the conclusion that witch-hunting for Communists among innocent American citizens was not the best way to keep America free from Communist influence. Such was the atmosphere of fear in our country, that it took nearly ten years and endless questioning of American citizens before the media stepped up to the plate to defend those under fire.

FASCISM IN THE UNITED STATES?

There are many definitions of Fascism. The Fascism that I understand is the opposite of Communism. In Communism, the State owns the means of production. In Fascism, the Means of Production own the State. Mussolini said, "Fascism should more properly be called Corporatism, since it is the merger of state and corporate power."

Fascism is indeed an undesirable form of government, but not for every entity in the society. Most corporations and media outlets thrive under Fascism. In a fascist state, the corporate-controlled and sometimes government-controlled media controls the flow of information. There is an overwhelming sense of "at all costs" patriotism, which can morph into all out nationalism. This love of nation can include excessive public display of images of the nation's leader. The love it or leave it mentality increases among the media and supporters of the leadership. A single unifying enemy is chosen, and all focus is put on that enemy, usually with racist motivations. At the same time, academics, journalists and other thinkers are vilified, in favor of encouraging blind support for whatever ill-conceived notions come through a media mostly dominated by government or corporate sponsored propaganda. We fought against six countries (Germany, Italy, Japan, Hungary, Romania and Bulgaria) which practiced some form of Fascism during World War II.

Using the above description as evidence, I believe our nation is nearing the jump off point between Democracy and Fascism. Attempting to prove a broad statement like this is difficult. All of the symptoms are present if we just take the time to try to notice them and piece them together into a logical conclusion. The Nazis used what they called the "Salami Tactic" to implement Fascism, which was used to minimize dissent and influence the citizens' thinking. The principle behind the Salami Tactic is to take civil rights and freedoms away in such thinly sliced pieces, that most people do not notice them slipping away. By the time the salami is completely gone, people will not realize anything has changed at all, when in fact nearly everything is different.

I am afraid that we are currently slipping into what might be best described as a soft Fascist state, where we maintain a façade of an actual Democracy. We still have the appearance of free press, political parties, right to sue, rule of law, and some free speech. But, is all of this window dressing, while the government continues to do pretty much whatever it wants regardless of the desires of the constituents?

To me, an analysis of Fascism does not necessarily need to go from the top down, from the leadership to the constituents. Rather, it can start with the chicken or the egg. In the case of America 2004, the Fascism I am witnessing almost seems to be self-motivated on the part of many American citizens. Rather than engage in critical thinking, they would prefer to use the media as a crutch for all of their information, and interpretation of that information. This is fascist. Rather than approach the War on Terror with common sense, appropriate perspective and Christian compassion, many people would like to see a "kill first, ask questions later" strategy. This serves to unite most Americans with strong nationalism against a common enemy, but this might also represent the beginnings of Fascism.

This is not the first time in our history that the possibility of an American form of Fascism has been discussed or even accused. In 1932, during the Great Depression, President Roosevelt (FDR) promised "a New Deal for the American people." This New Deal would regulate corporations, regulate the stock market, and empower workers and farmers to attempt to return their confidence in the economy. In many ways, Roosevelt's New Deal was the start of modern Liberal economic policies.

Of course, corporations and Wall Street were not big supporters of FDR or the New Deal. Some of the country's wealthiest industrialists formed a group called the American Liberty League in 1934 to combat FDR's policies, using donations of more than thirty-six billion dollars. Primary contributors were U.S. Steel, Chase National Bank, Goodyear Tire, the duPont family (duPont, General Motors), and Standard Oil. Social Security started during the New Deal, and was labeled by the American Liberty League as "the end of

Democracy." The American Liberty League believed, above all else, that Nazi-style Fascism was the way out of economic depression. The organization even distributed fifty million copies of Nazi pamphlets through a distribution network of twenty-six colleges and fifteen subsidiary organizations nationwide.

In 1936, economist Lawrence Dennis published a book called *The Coming American Fascism.* In his book, Dennis said that a form of economic Fascism in America would focus on "national spirit" to fuel "the enterprises of public welfare and social control." Of course, Dennis meant public welfare as defined by the state, which would almost certainly conflict with public welfare as defined by the public. However, Dennis recognized the biggest problem with Fascism in America, citing difficulties with "liberal norms of law or Constitutional guarantees of private rights." He also boasted that those who followed the policies of FDR and the New Deal would become the "laughing stock of their own countrymen." Is Rush Limbaugh related to this guy?

During World War Two, the New York Times asked Vice-President Henry Wallace to answer some questions for them. "What is a fascist? How many fascists have we? How dangerous are they?" On April 9, 1944, Wallace's answer was published.

> "The really dangerous American fascist is the man who wants to do in the United States in an American way what Hitler did in Germany in a Prussian way. The American fascist would prefer not to use violence. His method is to poison the channels of public information. With a fascist the problem is never how best to prevent the truth to the public, but how best to use the news to deceive the public into giving the fascist and his group more money or more power.
>
> Democracy, to crush Fascism internally, must...develop the ability to keep people fully employed and at the same time balance the budget. It must put human beings first and dollars

second. It must appeal to reason and decency and not to violence and deceit. We must not tolerate oppressive government or industrial oligarchy in the form of monopolies and cartels."

It seems that there is an identifiable pattern in 20th Century world history. Following a stock market crash accompanied by a depression or recession, countries have a tendency to be drawn to the siren's sweet lure of Fascism. It is actually somewhat understandable. In a period of economic instability, Fascism offers comfortable, ready-made opinions on every channel, a common enemy to vilify together around the campfire, and economic safety through empowerment of the Corporation. During the 1930s and 1940s, Fascism in America was rebuffed by leaders with fortitude; even during a time of economic and global instability, while many countries, including Italy, Japan and Germany, slipped into Fascist states. FDR bravely chose empowerment of the individual over empowerment of the corporation, and his plan worked for over fifty years. Today we may not be so fortunate to have the visionary leadership to avoid the pitfalls of corporate-driven government.

For the sake of argument, let me use an example from modern political discourse. President Bush's famous "Ownership Society" is a code word for Fascism. To own, you need to consume. And what will you own? Things. All kinds of things. Property. Stocks. Bonds. And when you own these new things, you will want to support those things so they do not drop in value. How does one support Property, Stocks, and Bonds? By supporting Corporations and Government. Corporatism is a clear side-effect of a true "Ownership Society." Privatizing Social Security is also a code word for Fascism, because it will give all Americans (including those on lower incomes) a sense of "Ownership" in Corporate America. Who will speak out against corporate fraud? Who will raise issues of fairness in employment? Who will support labor unions? Bush says this is good for America. I disagree, because America is not large corporations. America is people.

LOOKING BACK AT THE PRESENT DAY

Someday, the 2004 Presidential Election will be taught in American History class. Kids with hologram-glasses or something not yet imagined, will watch in three or four dimensions as they are "transported" into the audience of a debate between John Kerry and George W. Bush. What will they hear in retrospect? Will they hear the shame of a country driven by intense irrational fear, as it throws away more than two hundred and twenty-eight years of the mostly proud history of freedom? Will the teacher explain to them that this was America's last chance to escape the coming years of Fascism or Corporatism, and it was an opportunity missed? Will these kids of the future sit in their boring history class, and wonder how we could have let it all slip away for some temporary perceived safety?

I look back at the Alien and Sedition Act supporters, and I think, "Shame on you for your cowardice." I look at the circumstances and read the quotes from judges justifying the imprisonment of innocent people exercising their First Amendment rights during World War I, and I think, "Shame on you for imprisoning innocents." I look at the era of Japanese Internment and McCarthyism, and I think, "Shame on you for so many cowardly wrongdoings." Then I look to my own Red acquaintances, and I cannot help but wonder, "What will future school kids think of you, for your brazen support of the sacrifice of liberties in the name of escaping from your irrational suburban fear of everything, and yet nothing?" Will the name of the History book's chapter on the 2004 election be called, "Death by Silence"?

I am afraid of the sheer volume of otherwise intelligent people who simply follow President Bush, Rush Limbaugh, and Ann Coulter blindly, with undying trust and almost God-like adoration. When I discuss issues with these people, I hear nothing but talking points. If I use an analogy, I get a talking point straight from Limbaugh. If I ask a follow-up question, I get a talking point from

Coulter that has nothing to do with the follow-up question. Then, if all else fails, I get "War on Terror" or "They started it." Will these Americans be looked at as accomplices by future history students, as we look with confusion at many German and Italian citizens from the 1930s and 1940s?

I am afraid of the hatred that comes back at me from my own friends for expressing contrary opinions. This response has been conditioned, by talk radio, television news, and President Bush himself. Just think of that. Hate as a conditioned defense mechanism! Like a society of caring Christian rotweillers, or mutated Pavlov's dogs bred to attack every Liberal mailman who rings a bell of fact and starts to approach with an attempt to deliver a message.

I am afraid of the level of nationalism in America. This sounds strange, but it is based in a legitimate concern. I have not seen this level of overt nationalism in my lifetime. Flags are everywhere, and so are ribbons on the backs of cars. Patriotism by itself is fine, but using raw love of country to irrationally justify otherwise immoral or unjust actions by the country's government is a fascistic action. I support the troops, but not unconditionally. I do not support the war in Iraq or the strategy of the current War on Terror, and I am an extremely patriotic American.

I am not a jingoistic nationalist when it comes to the actions of my country's government. Blind faith in bad government is not patriotism. But for many people, the love of America and the unlimited support for actions of its government *are not* distinguishable. So with these distinctions in mind, is there such a thing as too much patriotism?

"I don't know the answer to that, but I do think that we'll know when there's too much patriotism," said Roger Rosenblatt, author of *Where We Stand, 30 Reasons for Loving Our Country*. "I really trust people to work out balances in their lives, to have a kind of sense of things. Certainly, we'd know there's too much patriotism if it becomes simple minded and jingoistic."

I am afraid for Muslim-Americans, and not afraid *of* them. Hatred of Muslims is on the rise. I fear that internment camps will be next—just ask Japanese-Americans about those. Many Muslims are already being held without charges, and nobody seems to care. Nearly half of all Americans think that Muslims should have restricted rights. This is what Hitler did to the Jews, in order to create a common enemy and unite the people behind his every move. It worked then, and it is working now. Think about it.

I am afraid of the influence that corporations and wealthy executives have on American government. The amount of money spent on lobbyists every year is staggering. The disparity between CEO pay and the average worker's pay is similarly hard to comprehend. The biggest beneficiaries of the War on Terror are American corporations and the old school banking families. This is a recipe for never-ending war, and the eventual bankruptcy of America, driven by fear of a common, yet strangely hard-to-define enemy.

In researching the characteristics of Fascism, I have realized that I am afraid after all. Only, I am not afraid of Muslims. I am not afraid of dirty bombs and model airplanes with bio-chemical agents and laser beams aimed at pilots. In this age of irrational fear, I am actually now only afraid of one thing: My own government.

10

On the Front Lines of Class Warfare

"Pale Death with impartial tread beats at the poor man's cottage door and at the palaces of kings."
—Horace, *Odes*

"In a Democracy the poor will have more power than the rich, because there are more of them, and the will of the majority is supreme."
—Aristotle

THRIVING IN MIDDLE AMERICA

When I was young, my family was economically situated smack dab in the middle of the suburban middle class. My father was a teacher and my mother stayed at home, with my older sister and me. He worked so hard, spending hours every night after school on lesson preparation, and working various other jobs during every available minute during summer vacations. Despite all of this hard work, money was tight, and there were not a lot of non-essential items in our home. During my childhood, I was well cared for, and someone was always there for me. However, looking at the harsh economic reality of life in the "middle class", and contrasting it to larger economic and voting trends, there is a valuable lesson to be learned.

We had food, but it was often spam and peanut butter and jelly sandwiches. Yes, I ate spam many times as a child. We had clothes, but each school year I was allowed two pairs of pants and two shirts. This usually resulted in repeatedly wearing the same three or four outfits to school, all year round, regardless of the weather, like short sleeve shirts in January. There was no choice in the matter.

Our vacuum cleaner was so old—I think it was inherited—and at least ten years past its effective life span by the time I was born. You could place a small scrap of paper on the carpet, and run that vacuum over it fifteen times, and it would still not pick up the scrap. When it was finally sucked up, you could turn the base upside down and see the piece of paper stuck in the turning bristles. Each purchase, no matter how small, was carefully scripted into a budget which included a small amount for food for the week, the house and car payment, insurance premiums, utility bills, and not much else. We were not poor, but we did not have much outside of basic necessities. We had no shower, only a bathtub. We had a television, but the knob broke off and the channels had to be changed with a wrench.

My family owned one car for most of my early childhood, and it was always the cheapest straight off the assembly line Chevrolet, with absolutely no extras. Every eight years the car would be swapped out for another base model. My mother finally got a car, and it was a used Ford Pinto. One year, my dad upgraded the next generation Chevy to add a sunroof, and I thought we were really living the dream. When I entered high school, my mom got a job working at a library, and she was allowed to get another car—a Ford Escort.

We took about one family-subsidized vacation per year, and it was usually a car trip to a run down hotel within a two hour drive from our home. I was so happy to get away from the house, that I would spend hours playing on the rusty, worn out playground equipment in front of the hotel, all the while thinking how wonderful vacations were. I went to Florida four times via plane before the age of eighteen, but these trips were always paid for by my grandfather, a successful entrepreneur and a wonderful man, who died all but penniless in a rather nice government-subsidized care facility in Minnesota.

On Christmas Eve, I would receive plenty of presents, most of which were small tokens. Quantity was definitely emphasized over quality. One year I got a few coloring books, a couple of puzzles, a board game, and a clearance sale electronic game from the local penny store. I would play that game for months and love every minute of it. I was so grateful to have a new toy, and I so seldom got one. My mother used to save grocery money and take me to get a small one dollar toy after every doctor appointment, but I was not really allowed to show it to my dad. I had some toy houses and building blocks, but most of those were handed down from my sister or from other relatives. One Christmas, when I was about eleven, Texas Instruments phased out its TI computer, and we went to buy one at Sears for fifty dollars. This was by far the best Christmas present I ever got. I was still excited about it two years later. Of course, we could not afford a monitor to go with the console, so I had to plug it into the television set, and cram myself onto the floor about two feet from the TV, while cocking my head straight up toward the screen.

Meanwhile, my father boasted with pride about being part of the middle class. He saved money every week, and eventually paid for college for his two kids. He tithed a full recommended ten percent to the local Lutheran church every paycheck, despite his family's direct financial needs. He retired at age sixty, with a nice pension from the State of Wisconsin and full benefits throughout his retirement, but in order to achieve this goal, there were many economic sacrifices. During his teaching career, my father would come home from teaching in the city of Milwaukee, and complain about his students and their families. "They are so poor and lazy," he would say.

"They have nothing, and they are so unmotivated," he would say. Ummm…Dad? Last I checked, you were pretty motivated and we didn't have a whole hell of a lot.

Don't get me wrong, I am eternally grateful to my parents for cutting corners and making it possible for me to attend college. It has benefited me in many ways, made me a more responsible and informed citizen, and raised my own standard of living. But how can it be that a single-income family smack dab on the median line of the middle class needs to resort to such bare necessities to make ends meet? In my opinion, this is the result of many decades of war against the middle class. In many ways, it is a self-waged war. The very political party that most perpetuated this not quite visible war of the classes was elected year after year by the same people who were repressed by their fiscal policies.

Based on income alone, we were considered a middle class family by the standards of the 1970s, but we lived with only basic necessities, just like the families of the kids in my dad's sixth grade classes. Every two years he would go the polls on election day, and he would make me come with him to watch him cast his middle class autovote for whichever Republicans happened to be on the ballot. The first term I ever learned about the voting process was "Straight Party Ticket." It wasn't until I was in my early twenties that I finally realized you did not have to vote for everyone from the same political party.

The teachers union would usually support Democrats for local positions, and my father would rant on and on about this. He even refused to pay the portion of his union dues that went toward political contributions. But in supporting Republicans throughout his life, was my father voting against his own best interest as a member of the middle class? Should members of the middle class have to sacrifice nearly everything in order to pay for college for their kids or avoid working into their seventies? If the living standard for the middle class was limping along in the 70s and 80s, try raising a family of four on a single "middle class" income in 2005.

TAX BREAKS FOR THE MIDDLE CLASS!

Under the leadership of Ronald Reagan in 1981, the biggest tax cut in United States history was passed by Congress. The vast majority of the cut went straight to those making over $200 thousand dollars per year. Reagan said that the cut would allow the "dynamics of the free market" to take hold, as the money flowed from super-wealthy to wealthy, from wealthy to upper middle class, from upper middle class on down. There was also a pittance of a tax cut included for the lower and middle classes, but even one of Reagan's own aides accidentally admitted that this portion of the cut was a "trojan horse", designed to get the bill through Congress.

Combined with extreme defense spending due to the nuclear arms race, the national debt began to balloon, and the following year saw the largest tax increase in United States history—$98 billion dollars. Unfortunately, someone forgot to implement the tax increase for the upper one percent of taxpayers, as their 1981 tax cut was not rolled back as much as the other 99 percent of us, who lost our tax cut entirely by 1984.

Again in 1986, Congress passed a "Tax Reform Act." This bill was marketed by supporters as a way to even out the tax code, to make millionaires pay more of their fair share. This was to be accomplished by forcing more of them to pay the Alternative Minimum Tax (AMT). But, so many loopholes were put into the text that the net result was a massive tax cut for those making over $500 thousand dollars per year. There was even language intended for specific wealthy individuals, such as a targeted tax break for a "taxpayer who incorporated on September 7, 1978, which is engaged in the business of manufacturing dolls and accessories." In other words, Xavier Roberts, the inventor of Cabbage Patch dolls, got his own personal $6 million dollar tax break enacted into law.

The net result in actual tax paid showed tax savings across the board, but what most people missed then, and continue to miss today is this: The vast majority of the cut, in both percentage and dollars, went to those making more than half a million dollars per year. This is true both in dollar terms and percentage terms. A family of four with one income on the lower end of middle class in 1986 received a $69.00 tax cut, which was about six percent of their overall federal tax payment. A wealthy individual making between $500 thousand dollars and one million dollars received a thirty-four percent tax cut. Thirty-four percent!

The standard tax cut argument from the Reds always centers around "Trickle-down Economics." That is, tax cuts to the wealthy trickle down through the economy, resulting in more jobs and better paying jobs for the middle class and the poor. Yada yada yada, blah blah blah. Reagan's own vice-President coined the term so well during the Republican primaries, when he called this theory complete and utter "Voodoo"!

Defense of trickle-down economics is rationalization at its absolute most apathetic, especially because it is so easy to disprove. The result of this type of tax cut, as proven repeatedly, is further exaggeration of the gap between the upper one percent and the rest of society. The wealthy keep more money, sure. But the wealthy also *save* more money. For the most part, this money sits in bank accounts and in stocks and bonds, while the twenty-two year old kid trying to support his new baby by working at Burger King continues to make four dollars an hour (in 1986 money). The owner of the Burger King franchise got a nifty tax cut and built a new house in that gated community down the street, while he gave the hard working kids behind the counter making hamburgers a fifty dollar bonus in their Christmas paychecks. Those in the upper middle class who are fortunate enough to have substantial investments in the stock market also benefit indirectly, but this type of economic theory does little nothing for a family trying to make it on twenty thousand dollars per year. The trickle slows to a drip, and gradually to water vapor, and finally there is nothing left for those who really need it.

If tax cuts for the wealthy really trickled down, there should have been a tremendous surge in the ranks of the middle class a few years following 1981 and 1986, and a surge in incomes for the poor after that, as the tax cuts for the upper one percent trickled down through the rest of the economy. This did not happen. Each time a tax cut of this variety is implemented, the middle class stagnates, the lower class grows, the stock market sometimes rises and the rich get richer.

Between 1980 and 1989, wages for those making under $20,000 per year rose only 1.4 percent, from a median of $8,528 to $8,651. During that same time period, the middle class shrunk from thirty-nine percent of taxpayers to thirty-four percent. The middle class raised their combined salaries an average of two percent per year under Reagan, for a total of forty-four percent during the 1980s. To many Fiscal Conservatives, this period of steady monetary growth for the middle class confirmed the modern theory of supply-side economics—Cut taxes and raise government spending (preferably defense spending in the case of both Reagan and Bush) to stimulate the economy.

However, during this same decade, combined salaries for millionaires rose a total of 2,184 percent! So the pattern is consistent. A small increase for the middle class is used to rationalize an entire fiscal policy, while the massive benefits for the upper class are marginalized or ignored entirely.

FOLLOWING IN REAGAN'S FOOTSTEPS

History does indeed repeat itself—usually more than once. The tax cuts signed into law by President Bush in May 2003 mirror the tax cuts of 1981 and 1986 in a remarkably similar fashion. According to

Citizens for Tax Justice, sixty-five percent of the benefit of the "Jobs and Growth Tax Relief and Reconciliation Act of 2003" went straight to the upper one percent of income earners. In 2003, forty-nine percent of all tax payers saved less than one hundred dollars from this tax bill. Planned reductions of tax rates for the four top income levels were accelerated from 2006 to 2003, but the minimum income level to qualify for one of these reductions was $311,951 dollars per year. I did not qualify. But I did get a nice check in the mail for eight hundred dollars (Four hundred dollars for each child). Ironically, when it came time to file my tax return in early 2004, I owed exactly eight hundred dollars to the federal government.

While I was "saving" my eight hundred dollars, estimates from the Congressional Budget Office from late 2003 indicated that a continuation of Bush's economic policies would triple the national debt by the year 2013. This is a $10 trillion dollar increase in just ten years. This jeopardizes social security for younger Americans, and threatens future economic viability for our children. If I had to choose between a tax cut that our country cannot afford, or the long term viability of social security, I would choose to minimize the national debt. That is an easy answer. If I have any second thoughts I only need to play with my kids for a few minutes. They need a future much more than any of us need a tax cut.

By the way, President Bill Clinton, that guy who had some form of sex in the oval office, was responsible for raising tax rates on those making over $200 thousand dollars per year. His 1993 tax increase even created a new higher tax rate (39.6 percent) for Americans who are not struggling to pay the bills (This tax increase was almost entirely undone in 2001 by President Bush). In fact, in August of 1999, Clinton prevented an additional tax cut, choosing instead to focus on fiscal stability for our nation's future through a budget surplus.

"Because this tax cut will not save and strengthen Medicare, because it will not add a day to the Social Security trust fund, because it will not pay down the debt and pay it off for the first time in 150 years, this tax cut will not become law," Clinton said. Damn those tax and spend Liberals. He raised taxes the most on those making the most money, and he subsequently presided over the biggest stock market boom in world history. I like to use this as an example of my theory of "Trickle-up Economics."

The National Low Income Housing Coalition releases an annual "Out of Reach" report, emphasizing the increasing difficulty for the average low-wage working family to obtain housing. The report from 2004 shows that, using standard formulas of no more than thirty percent of gross income of rent and utilities, Americans need the equivalent of more than two full time jobs at minimum wage to afford a two bedroom apartment. In other words, it takes a pay rate of $15.37 per hour to provide a cheap apartment for your family. There is a serious problem with these requirements. Over one quarter of American workers make less than $10.00 per hour. Most people living in two bedroom apartments make far less than $31 thousand dollars per year or equivalent in hourly pay. Therefore, assuming rent comes first, there is precious little remaining for the remainder of the essential bills.

In fact, there are only four counties in the United States where a worker making the minimum wage could afford a one bedroom apartment, taking into account all other mandatory living expenses.

Now, before you reinstate the House Committee on Un-American Activities to compel me to testify on Communist involvement, let me be perfectly clear. I am not a Communist. I believe that if you work hard and earn money, that you should be able to keep as much of it as possible, whether you make $20 thousand or $200 thousand. However, all I ask *first*, is that the lower and middle class can afford safe and comfortable housing, and nutritious food. Nearly fifty percent of Americans cannot afford these basic necessities. They work just as hard if not harder than the upper class, and they deserve a basic standard of living.

There are two options to meet this goal. Ideally, small business owners and large corporations could start paying a living wage to their employees, instead of $25 thousand dollars per year or far less. Or, we could do things the hard way. Small business owners, large corporations and the upper one percent of the Ownership Society can be compelled to contribute to a basic standard of living for the serfs below them. This can be accomplished through various means, including placing limitations on executive salaries and benefit packages, doubling or tripling the minimum wage, and reinstating the dividend tax. This is not Communism, it is simply humanitarianism. So when you are sitting on the sand at your inherited beach house, sipping a margarita and admiring your new dock and fifty-foot yacht and bitching about "Socialists", please remember that your hard-working employees and their children are sitting at home yet again, simply trying to make ends meet.

GEORGE BAILEY DEMOCRATS

In the movie *It's a Wonderful Life*, everyone loves George Bailey, and what's not to love. He is the ultimate working class hero, providing for his family while selflessly providing for hundreds of others in the community, at the expense of his own personal gain. My family loves *It's a Wonderful Life*. They always make it a point to catch the movie on television before the holidays, and my wife's parents own the movie on DVD.

On the opposite end of George Bailey you have Mr. Potter. When I first saw the movie, I wanted to jump through the screen and throttle the guy, sitting on his leather chair surrounded by riches, criticizing the people-first business practices of the Building and Loan. When he sat on the board of directors and berated George's father's loan qualification criteria, only one thought came to my mind. *Filthy Republican.*

In many ways, Potter is the ultimate Republican. He would have been the primary beneficiary of the tax cuts of 1981, 1986 and 2003, both through his massive property ownership and his extremely high income. A vote for Reagan turned out to benefit those like Potter, and not like Bailey. Likewise, a vote for Bush would be a hypothetical boon for Potter's pocketbook. Potter had more money than he would ever need. He had no family to support, and he already owned nearly the entire town of Bedford Falls, yet he wanted more. He would never take a risk on a family in need, with a reliable hard-working bread winner. He kept the townspeople burdened with high-rent, low-quality properties, while Bailey's company gave people mortgages to purchase their own houses. There are many George Baileys in every community across America. They are not asking for much—just an equal chance. Yet my own father, who worked so hard to save and provide for his family of four, repeatedly cast votes for candidates with policy slants enormously in favor of those like Potter, all so he could claim his $100 tax savings for a few years or less.

When debating the future of the Bedford Falls Building and Loan with the Board of Directors, Potter and Bailey had the following exchange.

Mr. Potter: Now, you take this loan here to Ernie Bishop...You know, that fellow that sits around all day on his brains in his taxi. You know...I happen to know the bank turned down this loan, but he comes here and we're building him a house worth five thousand dollars. Why?

George Bailey: Well, I handled that, Mr. Potter. You have all the papers there. His salary, insurance. I can personally vouch for his character.

Mr. Potter:	A friend of yours?
George Bailey:	Yes, sir.
Mr. Potter:	You see, if you shoot pool with some employee here, you can come and borrow money. What does that get us? A discontented, lazy rabble instead of a thrifty working class. And all because a few starry-eyed dreamers like Peter Bailey stir them up and fill their heads with a lot of impossible ideas…

While discussing the Building and Loan's liberal loan qualification policies, Bailey says, "Just remember this, Mr. Potter, that this rabble you're talking about…they do most of the working and paying and living and dying in this community. Well, is it too much to have them work and play and live and die in a couple of decent rooms and a bath?" George Bailey was most certainly one of the original bleeding heart Liberals. Yet which group loves *It's a Wonderful Life* the most? Conservatives in the suburbs. They love the concept of equal and fair lending opportunities, because it makes them feel good about themselves.

But, outside of dropping a couple of bucks in the Salvation Army bucket and donating a token hundred bucks to United Way in a fundraising drive at work (mostly for fear of losing their jobs), most of them do not translate this Christmastime feeling into actual year-round execution. They laugh at social welfare programs, throwing around terms like "lazy" and "worthless" and "It's all freakin' Socialism." They scoff at the union laborers and they revel in their perception of others' lack of adequate modern skills and training. They laugh at those who would criticize Wal-Mart's pay scales, while one by one, their own neighbors' jobs migrate to a blue vest and poverty-level wages. They go out for drinks with their buddies, who are very much like George Bailey and Ernie Bishop, and they all rip on the accelerating salaries of executives and professional athletes. Then they vote for Republicans, year after year, who give ever-expanding tax breaks to executives and professional athletes, while George and Ernie struggle to get by.

I believe this is because the vast majority of "Fiscal Conservative" voters view themselves as one of two things: Rich, or pre-Rich. They have a little money in the stock market, and they perceive a Republican president to be good for corporate profits, and in turn good for the market and their own income tax rates. Or, they do not have money yet, but they just know they will soon. And when they have it, they want a Republican president in office so they can keep more of it when they finally (soon) get into that upper tax bracket.

Another factor at work in the mind of the average Fiscal Conservative is the myth of the much-publicized "Ownership Society." If most Americans are the laborers and the ones who take out loans for possessions and property, then a select few are the primary owners and investors, holding possessions and investing instead of working; In short, owning instead of producing. This is class-warfare in its most basic form. An individual can make one thousand times more in a day from inherited fortunes, tax-free, than a hard working lower-class family provider who is employed in a 50-hour per week job. This theory is sadly proven by the Republican-led push to reduce or eliminate capital gains taxes and estate taxes. Instead of using the phrase "Ownership Society", we might as well revert to more traditional phrases, like Master and Slave, or Noble and Serf. An Ownership Society simply cannot work if every citizen is an "Owner." Somebody still has to pay the rent and do the actual work. These legislative efforts founded on modern myth will only exemplify the widening gap between the upper one percent (The *real* Ownership Society), and the rest of us.

Wages, over the last thirty years, after adjusting for inflation, have been flat for the lower eighty percent of America. That's right, flat.

During thirty years of stock market boom and economic boom, the standard of living for the vast majority of America is the same or worse than in 1974. Oh sure, the distribution of information has changed, we have technology and the drugs are certainly better, but income-based standard of living is unchanged or worse. This includes things like, how much house can you buy for the same amount of inflation-adjusted money? What type of car are you able to buy (not lease)? How many vacations can you afford to take with your family?

So for our friend George Bailey, it comes down to a simple decision. Does he vote Republican for the small pittance of a benefit that it will provide to the Building and Loan, and therefore to his family? He also knows full well that this vote will benefit his sworn enemy one hundred times more than it will benefit himself. He also knows that the one hundred fold benefit will be used to turn the screws even harder back down on the Building and Loan and the laborers of Bedford Falls. Or, does he vote Democrat, and possibly sacrifice his own pittance, in exchange for hurting his sworn enemy one hundred times greater than he hurts himself? George Bailey is a smart character, and I am quite sure he would not vote against his own long-term livelihood, and against his children's future well-being. Or would he?

OFF-SHORING THE AMERICAN DREAM

When I used to hear things like "Buy American" and "America First", I would roll my eyes and laugh. I used to believe in the free market. I walked around calling myself a "Fiscal Conservative and Social Democrat." I was so full of shit. The only reason I ever considered myself a "Fiscal Conservative" is because, frankly, I considered myself "Pre-Rich." I wanted to make sure that the stock market continued to boom, and corporations that paid my bills continued to succeed. In 1998, I was working as a consultant for a manufacturing company, and the union was threatening to picket some of the plant locations during a wage dispute. I was so ready for them to picket. "I'll run 'em down with my car, the un-American bastards," I would tell my coworkers. "They should get over it, and get an education. The company doesn't owe them squat."

Eventually, the dispute was settled, and there was no strike. But in 2004, things played out much differently. Since 1998, the original manufacturer was bought out by a huge Italian-based conglomerate. In April of 2004, the "shareholders" of this manufacturing company approved a dividend of $0.25 cents per common share, for a total of $33 million dollars. What the press releases failed to emphasize is a simple fact—the parent company owns over 90 percent of the shares of stock in this company. So, a $33 million dollar payout to the "shareholders" and approved by the "shareholders" amounts to approximately a $30 million dollar gift to the parent company, approved by the parent company.

Now, fast forward to late 2004, when talks began to break down between the manufacturing company and its more than six hundred remaining union employees. The company repeatedly offered a standard line—"Things have changed. Our non-union plants do not pay anywhere close to your inflated union salaries. Things are tight within the company. We can no longer pay you what you make in your current contract, because we need you to pick up a portion of the health care costs, and you will not get a raise. In fact, in some cases, you will get a pay cut."

Keep in mind; this is the same company that, just six months earlier, paid $30 million dollars of pure profit from its coffers to its parent company in the form of a dividend. This parent company is based in Europe, not America. Many of the union jobs from six years earlier are now filled by non-union laborers in Brazil, Italy, and France. The union employees, all six hundred of them, are trying to support families in America. And for me, this is the final straw in denouncing my Fiscal Conservative past.

$30 million dollars divided by six hundred workers equals $50 thousand dollars per worker. Let's say for the sake of argument that the difference between the union demands and the company's position was as high as $5 thousand dollars per worker. If they had simply cut the token stock dividend from $0.25 cents to $0.22 cents, this difference could have been easily resolved, and strong union families who have dedicated their professional careers and their families well being to this company could have received their fair reward for a lifetime of hard work.

The company in my example is certainly not alone in this dividend-based bait and switch maneuver. Wal-mart announced in March 2004, that it raised its annual dividend by forty-four percent to $0.52 cents per share. "Wonderful," you say. "Then the shareholders of Wal-Mart will benefit greatly, to the tune of $2.2 billion dollars!" However, thirty percent of Wal-Mart shares are owned by the founding family members, who would pocket near $700 million dollars just from a single year's dividend payout. Meanwhile, the average hourly wage for Wal-Mart employees is $8.00 per hour, a number that could be as high as $9.50 if the dividend for 2004 was diverted from the Ownership Society to the laborers. The difference between $8.00 and $9.50 over the course of a year could mean the difference between a new car and an unsafe used car. It could allow a single mother to afford better care for her children while she is at work. It could pay for a fully nutritious menu for families. But instead, it made the Walton family at least $700 million dollars wealthier. Helen, John, Alice, Jim, and Robson Walton are also indebted to President Bush for ending the tax on dividends, which makes for happy days at the Walton estates.

Back in the industrial Midwest, the union at my company did go on strike, and when the company brought in replacement workers, the union wanted to come back while an agreement was reached. But the company locked them out, and they remained locked out over the Thanksgiving and Christmas seasons of 2004. When I drive to work I often stop across the street from the picketers, and watch them for awhile. There is so much pride in those steps, as they walk back and forth, passively acknowledging angry stares and honks from the passing cars. Many of them have worked there for twenty years or more. Yet most of their own coworkers watch complacently as the leaders of an Italian conglomerate take away the well-deserved paychecks of hard-working blue collar Americans, in order to pad their own bonuses.

Denouncing My "Fiscal Conservativism"

I am no longer a "Fiscal Conservative." I cannot afford to be. When I started working for my current employer, there were over three hundred information technology employees at my location. Now there are only about one hundred. The rest of these jobs are being filled by outsourcing agreements with a handful of overseas outsourcing companies, billing out my work and the work of my coworkers at no more than $15.00 per hour, including commissions for the project pitchmen. They came for the union workers, and I did not care, because I was "educated", and my skills were in high demand. They came for the "seasoned" coworkers, and I did not care, because I was fresh out of college. Then one day, my high-demand tech job went to India for one quarter of my pay, and no one cared. Oh Crap!

So the answer to this crisis is training and education? Will we be training and educating on ways to support a family on close to minimum wage? Is a fifty-year-old lifelong assembly line forklift operator supposed to go to a technical college for two years, only to find that when he finishes there are no more tech jobs in America? How do you train someone for a job stocking shelves at Wal-Mart? Because that is about all this guy will find. This is still America, despite our many differences. We should stand up for each other, against the

Ownership Society, and against multinational corporations based in other countries, even if this means taking an "America First" attitude.

One might consider my position on this topic isolationist or overly patriotic. I would debate you by saying that this is not an isolationist view, but rather it is simply common sense, with an eye on the future of America. Myself, my friends and my neighbors will not accept an America of "Managers, Salesmen and Shelf Stockers", where you either manage or sell projects run by overseas consulting firms, or stock shelves at a store selling the imported goods that result from those projects. America needs to return (at least in part) to a society of producers, or we will become a society of unemployed, depending on the government for our every morsel, scrounging for scraps from the tables of the Ownership Society.

The real battle being waged on a worldwide basis is the battle between labor and ownership. In 2005, India may be the trendy place to go, but that will change. Five years ago Ireland was the hot trend in off-shoring IT work, but as demand increased so did salaries, and eventually the work all but disappeared. Next may be Mexico, or Brazil, or China. Regardless, this is a sprint to the bottom of a cesspool for the working class of the entire world. As increasingly multinational companies find more cheap and immoral ways to exploit the working class through loopholes in trade agreements in country after country, they will leave behind a wasteland of broken dreams and promises when it is time to move on. This happened in Ireland, it is happening in the United States, and it will happen in India. The real losers are not only the American working class, but all of the workers of the world.

A Bush Administration economic report from February 2004, claimed that outsourcing is a positive economic transformation that will have long term effects on the American economy. In July, Philip Bond, the Undersecretary of Commerce for Technology, confirmed the Bush Administration position on the issue. Bond said that the solution to the problem is more investment in training and education, and not legislation that would prohibit or restrict offshore outsourcing. "If we embrace isolation and reject working with the rest of the world, it will be to our detriment," Bond said.

What we have in place today is not a "free market." A truly "free" market does not include tax incentives for outsourcing work. The root cause of the outsourcing problem can be found in the same nefarious place as most other things—follow the money. There are corporate tax loopholes in place which encourage outsourcing over the use of American workers. Commonly known as "un-repatriated earnings", this loophole involves taking money made overseas and "reinvesting" it overseas. In other words, the money is made through a sale of a product in Asia, and it is "reinvested" into outsourced computer work in India. The money hypothetically never passes through United States soil. When the books are finalized for tax purposes, the money spent on outsourcing becomes a write off from gross income, resulting in significantly lower taxes.

For example, Pfizer had $9 billion dollars in un-repatriated earnings just for fiscal 2003 alone. This amount was in addition to $20 billion dollars that they logged prior to 2003. Why would Pfizer queue up all this money in unreported income from foreign soil? Well, in part because only thirty-seven percent of their workforce is located in the United States. That leaves a lot of salary which can be written off against foreign earned profits.

In 2003, the Congressional Research Service issued a report on un-repatriated earnings. This loophole predates the Bush Administration by decades, but apparently, abusing it is all the rage in George Bush's America. In 2002, $639 billion dollars of un-repatriated earnings were reported, a fifty-nine percent increase over a three year period. This translates into improved dividends and higher stock prices than they would otherwise have been if this loophole was appropriately closed. The upper one percent of the Ownership Society must absolutely *revel* in the outsourcing of American jobs. This loophole needs to be closed—Yesterday. Any trade or tax policy which encourages and almost demands outsourcing American jobs in order to remain competitive does not fit into my definition of free trade.

The European Union and the World Trade Organization agree. The WTO has long considered a portion of the United States policy on foreign earnings to be an illegal tax subsidy. The potential punishment carries a harsh price tag—a $4 billion dollar in trade sanctions by the European Union. This raises a logical question. Why is the World Trade Organization more interested in truly "free" trade than our own free-trade-oriented President? I guess when corporate tax breaks are involved, free trade takes a back seat, right next to the former American dream.

MY "FREE MARKET" COWORKERS

When I spoke to one of my Red coworkers about the plight of the striking union workers, he minced no words. "I don't feel sorry for the picketers. They brought this on themselves by demanding such high pay. Their skills are becoming commodities." I responded by asking him one simple question: "When was the last time you took a pay cut?" The conversation stopped quite abruptly.

In fact, the standard response of my Red coworkers on the issue of outsourcing is simple. "I thought you were a Liberal," they say with loads of sarcasm. "Don't you want to help the poor and downtrodden in India? They have so much less than you." I have compassion for my fellow man, regardless of where they may live. But on the issue of jobs and poverty, I will put myself and my fellow Americans first.

Besides, helping the poor in India is certainly NOT the primary goal of American outsourcing. The driving force behind the trend would be, of course, the almighty dollar, inspired by outsourcing tax loopholes and executive bonuses and health care premium savings and on and on. Also, the truly poor in India are not the ones manning call centers and computer programming sweat shops. So, to believe that the poor will benefit from Indian outsourcing, one must also believe that trickle-down economics will work in India, when it does not even work in America. A poor farmer making less than one dollar per day will likely not see any benefit whatsoever from the call center that employs college graduates in the city a few hundred miles away.

Critics of India's call centers, such as author Praful Bidwai, are also less than thrilled by the economic positives even within India. "They work extremely long hours badly paid, in extremely stressful conditions, and most have absolutely no opportunities for any kind of advancement in their careers. It's a dead end, it's a complete cul-de-sac. It's a perfect sweatshop scenario, except that you're working with computers and electronic equipment rather than looms or whatever." In fact, a yearly call center salary in India averages $2,100 dollars, and most of the employees have a college education. These are not Indian farmers picked up from their crops to work in the air conditioned offices. Assuming sixty hour weeks with little or no vacation, this level of pay computes to approximately $0.82 cents per hour. That sure sounds like the white collar equivalent of a sweatshop to me.

Let's face facts. There are at least thirty-six million people in poverty here in the United States. This represents 12.5 percent of the population. With the current cost of living in America, there are another twenty to thirty million Americans who are one or two paychecks away from joining this classification. Many of these "paycheck to paycheck" Americans are my IT coworkers. Many others are former union manufacturers. As an American, this has to be my top priority, and I would expect the same from my elected representatives. American poverty is what I would consider a "Tier One" issue. World poverty, while still an important issue, is frankly a "Tier Two" issue for any American.

As a former Pre-Rich Fiscal Conservative, I think it is safe to say that this version of free trade is not working. I may become a Fiscal Conservative again at some point in the future, but this version of the policy is not consistent with my idea of America. Trickle-down economics do not work. Un-repatriated earnings are morally reprehensible. America is being eaten alive from the inside by the Ownership Society. Nobody I talk to seems to care. The so-called middle class is just scraping by, and the Ownership Society is more concerned with the profitability of their assets than the ability of their fellow Americans to provide for their families.

This is not my America. My American dream has been hijacked right out from under me and traded to someone in Asia for one quarter the cost. While I'm on the topic, those popular "Support the Troops" ribbons are made in China. Go to Wal-Mart and see for yourself on the back of the package.

The Nicest Buildings in Every Small Town

Driving through rural middle-America, my wife and I have a running joke. When we drive through a downtown area on a State highway junction, it usually consists of just a few buildings, mostly run down. There will be a gas station, an abandoned factory or two, and a few abandoned cars parked on lawns here and there. Just as we get to the town proper, I turn to my wife and say, "What is the nicest building in every small town?"

And around the next corner, there it is—Usually a sprawling, beautifully ornate and spacious church. Even if it is not new, it's still the nicest building in town, whether it is Lutheran or Catholic or Episcopalian or Methodist or Assembly of God or one of many other denominations. The houses on all sides of it are leaning over, glorified trailers on top of concrete slabs. The house doors are falling off, and the paint peeled long ago, but the church next door is thriving.

After we see the church, we have a good laugh, although it really should not even be funny. Then, I say, "What is the second nicest building in every small town?" And, around the next corner, there it is. A huge concrete block building, no more than five years old, that looks prestigious and welcoming all at the same time. Above the door it says, "(Anytown) Bank." On the window, a brand new laminated sign reads, "We do home equity loans and reverse mortgages!" Next to the bank is a strip mall that once housed "Mabel's Diner" and "Penny a Day Thrift Shop", but they are both closed now, and their signs are worn and faded. Sometimes the windows are boarded up. These days people prefer to take a jaunt to the next town, and hit the Wal-Mart near the interstate highway. Most of them work there anyway, so that works out nicely.

After we see the bank, we are not in much of a laughing mood anymore, but we continue on. I almost hesitate to do it, but I have to retain some road trip tradition, so I look at my wife and hesitantly stammer, "Okay fine. What is the third nicest building in any town?" She rolls her eyes and points, and there it is just down from the bank—the City Hall and the Courthouse. Taxes and crime are just as consistent as religion and money, of course.

God, Country, and Republicans were the three foundations of my childhood upbringing in a strongly Red house. They are also the three foundations of millions of other good Christian families in middle-America, where the ten percent tithe often comes before school clothes and meaningless things like front doors that are falling off.

So when you drive through small town America, think of my road-trip tradition. You will be amazed how often it actually works.

But do yourself a favor. Do not think about it for too long, or you will want to turn around and go home. Like Russian Roulette, this is the kind of game that you can only play for about two rounds before it becomes far too morbid.

Epilogue: Bigger Than You Can Imagine

"What makes a King out of a slave? Courage. What makes the flag on the mast to wave? Courage. What makes the elephant charge his tusk in the misty mist or the dusky dusk? What makes the muskrat guard his musk? Courage. What makes the Sphinx the seventh wonder? Courage. What makes the dawn come up like thunder? Courage."
—The Cowardly Lion, *The Wizard of Oz*

"The America represented in this room is not the America he died defending... Your America is bitter, and cruel, and small. His America was big—bigger than you can imagine, with a wide open heart, where every person has a VOICE, even if you don't like what they have to say... And even though these contracts, the Constitution and the Bill of Rights, even though they're just pieces of paper with signatures on them, they're the only contracts we have that are most definitely not subject to renegotiation... Too many people have paid for this contract in blood."
—Peter Appleton, *The Majestic*

"Our enemies are innovative and resourceful, and so are we. They never stop thinking about new ways to harm our country and our people, and neither do we."
—President George W. Bush

THE CASTLE ON THE HILL

To truly understand why I wrote this book, it is necessary to understand my motivations. Why do I continue to press these "political" issues with my Red friends and family members? Why don't I mind my own business? Or, as my own family asks, "Why do you care who I voted for? I can vote for anyone I want to."

Let me try to explain why it is appropriate for me to care who they voted for. In my opinion, it is not only appropriate, but it is a moral imperative.

<Fade to Dreamlike Sequence and Cue Cloudlike Harp Music>

Once upon a time, there was a village in a hilly region of a far away land. Thousands of people lived in this foothill village, and the vast majority of the villagers were inherently good. If you were in need of help, they would welcome you in to their houses, and they would offer you warm food and a place to sleep, despite the reality of their meager incomes and possessions.

> *"Yes, there were some in our country who doubted the Iraqi people wanted freedom, or they just couldn't imagine they would be welcome—welcoming to a liberating force. They were mistaken, and we know why. The desire for freedom is not the property of one culture, it is the universal hope of human beings in every culture."—President George W. Bush*

> *Last year nearly 36 million Americans lived below the poverty threshold—defined as an income of just under $19,000 dollars for a family of four. That's also an increase of 1.3 million people from the previous year. The numbers of poor and uninsured have now risen for three straight years.*

Epilogue: Bigger Than You Can Imagine   213

On the top the largest hill in town sat a moderately-sized castle, situated near the center of town. It was a nice castle; not fully paid for, heavily taxed, but well maintained nonetheless. In order to obtain the maximum view of the valley below, the castle had been built to directly overhang the town square, where most of the villagers lived and conducted business. In this castle lived an old man. He was a reasonably sensible old man, who worked hard all his life and happily enjoyed the isolation and comforts of the castle. He was a very fortunate, and he knew it. Once a year, he would donate money to worthy causes, and he was generally well-liked around town.

> *But noting that most of the victims were Muslims, he pointedly elaborated on the American aid effort. "We'd be doing it regardless of religion," Powell said. "But I think it does give the Muslim world and the rest of the world an opportunity to see American generosity, American values in action—that we care about every individual and the dignity of every individual" as well as "the needs of every individual, regardless of faith."*
>
> *"If you don't want us in your community, let's be honest about why you don't want us. Don't say it's about our wages cause the facts are the wages are good. Don't say it's about our benefits, cause the facts are we have benefits. Don't say it's about dead-end jobs, because the truth is we promoted 90,000 people out of hourly positions to management."—Wal-Mart Chief Executive Lee Scott*

One winter, an unusually gripping cold, wet weather pattern overtook this small village. A line of successive snow storms passed through the region, covering the region in snow and ice and generally making everyone miserable. Nobody could remember anything like it in their lifetimes. Every time they thought the storms had passed, another dark cloud rolled over the hills and dumped another pile of snow and ice. In fact, the ice was so terrible that the moderately-sized castle on the hill began to form large icicles from every eave and overhang. With each passing storm and subsequent melt, the icicles grew bigger, heavier and more potent.

> "Saddam Hussein is a man who told the world he wouldn't have weapons of mass destruction, but he's got them. He's a man who a while ago who was close to having a nuclear weapon. Imagine if this madman had a nuclear weapon."—President George W. Bush
>
> Hailing "new tools" to fight terrorism, President Bush signed into law Friday a measure that grants federal authorities expanded surveillance and intelligence-gathering powers. On Thursday, both houses of Congress overwhelmingly passed the bill, crafted in the wake of last month's terrorist attacks and dubbed the U.S.A. Patriot Act. Attorney General John Ashcroft, who had lobbied hard for the legislation, said federal agents would immediately begin exercising their new capabilities.

One day, one of the largest icicles was ripped from the castle overhang, and it fell directly onto a crowded market in the valley below. People scattered, and children screamed and frantically dove for cover. Buildings and shops were destroyed, leaving people without homes and jobs, and in many cases, without loved ones. At least fifty villagers did not make it out alive. The man in the castle saw the tragedy on television, and he thought, "Why does God allow things like that to happen. It's tragic. Simply tragic." Then he turned off the news (He didn't like to think about such things too much), and looked out of his window instead, surveying the valley below. He could see the carnage in the village, far off in the distance below him. And as he looked out the window, he also noticed the most beautiful icicles hanging from the eaves of his roof. The icicles glittered and absolutely shone in the afternoon sunshine. "God works in mysterious ways," he thought. "Something that looks so beautiful to me can be so tragic to someone else." Then he sat down to a healthy and filling dinner, and tried to put the tragedy out of his mind.

> *What does Iraq look like now? What aren't the people in the United States seeing, and what do you feel they should be seeing? The devastation. The massive suffering and devastation of the people and their country. Baghdad remains in shambles 19 months into this illegal occupation. Bombed buildings sit as insulting reminders of unbroken promises of reconstruction. Bullet ridden mosques with blood stained carpets inside where worshippers, unarmed, have been slaughtered by soldiers. Entire families living on the street. 70% unemployment with no hope of this changing. Chaotic, clogged streets of Baghdad and 5 mile long petrol lines in this oil rich country. Engineers and doctors, unemployed, driving their cars as a taxi to try to feed their families.*

> *Six months after gay and lesbian couples won the right to marry in Massachusetts, opponents of same-sex marriage struck back Tuesday, with voters in 11 states approving constitutional amendments codifying marriage as an exclusively heterosexual institution. Voters in Arkansas, Georgia, Kentucky, Michigan, Mississippi, Montana, North Dakota, Ohio, Oklahoma, Oregon and Utah all approved anti-same-sex marriage amendments by double-digit margins.*

On subsequent days, the storms continued. The snow would fall at night, and partially melt during the warmth of the day's sunshine, and the icicles continued to grow in both size and number on the overhang of the castle overlooking the town square. More and more icicles fell, killing hundreds of villagers each day. Before long, the number of dead reached into the tens of thousands. All the while, the people of the village looked up to the moderately-sized castle on the hill, wondering when the owner would simply dispose of the icicles.

They could not understand why the owner kept the icicles around, when they provided little or no inherent value.

> *I see more bloodshed and chaos. Sending more troops will only speed up the spiral here; increase the fighting. I see a continuing degradation of the infrastructure and failing of the occupation. It has already failed. It had failed even before the April siege of Fallujah and the Abu Ghraib scandal (which is ongoing). The real question is, how many more Iraqis and soldiers die before the U.S. admits to its colossal failure, makes reparations for the countless war crimes that have been committed and pulls out. The long term-that depends on how long the U.S. stays here. It is rare when I speak with an Iraqi who wants the U.S. to stay-they say, "Civil war? It can't possibly be worse than this-so the U.S. should leave. Then we'd at least have the chance to run our own country." Another man pointed out that if there were a civil war, no Shia or Kurdish attack on Fallujah could ever possibly compare to the devastation the U.S. military has caused there.*
>
> *Bush would chop farm programs by 2.9 percent and squeeze $45 billion in savings from the Medicaid health program for the poor...Even if Bush meets the goal, the total federal debt would swell to $11 trillion in 2010 from $8 trillion this year...Within days, Bush will ask for another $80 billion to fund the conflicts in Iraq and Afghanistan this year, on top of the $25 billion provided for 2005. Another big supplemental request for the Iraq war is expected to be sent to Congress next year.*

One day, a wise man wandered into this village as he was touring the far away land. He was shocked at the carnage and tragedy. He spoke to the villagers and researched their problem, and came to the only reasonable conclusion. "He should knock down those icicles," he thought. "It would only be the humane thing to do. Maybe I'll go have a talk with the guy."

Epilogue: Bigger Than You Can Imagine

So he trudged up the hill to the castle, and met with the old man. The old man was polite and cordial, and they had a hot toddy in the foyer. Eventually, the traveler got to the point.

"Sir, I'm sure you realize, those are *your* icicles that are killing the villagers in the valley below. They are falling from *your* castle. You are responsible for actions that originate from your property."

"Yes, they are beautiful icicles, aren't they? Did you hear what happened to those villagers in the valley down below? Why would God allow such a thing to happen?"

"Sir, I must repeat myself. Those icicles are falling from your castle. Any chance you might get rid of them before any more have to suffer and die, or lose their loved ones and homes? Please!"

"Hmmm..." he said. "I am sure you must be mistaken. Those villagers are always killing each other. I'm quite sure that is what happened. It is wonderful that you have so much compassion, though. More people should be like you. Thanks for stopping by." Despite my strenuous objection, he showed the traveler the door.

> *"President Bush ran forthrightly on a clear agenda for this nation's future and the nation responded by giving him a mandate," said Vice President Dick Cheney. Bush voters echoed that sentiment, saying their majority is strong and clear: Godspeed and full steam ahead.*

As the days passed, the icicles on the castle grew larger still, and they continued to break off and fall on the village below, killing hundreds more villagers. The villagers wanted to leave, but they had nowhere else to go.

Again, the traveler reluctantly trudged back up to the castle on the hill. He thought he would try one more time to get through to the old man. Though, in many ways, it was already too late. He knocked at the door.

"Go away", said the castle-dweller.

"But sir, your icicles are *still* breaking off from the roof and people are still dying," he pleaded.

"No, they aren't," said the old man. "I watch the news every night, and they haven't said anything about it."

"Damn it! Listen to me; your icicles are killing these innocent people. All you had to do was knock the things off your roof and we could have started to put an end to this tragedy by now!"

> *"If it takes 10 years, let's blow them all away in the name of the Lord...I don't care where they came from."—Jerry Falwell*
>
> *Stem cells are "blank" cells that can potentially form any kind of tissue in the body. Doctors say harnessing the power of those cells could one day lead to treatments—or even cures—for a number of diseases. For instance, they might be used to regenerate nerve cells to repair damaged spinal cords, helping paralyzed people walk again. Or they might be used to slow or reverse the damage done by Parkinson's disease. Some doctors even hold out the hope that stem cell research could be used to create an unlimited supply of organs for transplant.*

"Look buddy," he said, "I have no control over those icicles. I just live in the castle, I'm not responsible. God must have put them there for a reason, and they are so beautiful. Who I am to interfere with God's will? Besides, if you are so convinced my icicles are causing this tragedy, then why don't you just knock them off yourself?"

"I can't do it by myself," said the traveler, looking down at the village one last time with shame, frustrated by his complete failure to help. "If you won't do something so simple, that comes at such a small price to you, then what more can I say. Enjoy your icicles."

> *There was support by most Iraqis for the removal of Saddam Hussein. But that started to ebb quickly on in the occupation as people watched family members killed, detained, tortured and*

humiliated by the occupation forces. Then there was Abu Ghraib. I cannot stress enough how devastating this was to U.S. credibility in Iraq, and the entire Middle East. Throw on top of that the April siege of Fallujah, nearly complete lack of reconstruction, importation of foreign workers to do jobs Iraqis are far more qualified for, the installation of an illegal interim government, and you have a complete PR disaster for the U.S. here. Any credibility for the occupiers, and I doubt there was much to speak of, after the destruction of Fallujah has been lost. Iraqis I speak with are infuriated at the U.S. government. While they are well aware that what is most likely the majority of people in the U.S. being in opposition to the Bush regime, they believe the U.S. government and those who support it are guilty of war crimes of the worst kind. I see rage, grief, and the desire for revenge on a daily basis here.

About 44 million people in [America] have no health insurance, and another 38 million have inadequate health insurance. This means that nearly one-third of Americans face each day without the security of knowing that, if and when they need it, medical care is available to them and their families. Having no health insurance also often means that people will postpone necessary care and forego preventive care—such as childhood immunizations and routine check-ups-completely. Because the uninsured usually have no regular doctor and limited access to prescription medications, they are more likely to be hospitalized for health conditions that could have been avoided.

As he slowly walked down the hill, kicking rocks and thinking, he began to hear a sound. It was quiet, at first, then louder. Soon, the sound was a roar. A glow appeared on the horizon, and it was getting closer. He ducked into the bushes and watched in horror. The villagers from the valley were running up the hill at full speed, and they were pissed. They had torches and long poles and terrible grimaces. They were headed to the castle, and its walls would never be sufficient to defend against the rising hoard of hundreds of thousands of innocents.

Soon, inevitably, the beautifully-perceived icicles were smashed to pieces, and the castle was no more.

The Moral of the Story: It is perfectly acceptable to believe that God has a master plan for America, but not at the expense of personal responsibility for every one of America's actions. It is also ok to be apathetic in most areas of your life. Personal responsibility and American freedoms give you that right. But considering the availability of information regarding what has transpired over the last four years, you are fully responsible for your own hand as it casts a vote. If you chose not to pay attention for four years, you are still responsible. If you chose to vote based on your own primary issues over the stark reality of the larger picture, you are still responsible for the larger picture. As Americans, we are personally responsible for the actions of the Bush Administration; humane or inhumane, domestic or international. Belief in Manifest Destiny is not a valid defense, and nor is willful ignorance or beautifully-perceived icicles of "Freedom", "Democracy", and the "Ownership Society." As they say, the road to Hell is paved with good intentions.

The people in the angry mob have various motivations. One man lost his health care when his company laid him off. Now his child is sick and he cannot afford the proper medical treatment. A woman in the mob watched her grandfather waste away from Parkinson's disease, and she doesn't understand why stem cell research is being limited. There are Iraqis in the crowd as well—children who have no parents and parents who lost their children to cluster bombs. Many in the crowd are poor Americans, who took the brunt of small tax cuts and small wage increases year after year since Republicans regained power.

I would not have protested a vote for Ford. I would not have protested a vote for Reagan. Bush, Sr. was an acceptable vote his first time around. If you wanted to fill the ballot for George W. Bush in the 2000 election, even that was ok with me. But voting for him this time? This time the good people in the Castle on the Hill should have known better. Instead, they sat in their comfortable homes, isolated from reality, admiring only their view of the issues, and never once applying the Golden Rule. For them, this is simply Election Day tradition. This is how they determined their vote in every election for the past twenty or thirty years, and it never mattered before.

Unfortunately, this time it really mattered, for the future of America and millions of people around the world.

And this time they blew it.

About the Election

I have covered just about every topic imaginable, and I still have not explained why over sixty-one million people voted for Bush. I am not going to discuss the ten hour lines in urban areas of Ohio, or the lack of adequate voting trails on many electronic voting machines. I am also not going to explicitly get into the consequences of America's decision. If you have read the book, the consequences should be obvious by now. But I would like to get into my understanding of the motivations of Bush voters, based on my experiences of talking with hundreds of them personally. I have found that Bush voters fall into six main categories, with some cross-category hybrids. I have given you plenty of reasons not to have voted for Bush in November 2004. Lest you think I have tunnel vision, here are the reasons why Americans did vote for him.

Category One: The Old Testaments (Estimated 15 Million Bush votes)

This group can alternatively be called the "Intercessor's Elephants." Their primary motivation is a Holy War against the

Muslims, which God apparently mandated in the Old Testament in some rant about fire and brimstone raining down on the heathens. Yes, these people still exist. They sit around my Thanksgiving dinner table and they send me emails with Old Testament Bible passages, reminding me to pray to God to strike down "His" enemies. To them, Jesus is fun to talk about on Sundays, but he's nothing but a hippie freak loser when Ann Coulter's on the television set. Hell, Ann Coulter is proudly part of this group.

These people have secondary issues too—Pro-Life, which is really Pro-Birth, since these people are invariably racist as well, and they do not support anything that could be perceived as helpful to others, such as social welfare programs or the proper funding of primary education. They are all, of course, Pro-Gun, which I would have no problem with if they did not consistently make me think they were about to go shoot up a Mosque. These are the tough guys and a handful of slightly-testosterone-imbalanced security moms, you know, the ones whose voices are a little too deep. If you challenge them on their positions the bravado really comes out, and you will hear empty phrase after empty phrase as Rush Limbaugh and Sean Hannity regurgitate bile on auto-drivel through their lips.

Category Two: The Jessica Simpson Moderates (Estimated 6 Million Bush votes)

"Ummm…I know there's an election, but I haven't really been paying attention. I could go either way. Isn't Kerry that flip-flopper guy? I heard that Bush will keep me safe from terror, and I'm not in favor of terrorism. I lost my job, but I've started playing online scrabble, and soap operas really aren't all bad these days, so it's cool, man. I guess you could say I'm undecided. But I'll probably vote for Bush when push comes to shove. Some of the things I've heard about Kerry make me uncomfortable, like how he's anti-American and how he used botox. That's just creepy.

I've been thinking about joining the military, since they'll pay for my college, and I've heard they have some great career options. The media always says that things are bad over in the Middle East, but I know it's not really that bad, because the media is full of anti-American Liberals and they'll say anything. I can't find a job anyway. I love *Desperate Housewives*. The Interior Secretary did a great job decorating the White House."

Category Three: The Magnets (Estimated 12 Million Bush votes)

These people define the status quo. If Bush is leading in the suburban polls, then they are Bush supporters. They are also easily influenced by their friends, family, and coworkers. These people have a very simple life philosophy: Go with the flow. Don't rock the boat. Status quo is status one. The war in Iraq was a problem for The Magnets, because they heard more and more bad things about it as the election got closer, but ultimately to go against a war means to go against the President, and that would be conflict, and by definition not status quo. Choppy waters there bucko, float on back to shore. Magnets also oppose gay marriage, because their neighbor hates "flamers," and they cannot think of any good reason to disagree. They hate abortion, because their pastor said it was wrong. And they especially hate "Holywood Liberals" and the "Liberal Media" because they heard on the radio that everyone in the media is becoming anti-American. But they will vote for a Democrat if a few friends do it first. They "just don't like politics", and they think it doesn't really impact them anyway. But once every two years (a few weeks before the election), they wet a finger and hold it up to the wind.

Category Four: The Ownership Society (Estimated 1 Million Bush votes)

This is the famous Upper One Percent—The primary beneficiary of every single Republican president tax cut since 1980. Because of this, they are 99.9 percent likely to vote Republican, period. The Republicans could put up a combination of Pee Wee Herman and the Where's the Beef Lady, and they would garner at least 95 percent of the vote from this group. For these people, a Presidential election is about four things. Dividend taxes, upper bracket tax rate, stock market outlook, and minimal redistribution of wealth (translated "Socialism" or "Communism"). This means a Bush vote, and who can blame them. Greed makes for a great three-month-long trip to the Hamptons.

Category Five: Traditionalists (Estimated 16 Million Bush votes)

This group is similar to The Magnets, with one major difference. While Magnets can be influenced under certain conditions, this group will never waiver from its generations of historical Republican voters. Grandpa Frank voted straight ticket Republican, and so did Frank Jr. And for Frank III, there is not even a consideration. To Frank III, a vote for Bush is a proud memorial to past generations of the Frank lineage. As a former third or fourth generation Republican traditionalist, I find this group offensive, since they are not even approachable for basic discussion about their motivations. For a Traditionalist, asking if they will vote for a Republican is like asking if they will get up in the morning. Checking the straight party box on the ballot is like checking "male" or "female." There is no thought in the process whatsoever. These people love Conservative talk radio because it gives them the latest round of ready-made opinions to throw around, just in case anyone asks.

Traditionalists also tend to be the first to bash the "Hollywood Liberals", and classify anyone who disagrees with them as an "anti-American" or "Atheist" Democrat. You can identify a Traditionalist because they can't stop obsessing about Michael Moore and how "anti-American" he is. If it were up to them, creating or viewing movies like *Fahrenheit 9/11* would result in immediate incarceration for treason. I have emails from Traditionalists that explicitly state that goal.

Category Six: The Pre-Rich Consumers (Estimated 11 Million Bush votes)

This is my favorite group of them all. The anti-Socialist anti-Communist anti-Liberal pro-NOW crowd. For these sorry suburbanites, the America of the future is no time like the present. Budget deficits be damned. War cost be damned. Social programs be damned. To hell with reality and anything that reminds them of it. I want my, I want my, I want my S. U. V. These people are typically workaholics. They have investments and other savings, but they also have mountains of debt. These people despise the Upper One Percent, and they regularly bitch about how CEOs and Professional Athletes are overpaid, but they would sacrifice anything to join that group themselves. They will vote Republican just as frequently as The Ownership Society, because they believe that the only way to go from Pre-Rich to the elusive Upper One Percent is to vote Republican, election after election. The first words these people are ever taught, usually while still in the womb, are "Straight…Party…. Ticket."

Along with the Old Testaments, the Pre-Rich are the absolute worst at moral relativism and hypocrisy. They can be persuaded to the extremism of The Old Testaments, because they are willing to say or do almost anything to see a Republican in office. However, some can also be persuaded into The Magnets, since they are easily influenced by neighborhood and workplace trends.

LETTER TO THE RED STATES

This letter was posted on the Internet two days after the 2004 Presidential Election. The raw passion for the subject and the coherent agreement with my subject matter warrants its inclusion here in the Epilogue. I have left the text unedited to retain the original intent.

Sorry, I try not to deluge people with my ramblings. But I had to write this and, having written it, had to send it. Even though I don't know anyone I can send it to (without alienating my Republican in-laws, who are the only "middle country" people I know.)

I am writing this letter to the people in the red states in the middle of the country—the people who voted for George W. Bush. I am writing this letter because I don't think we know each other.

So I'll make an introduction. I am a New Yorker who voted for John Kerry. I used to live in California, and if I still lived there, I would vote for Kerry. I used to live in Washington, DC, and if I still lived there, I would vote for Kerry. Kerry won in all three of those regions.

Maybe you want to know more about me. Or maybe not; maybe you think you know me already. You think I am some anti-American anarchist because I dislike George W. Bush. You think that I am immoral and anti-family, because I support women's reproductive freedom and gay rights. You think that I am dangerous, and even evil, because I do not abide by your religious beliefs.

Maybe you are content to think that, to write me off as a "Liberal"—the dreaded "L" word—and rejoice that your candidate has triumphed over evil, immoral, anti-American, anti-family people like me. But maybe you are still curious. So here goes: this is who I am.

I am a New Yorker. I was here, in my apartment downtown, on September 11th. I watched the Towers burn from the roof of my building. I went inside so that I couldn't see them when they fell. I had friends who were inside. I have a friend who still has nightmares about watching people jump and fall from the Towers. He will never be the same. How many people like him do you know? People that can't sit in a restaurant without plotting an escape route, in case it blows up?

I am a worker. I work across the street from the Citigroup Center, which the government told us is a "target" of terrorism. Later, we found out they were relaying very old information, but it was already too late. They had given me bad dreams again. The subway stop near my office was crowded with bomb-sniffing dogs, policemen in heavy protective gear, soldiers. Now, every time I enter or exit my office, all of my possessions are X-rayed to make sure I don't have any weapons. How often are you stopped by a soldier with a bomb-sniffing dog outside your office?

I am a neighbor. I have a neighbor who is a 9/11 widow. She has two children. My husband does odd jobs for her now, like building bookshelves. Things her husband should do. He uses her husband's tools, and the two little girls tell him, "Those are our daddy's tools." How many 9/11 widows and orphans do you know? How often do you fill in for their dead loved ones?

I am a taxpayer. I worked my butt off to get where I did, and so did my parents. My parents saved and borrowed and sent me to college. I worked my way through graduate school. I won a full tuition scholarship to law school. All for the privilege of working 2,600 hours last year. That works out to a 50 hour week, every week, without any vacation days at all. I get to work by 9 am and rarely leave before 9 pm. I eat dinner at my office much more often than I eat dinner at home. My husband and I paid over $70,000 in federal income tax last year. At some point in the future, we will have to pay much more—once this country faces its deficit and the impossible burden of Social Security. In fact, the areas of the country that supported Kerry—New York, California, Illinois, Massachusetts—they are the financial centers of the nation. They are the tax base of this country. How much did you pay, Kansas? How much did you contribute to this government you support, Alabama? How much of this war in Iraq did you pay for?

I am a Liberal. The funny part is, Liberals have this reputation for living in Never-Neverland, being idealists, not being sensible. But let me tell you how I see the world: I see America as one nation in a world of nations. Therefore, I think we should try to get along with other nations. I see that gay people exist. Therefore, I think they should be allowed to exist, and be treated the same as other people. I see ways in which women are not allowed to control their own bodies. Therefore, I think we should give women more control over their bodies. I see that people have awful diseases. Therefore, I think we should enable scientists to try to cure them. I see that we have a Constitution. Therefore, I think it should be upheld. I see that there were no weapons of mass destruction in Iraq. Therefore, I think that Iraq was not an imminent danger to me. It seems so pragmatic to me. How do you see the world? Do you really think voting against gay marriage will keep people from being gay? Would you really prefer that people continue to die from Parkinson's disease? Do you really not care about the Constitutional rights of political detainees? Would you really have supported the war if you knew the truth, or would you have wanted to spend more of our money on health care, job training, terrorism preparedness?

I am an American. I have an American flag flying outside my home. I love my home more than anything. I love that I grew up right outside New York City. I first went to the Statue of Liberty with my 5th grade class, and my mom and dad took me to the Empire State Building when I was 8. I love taking the subway to Yankee Stadium. I loved living in Washington DC and going on dates to the Lincoln Memorial. It is because I love this country so much that I argue with my political opponents as much I do.

I am not safe. I never feel safe. My in-laws live in a small town in Ohio, and that town has received more federal funding, per capita, for terrorism preparedness than New York City has. I take subways and buses every day. I work in a skyscraper across the street from a "target." I have emergency supplies and a spare pair of sneakers in my desk, in case something happens while I'm at work. Do you? How many times a month do you worry that your subway is going to blow up? When you hear sirens on the street, do you run to the window to make sure everything is okay? When you hear an airplane, do you flinch? Do you dread beautiful, blue-skied September days? I don't know a single New Yorker who doesn't spend the month of September on tip-toes, superstitiously praying for rain so we don't have to relive that beautiful, blue-skied day.

I am lonely. I feel that we, as a nation, have alienated all our friends and further provoked our enemies. I feel unprotected. Most of all I feel alienated from my fellow citizens, because I don't understand what you are thinking. You voted for a man who started a war in Iraq for no reason, against the wishes of the entire world. You voted for a man whose lack of foresight and inability to plan has led to massive insurgencies in Iraq, where weapons are disappearing into the hands of terrorists. You voted for a man who let Osama Bin Laden escape into the hills of Afghanistan so that he could start that war in Iraq. You voted for a man who doesn't want to let people love who they want to love; doesn't want to let doctors cure their patients; doesn't want to let women rule their destinies. I don't understand why you voted for this man. For me, it is not enough that he is personable; it is not enough that he seems like one of the guys. Why did you vote for him? Why did you elect a man that lied to us in order to convince us to go to war? (Ten years ago you were incensed when our president lied about his sex life; you thought it was an impeachable offense.) Why did you elect a leader who thinks that strength cannot include diplomacy or international cooperation? Why did you elect a man who did nothing except run away and hide on September 11th?

Most of all, I am terrified. I mean daily, I am afraid that I will not survive this. I am afraid that I will lose my husband, that I will never have children, that I will never grow old and watch the sunset in a backyard of my own. I am afraid that my career—which should end with a triumphant and good-natured roast at a retirement party in 2035—will be cut short by an attack on me and my colleagues, as we sit sending emails and making phone calls one ordinary afternoon. Is your life at stake? Are you terrified?

I don't think you are. I don't think you realize what you have done. And if anything happens to me or the people I love, I blame you. I wanted you to know that.

Blueness is a State of Mind

Some will say this is a politically-motivated book. I firmly disagree. Instead, I see this effort as an exercise to explore the psychology and philosophy of the mental condition of America at the turn of a new millennium, and to encourage proper historical perspective on current events.

I am not a politician, and I am not a historian. I am not a journalist or a professional communicator by trade. I am not a psychologist or a philosopher. When it comes down to basics, I am just a regular middle class guy, who loves my family and my country more than I love my extended family's strong Republican traditions. If you haven't figured it out by now, I was raised a strong Republican Traditionalist, with a sprinkle of Old Testament and plenty of Pre-Rich, without the related consumerism.

I spent nearly every moment outside of work or family time on this effort, since November 3rd. Will this book convince anyone outside my own family? Probably not. But in early 2005, I thought all of my effort paid off in a way that I could never have imagined. My mother called me, and she was talking sort of quietly, in hushed undertones.

"Your father is outside shoveling snow," she said. "I just wanted to tell you, I've been reading your manuscript and thinking for two hours. I've just been thinking. And I think I am *Blue*. Didn't you say that the Red's don't think?" There was some uncomfortable laughter from both of us. "I think you are right, Tim. I've been thinking about things for two hours, and I've decided that I am Blue."

I choked back tears. Seriously. No longer did I have to try to reconcile the discrepancy between my wonderful mother and the industrial war complex. No longer did I have to debate, endlessly, with my father, in the hope that the message would make it through his fact-bouncing filter and some portion of it would reach my mom. I succeeded in my goal of reaching just one person with unfiltered information, and with a timely message.

And after all of the work, and all of the research, and all of the what if scenarios and 'How Does This Sound' sessions with my wife, it was all worth it to hear those words from my mom. "I think I'm *Blue*," she said.

And *of course* she is Blue. I knew that all along, even if she did not. There is no room for moral relativism or ethnic hatred in my mother's America. There is no room for persecution of the poor of any country, in the name of greed, selfishness, and self-righteousness. And there is no room for wars of questionable morality, with a neat and clean nametag slapped on for good measure.

I wish that could be the end of the story. It would be such a fitting, satisfying ending to a tale of political family conflict. Unfortunately, the story does not end there. In the end, my mother was being sarcastic. "You said that Bush supporters don't think. Well, I'm thinking, so I must be Blue," she said with a written smirk. It was a joke. She is not Blue. She is as Red as ever, and she is proud of it. She says it is unfair for me to say she supports the "War Machine" of George W. Bush. She voted for him, so I do not see how she could not support his actions. Simply, a vote for a sitting President is an active mandate of the actions of that President's first term in office; not just some of the actions, but all of them.

As for me, I am headed back to the very same place where I started this journey.

Moderator: "Please state your name, and what brought you here."

Me: "My name is Tim, and every member of my family is a Bush voter."

Group: "Welcome Tim."

AMERICA THE BEAUTIFUL

For me, breaking the chains of my upbringing changed my life. Through the process of "Growing Up", love of country appropriately gained separation from misplaced love of government. Over time, love of God painstakingly tore away from misplaced love of organized religion.

Most of my extended family changed too. But for them, September 11th changed everything. It started the War on Terror. It created a new enemy for America. Obsessive nationalism was trendy again, with flags and ribbons on every available surface. To most of my family, "America is back."

To me, America never left. America is not a ribbon on the back of an SUV or an inappropriately huge flag waving outside a used car dealership. The process of breaking free from my upbringing made me appreciate America more than ever, flaws and all. Having children of my own allows me to experience "finding America" all over again, through the amazement in their own eyes at their first Fourth of July parade, their first baseball game, and their first trip to Disneyworld. The childhood of my own kids is quite different from my own. They appreciate true diversity and true freedom, and they don't even know it. That is because they have never heard a negative thing about anyone who doesn't look like them or think like them. They are not afraid of shadows, because they have never been told to fear mysterious evildoers who might blow up their suburban home. My oldest child is beginning to understand that his parents don't always agree with the actions of our American leadership, and that is just fine. My children will understand appropriateness, and perspective, and common sense, for they see it evidenced in their parents actions daily.

I loved this country when I was a kid. I had a stars and stripes tank top that I wore all summer long. I wore it playing flashlight tag in my backyard, chasing my sister through the trees while swatting mosquitoes away. I wore it to baseball games, cheering for the Milwaukee Brewers at old County Stadium, as summer days wore on and Paul Molitor delivered hit after hit. I wore it while watching the summer Olympics, with my McDonalds "free hamburger" gold medal stickers spread out in front of me, cheering for each and every American competitor, and booing the Soviets. I wore it to Fourth of July parades, clapping and waving to every good American that passed by. I wore that tank top almost every day, because America meant something. To me, America was comfort and reassurance, like a secret that you just cannot wait to tell your best friend when you get home from school.

I don't know what happened to my America. Maybe it was morphed by the things I have described in this book. Maybe we have become so obsessed with thinly veiled greed and ethnic hatred, that we have simply forgotten the _American_ values we used to hold in such high regard. Or maybe America never was the great country of my youthful perception. Maybe I was dealing in unrealized potential, or the rose coloring of my perceived ideal suburban upbringing. But whatever the reason, my America is gone, or at least buried under a heap of discolored ribbons and oversized flags, with a strange, distinctly fascist stench.

When I talk to my father or my uncle about America, they disagree. They still see our country on the road to the famous Shining City of Ronald Reagan. To much of Red America, Reagan's dream is on the verge of being realized. America has returned to its "predestined" role as moral guide for the rest of the world, and we are going to do whatever it takes to fulfill this God-given duty. According to many of the Reds, America is a more free and moral nation than ever before, we are spreading *Democracy* and *Freedom* to the Middle East, and we got a tax cut to boot.

In 1852, Frederick Douglass was invited to speak at a meeting of the Rochester Ladies' Anti-Slavery Society on July 5th. Douglass was a former slave, who became an advisor to President Lincoln and one of the leaders of the abolitionist movement. His speech is so relevant, over one hundred and fifty years later, that it warrants printing here, in this very different era and context. For Douglass has touched on an important conclusion.

> "This, for the purpose of this celebration, is the 4th of July. It is the birthday of your National Independence, and of your political freedom. This, to you, is what the Passover was to the emancipated people of God. It carries your minds back to the day, and to the act of your great deliverance; and to the signs, and to the wonders, associated with that act, and that day…
>
> What, to the American slave, is your 4th of July? I answer: a day that reveals to him, more than all other days in the year, the gross injustice and cruelty to which he is the constant victim. To him, your celebration is a sham; your boasted liberty, an unholy license; your national greatness, swelling vanity; your sounds of rejoicing are empty and heartless; your denunciations of tyrants, brass fronted impudence; your shouts of liberty and equality, hollow mockery; your prayers and hymns, your sermons and thanksgivings, with all your religious parade, and solemnity, are, to him, mere bombast, fraud, deception, impiety, and hypocrisy—a thin veil to cover up crimes which would disgrace a nation of savages. There is not a nation on the earth guilty of practices, more shocking and bloody, than are the people of these United States, at this very hour."

Douglass was right. What is the Fourth of July, in a disgraceful period of American history? What is the Fourth of July, when the values that our nation was founded on are being breached on a daily basis through Patriot Act rights infringements, unjust warfare, and politicians hiding their indefensible actions behind empty language and the stars and stripes of the flag? What is the Fourth of July, when more than half of all voters don't even know that they already lost what their parents and grandparents spent lives and destinies fighting for? Morality, freedom, equality, civility, opportunity, compassion, tolerance, respect, honor, dignity, and finally, *Greatness*.

Don't get me wrong, the country that I love is still here. Like I said, it never left. But it is not represented in Washington, or through bile-spewing talk radio bigots and hypocrites. It is represented in the strong and proud voices of the dissenters, who will never agree to a mandate of thirty-one percent of eligible voters. My America lives on in my memory, as I remember my hard working grandfather, who literally built his successful motel business with his own two hands, starting with the remnants of an old barn. And it lives every time I recall the memory of my wife's grandfathers, both of whom served proudly in World War Two. It survives in the smiles of my children, who are not afraid of dark-skinned shadows. My son will run for President, he says, when he is a daddy, and he will bring America back. That is what he told me anyway.

Memories of what America used to be before military industrial and corporate greed stole it from us, still live on in me and millions like me. And the day will come when I will find myself joined by millions of others who have been pushed too far. For some, the trigger will be the military quagmire in Iraq, or a pre-emptive invasion of Iran, or a picture of a small Arab child, with her mother's blood smeared on her upturned questioning hands. Others will be triggered by an outsourcing deal that takes their job and nets their company's CEO a ten million dollar stock option payout. And for still others, the trigger may unfortunately need to be a military draft notice for one of their own children, as the War on Terror drags on, and on…and on.

My country does not endorse unjust wars against nebulous poorly-defined enemies. My country does not accept misleading explanations based on empty language from our leaders. My country demands truth and justice for evildoers, at home and abroad, and in seats of power. My country revels in real freedom and real civil rights, not just spoken words, regardless of appearance, ethnicity or thought. My country is America, and it is here to stay. Even the far-reaching roots of Fascism and Consumerism cannot kill it. For America is not about corporate profits or real estate or stock options. America is not about becoming an "Ownership Society", as our President would have us believe. America is about people, and I still believe they are good people, even if some of them have temporarily forgotten this fact.

For me, it is not just about the Fourth of July anymore. Someday soon I hope to walk down to my spot on the sidewalk and stand and salute my flag with pride. I will sip a drink as the parade rolls by, and laugh with my kids as they fill their bags with candy and memories. And I will stand and honor our veterans—every last one of them, not just the ones who march under a Republican or Democrat banner. But rather than limiting my expression to the Fourth of July, I choose to rejoice in America on a daily basis, so my children will grow to love my country as much as I do.

Growing Up Red, I learned one thing above all else—"Have Faith, son. Especially have faith in the goodness of the American people."

Let's get started in the right direction by properly reflecting the goodness of the American people, represented in the White House, the Congress and through our collective actions around the world.

Amen.

Notes and References

Chapter 1: Born on the 16th of January

- If you really want to learn more about Evolutionary Creationism (and I cannot for the life of me understand why you would want to), try the Wikipedia on the topic: en.wikipedia.org/wiki/Evolutionary_Creationism

- The January 9, 1991 *Open Letter to College Students on the Persian Gulf Crisis* from George Bush can be found at the George Bush Presidential Library and Museum: bushlibrary.tamu.edu/research/papers/1991/91010906.html

- On October 10, 1990, the *Congressional Human Rights Caucus* held a hearing on Capitol Hill. Nayirah's quotes are from her testimony at this hearing.

- "In addition, over 300 premature babies were reported to have died after Iraqi soldiers removed them from incubators, which were then looted." This text was included in an 84-page *Amnesty International report* from December 19, 1990 on human rights violations in occupied Kuwait.

- On October 15, 1990, President Bush reported that he had met with the Emir of Kuwait, who had told the President stories about "newborn babies thrown out of incubators and the incubators then being shipped to Baghdad." He referred to the story five more times during the next five weeks.

- Citizens for a Free Kuwait, organized by the exiled Kuwaiti government, had hired Hill & Knowlton to gain support for the U.S. counterstrike; Hill & Knowlton was paid U.S. $14 million by the U.S. government for its help in promoting the Gulf War.

- The Columbia Journalism Review from Sept/Oct 1992, reports that ABC's John Martin, who interviewed key Kuwaiti hospital officials in March 1991, shortly after the war ended; they acknowledged that some infants had died as the result of a chaotic conditions, including a shortage of nurses, but said no infants had been dumped from their incubators. Reuters was the only news service to pick up the story, even though the AP and others were notified in advance by ABC.

- Writing in the New York Times on Monday, January 6, 1992, John MacArthur noted that Amnesty International later retracted its support for Nayirah's story.

- Macarthur also wrote, "Nayirah, her real name, is the daughter of the Kuwaiti Ambassador to the U.S., Saud Nasir al-Sabah. Such a pertinent fact might have led to impertinent demands for proof of Nayirah's whereabouts in August and September of 1990, when she said she witnessed the atrocities, as well as corroboration of her charges. The Kuwaiti Embassy has rebuffed my efforts to interview Nayirah."

- The Topps *Desert Storm* trading cards can still be found on the company web site, at www.topps.com/Entertainment/Flashback/DesertStorm/desertstorm.html

Chapter 2: Growing Up Red

- Nearly all Reagan history obtained from CNN.com's *Reagan Remembered* section at www.cnn.com/SPECIALS/2004/reagan/index.html

- Bergsten and Stockman quotes are from "*A Fresh Look at Reaganomics*" story on CBS Evening News on June 9, 2004 by CBS News Correspondent Anthony Mason.

- "My fellow citizens, our nation is poised for greatness. We must do what we know is right and do it with all our might. Let history say of us, 'These were golden years when the American revolution was re-born, when freedom gained new life and America reached for her best.'"—President Ronald Reagan, Second Inaugural Address, January 21, 1985.

Chapter 3: Facing Red House Ghosts

- Everything you ever wanted to know about Imprecatory Prayers can be found here: www.hyperbible.com/articles/imprecatoryprayers.asp

- Jerry Falwell said, "If it takes 10 years, let's blow them all away in the name of the Lord" on CNN's Late Edition on October 24, 2004.

- Read Dr. Henry Blackaby for yourself at www.blackaby.org

- Dr. Charles Stanley's "Special Message" about the war is at his web site: www.intouch.org/War/index_38027182.html

- Major General Antonio M. Taguba's fifty-three page report on torture was mentioned and cited in *the New Yorker* on May 10, 2004.

- The Geneva Convention relative to the Treatment of Prisoners of War was adopted on August 12, 1949 by the Diplomatic Conference for the Establishment of International Conventions for the Protection of Victims of War, held in Geneva from April 21 to August 12, 1949. Full text is here: www.unhchr.ch/html/menu3/b/91.htm

- The Aiden Delgado quotes are referenced from an article called, "*In Good Conscience*", Scott Fleming, LiP Magazine, January 10, 2005. Full article can be found here: www.alternet.org/waroniraq/20935

- Alberto Gonzales "Torture Memo", dated January 25, 2002, can be viewed at MSNBC: www.msnbc.msn.com/id/4999148/site/newsweek/

- Alberto Gonzales called the Geneva convention "quaint" in the Memo for the President of January 25, 2002: "The nature of the new war places a high premium on other factors, such as the ability to quickly obtain information from captured terrorists and their sponsors in order to avoid further atrocities against American civilians…In my judgment, this new paradigm renders obsolete Geneva's strict limitations on questioning of enemy prisoners and renders *quaint* some of its provisions…"

- August, 2002 Torture Memo information from The Washington Post, *"Memo Offered Justification for Use of Torture."* Dana Priest and R. Jeffrey Smith, June 8, 2004. "In the 2002 memo, written for the CIA and addressed to White House Counsel Alberto R. Gonzales, the Justice Department defined torture in a much narrower way, for example, than does the U.S. Army, which has historically carried out most wartime interrogations. In the Justice

Department's view—contained in a 50-page document signed by Assistant Attorney General Jay S. Bybee and obtained by The Washington Post—inflicting moderate or fleeting pain does not necessarily constitute torture. Torture, the memo says, "must be equivalent in intensity to the pain accompanying serious physical injury, such as organ failure, impairment of bodily function, or even death."

- "And by the way, there's a reason—I'll conclude by saying—there's a reason why we sign these treaties: to protect my son in the military. That's why we have these treaties. So when Americans are captured, they are not tortured. That's the reason, in case anybody forgets it. That's the reason."—Senator Joe Biden, Questioning John Ashcroft on anti-terror policy, June 8, 2004. www.washingtonpost.com/wp-dyn/articles/A25211-2004Jun8.html

- Information on the new and improved torture memo from The New York Times, "*With No Fanfare, Justice Revamps Torture Definition*", January 1, 2005. "'Torture is abhorrent both to American law and values and to international norms,' states the new memorandum, written by Daniel Levin, the acting assistant attorney general in charge of the Office of Legal Counsel, which produced the earlier definition."

- Aidan Delgado quote on types of prisoners at Abu Ghraib prison: "*In Good Conscience*", Scott Fleming, LiP Magazine, January 10, 2005. Full article can be found here: www.alternet.org/waroniraq/20935

- Christian Peacemaker teams information and quote from Peggy Gish are referenced from BBC News, "*Eyewitness: Taking detainee testimony in Iraq.*" December 24, 2004. news.bbc.co.uk/2/hi/middle_east/4066835.stm

- Lynndie England quote and information from CBS News, "*Female GI In Abuse Photos Talks.*" May 12, 2004. www.cbsnews.com/stories/2004/05/12/iraq/main616921.shtml

- Charles Graner quote and information from cbsnews.com, "*Graner Gets Ten Years*", January 15, 2005.

- FBI Emails released by the American Civil Liberties Union came from an ACLU Press Release, "*FBI E-Mail Refers to Presidential Order Authorizing Inhumane Interrogation Techniques*", December 20, 2004. www.aclu.org/SafeandFree/SafeandFree.cfm?ID=17216

- 27 percent of voters listed "Moral Values" as their number one issue in a fixed answer poll from The Pew Research Center, "*Summary of Findings: Voters Liked Campaign 2004, But too Much 'Mud-Slinging'*", November 11, 2004. people-press.org/reports/display.php3?ReportID=233

- State by State divorce rates from *Divorce Magazine*, www.divorcemagazine.com/statistics/statsUS2.shtml

- Supreme Court decision to not hear Massachusetts Gay Marriage law case from Associated Press, "*Supreme Court turns aside challenge to gay marriage law*", Hope Yen, November 29, 2004.

- Embryonic Stem Cell Research information from the University of Wisconsin, Madison: www.news.wisc.edu/packages/stemcells/

- Isaiah 58:9, "Then you will call, and the LORD will answer; you will cry for help, and he will say: Here am I. 'If you do away with the yoke of oppression, with the pointing finger and malicious talk,"

- Clinton budget surplus from CNN.com, "*President Clinton announces another record budget surplus*", September 27, 2000.

- Center for Moral Clarity information from their web site: www.centerformoralclarity.org

Chapter 4: War and Country and The American Media

- "*Life Under Saddam Hussein: Past Repression and Atrocities by Saddam Hussein's Regime*" was a Fact Sheet, released by the Office of the White House Press Secretary on April 4, 2003. www.state.gov/p/nea/rls/19675.htm

- Details of the Shi'a Uprising are available, as referenced from the State Department's own document, from the Human Rights Watch, "*Iraq and Occupied Kuwait: Human Rights Developments*", 1992. www.hrw.org/reports/1992/WR92/MEW1-02.htm

- The Human Rights Watch, as referenced by the State Department's own document, did not condone the Iraq War as a humanitarian invasion, in "*War in Iraq: Not a Humanitarian Intervention*", Ken Roth, January, 2004. www.hrw.org/wr2k4/3.htm

- John Hopkins University report on civilian deaths in Iraq referenced in The Washington Post, "*100,000 Civilian Deaths Estimated in Iraq*", October 29, 2004. www.washingtonpost.com/wp-dyn/articles/A7967-2004Oct28.html: "The estimate is based on a September door-to-door survey of 988 Iraqi households—containing 7,868 people in 33 neighborhoods—selected to provide a representative sampling. Two survey teams gathered detailed information about the date, cause and circumstances of any deaths in the 14.6 months before the invasion and the 17.8 months after it, documenting the fatalities with death certificates in most cases. The project was designed by Les Roberts and Gilbert M. Burnham of the Center for International Emergency, Disaster and Refugee Studies at the Johns Hopkins Bloomberg School of Public Health in Baltimore; Richard Garfield of Columbia University in New York; and Riyadh Lafta and Jamal Kudhairi of Baghdad's Al-Mustansiriya University College of Medicine. The researchers called their estimate conservative because they excluded deaths in Fallujah, a city west of Baghdad that has been the scene of particularly intense fighting and has accounted for a disproportionately large number of deaths in the survey."

- Information on cluster bomb usage in Iraq and quotes from Dr. Sa'ad al-Falluji from Human Rights Watch, "*Off Target: The Conduct of the War and Civilian Casualties in Iraq*", December, 2003. www.hrw.org/reports/2003/usa1203/5.5.htm

- "Who is the enemy?" quote from an anonymous U.S. Marine in Fallujah, obtained through forwarded email. Authenticity verified anonymously.

- "Weapons-Free" documented from numerous sources, including Kevin Sites, NBA cameraman who heard it referenced during battle. www.kevinsites.net/2004_11_07_archive.html

- Donald Rumsfeld quote from The Washington Times, "*Coalition Uses Divide-Conquer Plan in Fallujah*", Rowan Scarborough and Bill Gertz, November 9, 2004. "They are well-led. They're well-trained. They are using precision. And they have rules of engagement that are appropriate to an urban environment."

- The AP Photographer's fascinating Fallujah story documented at ABC News, "*AP Photographer Flees Fallujah*", November 14, 2004.

- Captain Robert Johnson quote from the "*Dellums Committee Hearings on War Crimes In Vietnam*", April 25, 1971. Johnson's story was verified by numerous individuals testifying at those hearings.

- Jules Lobel was interviewed on Democracy Now!, "*U.S. War Crimes in Fallujah*", November 19, 2004.

- Most Jessica Lynch detail from the BBC, "*Saving Private Lynch Story Flawed*", John Kampfner, May 15, 2003.

- "Disproportionately strong encouragement" to cover the Lynch story over other stories on that day, and Tom Mintier and Donald Rumsfeld quotes, seen on video in the documentary, "*Control Room*", Jehane Noujaim, 2004.

- Army report of the Lynch incident released in July 2003, documented in The Washington Times, "*Crash Caused Lynch's 'horrific injuries'*", July 9, 2003.

- Diane Sawyer interviews Jessica Lynch, *ABCNews Primetime*, November 11, 2003.

- Draft Bills: House bill, HR 163; and Senate bill, S 89.

- Stop-Loss Program from the Department of Defense, "*Army to Expand Stop-Loss Program*", January 2, 2004. www.defenselink.mil/news/Jan2004/n01022004_200401023.html

- Information about the Individual Ready Reserve from the Department of Defense, "*Frequently Asked Questions,*

Reserve Components". www.defenselink.mil/ra/secondary/componentsfaq.html

- Information about specific IRR call up from The Houston Chronicle, "*Army to Recall 5,600 Troops Involuntarily*", June 29, 2004. www.chron.com/cs/CDA/ssistory.mpl/nation/2653148

- Military recruiting shortfalls from The New York Times, "*Guard Reports Serious Drop in Enlistment*", Eric Schmitt, December 17, 2004.

- The November/December 2003 Selective Service newsletter clearly outlines strategic planning for a skills-based draft, including the hiring of Alpine Magic, Inc, "A small firm that specializes in change management and has professional expertise in applying business process review techniques to government entities." www.sss.gov/PDFs/NovDec2003-Register.pdf

- Draft Board reactivation from USA Today, "*Selective Service notice creates flurry of press reports suggesting return of draft*", November 10, 2003.

- Richard Flahavan quote from Hearst Newspapers, "*'Special Skills Draft' on Drawing Board*", Eric Rosenberg, March 13, 2004.

- "I heard there's rumors on the Internets that we're going to have a draft."—President George W. Bush, Presidential debate, Oct. 8, 2004.

- Saving Private Ryan pulled from ABC, information from CNNMoney, "*ABC Affiliates pulling 'Private Ryan'*", November 11, 2004. money.cnn.com/2004/11/11/news/fortune500/savingpvt_ryan/

- OneMillionMoms.com, if you are so inclined. I cannot imagine why you would be.

- Armstrong Williams information from USA Today, "*Education Department Paid Commentator to Promote Law*", Greg Toppo, January 7, 2005.

- "There are others" quote attributed from David Corn, *The Nation*, quoted on Yahoo News, "*Armstrong Williams, I am Not Alone*", January 10, 2004.

- Ralph Neas quote from CNN.com, "*Feds Paid Pundit to Push Bush Policy*", January 7, 2005.

- Karen Ryan information from the Milwaukee Journal/Sentinel, "*Medicare Video News Release Raises Media Hackles*", Jan Uebelherr, March 18, 2004.

- GAO decision on Video News Releases, like Karen Ryan's, at "*Department of Health and Human Services, Centers for Medicare & Medicaid Services—Video News Releases, B-302710, May 19, 2004*", available here: www.gao.gov/decisions/appro/302710.htm

- Sinclair's corporate web page clearly shows twenty-four percent ownership of the national television market. www.sbgi.net/business/television.shtml

- Sinclair's statement of Bush support, KACV-TV, "*Media Face Dilemma in Patriotic Displays*", David Folkenflik, September 18, 2001. www.kacvtv.org/local/media/media10.shtml

- Sinclair's Statement on refusal to air Nightline Special on fallen soldiers, "While the Sinclair Broadcast Group honors the memory of the brave members of the military who have sacrificed their lives in the service of our country, we do not believe such political statements should be disguised as news content," April 30, 2004. The statement went on to question why ABC had not read "the names of the thousands of private citizens killed in terrorist attacks since and including the events of Sept. 11, 2001." The statement did not mention that there was no connection between Iraq and the attacks of September 11th, 2001.

- McCain's letter to Sinclair, over Nightline Special, on John McCain's Congressional Web Site: "I write to strongly protest your decision to instruct Sinclair's ABC affiliates to preempt this evening's Nightline program. I find deeply offensive Sinclair's objection to Nightline's intention to broadcast the names and photographs of Americans who gave their lives in service to our country in Iraq." mccain.senate.gov/index.cfm?fuseaction=Newscenter.ViewPressRelease&Content_id=1276

- Read Mark Hyman's *The Point* archives on his web site: www.newscentral.tv/thepoint/editorial.shtml

- Russ Feingold comments on Telecommunications Act of 1996 and resulting trends, from Feingold's Senate Web Site, "*Feingold Calls FCC's Easing of Media Ownership Rules Harmful to Local Diversity*", June 2, 2003. feingold.senate.gov/~feingold/releases/03/06/2003602626.html

Chapter 5: America on a Bumper

- Phatic communication is defined on dictionary.com as "conversational speech used to communicate sociability more than information".

- Other Phatic communication definitions from DHinMI blog on dailyKos, "Liberals are from Conceptual, Conservatives are from Phatic", November 21, 2004.

- I got the term empty language, and comparisons between words and nutritional value from the Sommet Institute article "*The Fairy Tale Presidency*".

- "We will answer every danger and every enemy that threatens the American people."—President George W. Bush, State of the Union address, January 28, 2003.

- "Saddam Hussein now sits in a prison cell. America and the world are safer for it."—President George W. Bush, Presidential Debate, September 30, 2004.

- "No one has ever been healed by a frivolous lawsuit."—President George W. Bush, State of the Union Address, January 28, 2003.

- "The best and fairest way to make sure Americans have that money is not to tax it away in the first place."—President George W. Bush, State of the Union Address, January 28, 2003.

- "September the 11th changed how America must look at the world."—President George W. Bush, Presidential Debate, September 30, 2004.

- "This nation of ours has got a solemn duty to defeat this ideology of hate."—President George W. Bush, Presidential Debate, September 30, 2004.

- "We have a duty to our country and to future generations of America…to rid the world of weapons of mass destruction."—President George W. Bush, Presidential Debate, September 30, 2004.

- References to the Childish nature of political discourse from smintheus blog on dailyKos, "*Infantilization of Politics in America*", November 18, 2004.

- "States like these, and their terrorist allies, constitute an Axis of Evil, arming to threaten the peace of the world."—President George W. Bush, State of the Union Address, January 29, 2002.

- "Axis of Evil" referenced to David Frum from The Washington Times, "*'Axis of Evil' Writer Leaves Bush Staff*", dated 2/26/2002 by Robert Stacy McCain.

- David Frum linked to Manhattan Institute on the organization's website, www.manhattan-institute.org. Search for Frum.

- William Casey references to support of Afghan mujaheddin from MSN Slate article by Fred Kaplan, "*Reagan's Osama Connection—How he Turned a Jihadist into a Terrorist Kingpin*", June 10, 2004. slate.msn.com/id/2102243

- In a January 5, 2000 article, *The Wall Street Journal* asked President Bush to name the book (excepting the Bible) that has been most important to him. He said: "The Dream and the Nightmare by Myron Magnet crystallized for me the impact the failed culture of the '60s had on our values and society."

- A June 12, 2000 article in The New York Times, titled "*Bush Culls Campaign Theme From Conservative Thinkers*", states, "Gov. George W. Bush has said his political views have been shaped by the work of Myron Magnet of the Manhattan Institute."

- Project for a New American Century can be found at: www.newamericancentury.org

- Statement of principles of the PNAC, with signatures, can be found at: www.newamericancentury.org/statementofprinciples.htm

- "I believe today that my conduct is in accordance with the will of the Almighty Creator."-Adolph Hitler, *Mein Kampf*, page 46

- "I trust God speaks through me. Without that, I couldn't do my job."—President George W. Bush, quoted in the *Lancaster New Era*, from a private meeting with an Amish group in Pennsylvania on July 16, 2004.

- "Those who want to live, let them fight, and those who do not want to fight in this world of eternal struggle do not deserve to live."—Adolph Hitler, *Mein Kampf*, Chapter XI.

- "Every nation and every region now has a decision to make. Either you are with us, or you are with the terrorists."—President George W. Bush, to the United States Congress on September 21, 2001.

- "Strength lies not in defense but in attack"—Adolph Hitler, *Mein Kampf*.

- "But the truth of the matter is, in order to fully defend America, we must defeat the evildoers where they hide. We must round them up and we must bring them to justice. And that's exactly what we're doing in Afghanistan, the first battle in the war of the 21st century."—President George W. Bush, News Conference, October 11, 2001.

- On January 17, 1961, in his farewell address to the nation, President Dwight D. Eisenhower said, "The conjunction of an immense military establishment and a large arms industry is new in the American experience," said Eisenhower. "We must guard against the acquisition of unwarranted influence, whether sought or unsought, by the military-industrial complex. The potential for the disastrous rise of misplaced power exists and will persist."

- Albert J. Nock, *Memoirs of a Superfluous Man*, 1943.

- "They that can give up essential liberty to obtain a little temporary safety deserve neither liberty nor safety."-Benjamin Franklin, *Historical Review of Pennsylvania*, 1759.

- United States Supreme Court, *TINKER v. DES MOINES SCHOOL DIST.*, 393 U.S. 503 (1969).

- First Amendment study results from the Associated Press, "*U.S. Focus: Free Speech. Study has 'dangerous' results.*", Ben Feller, Feb. 1, 2005.

- "That's just the nature of Democracy. Sometimes pure politics enters into the rhetoric."—President George W. Bush, Crawford, Texas, Aug. 8, 2003

- Details on *No Child Left Behind* proposed benefits from the United States Department of Education. www.ed.gov/nclb/accountability/index.html

- NEA statement on Federal education spending gaps, from National Education Assocation, "Statement by National

Education Association President Reg Weaver on 2004 Spending Legislation", January 22, 2004.

- NEA funding information and comments from an article in the Northwest Indiana Times, "*Are Schools Being Left Behind,*" Gunder Rask, February 8, 2004.

- Walter Cronkite comments from The Miami Herald, "*Now Outspoken, Cronkite Rips Bush's Record.*" Glenn Garvin, November 19, 2004.

- Students for Academic Freedom information and case studies from www.studentsforacademicfreedom.org

- United States Supreme Court, *KEYISHIAN v. BOARD OF REGENTS*, 385 U.S. 589 (1967).

- Ohio Academic Bill of Rights, 126th General Assembly, S.B. No. 24. www.legislature.state.oh.us/bills.cfm?ID=126_SB_24

Chapter 6: The Reality-Based Chapter

- If you want to play "America's Army", go to www.americasarmy.com

- Additional information and quotes about America's Army game is from the San Francisco Chronicle, "*Army's War Game Recruits Kids*", Joan Ryan, September 23, 2004.

- More information and quotes from newsreview.com, "*The Killing Game*", Gary Webb, October 14, 2004. www.newsreview.com/issues/sacto/2004-10-14/cover.asp

- Lan parties listed on the Americas Army Web Site, "*America's Army, Events Home Page*". www.americasarmy.com/events/events.php

- Information on GAMES summit from the Orlando Sentinel, "*Game Face*", Chris Cobbs, January 29, 2005.

- Information on Andres Raya from the Modesto Bee, "*Raya's Family, Friends Stunned by Deadly Act*", Joel Hood, January 12, 2005.

- 5,500 American soldiers in Canada, and quote, from the News Telegraph, "*US Deserters Flee to Canada to Avoid Service in Iraq*", Charles Laurence, September 1, 2005.

- Ninety percent of Americans had PTSD symptoms after September 11th. This came from the New England Journal of Medicine, "*A National Survey of Stress Reactions after the September 11, 2001, Terrorist Attacks*", AU Schuster, Mark A; Stein, Bradley D; Jaycox, Lisa H; Collins, Rebecca L; Marshall, Grant N; Elliott, Marc N; Zhou, Annie J; Kanouse, David E; Morrison, Janina L; Berry, Sandra H., November 15, 2001.

- PTSD symptoms from the National Center for PTSD, "*Common Reactions to Trauma*", Edna B. Foa, Elizabeth A. Hembree, David Riggs, Sheila Rauch, and Martin Franklin. www.ncptsd.org/facts/disasters/fs_foa_handout.html

- Manhattan voting results from New York Metro, "*New York City's Democratic Leaning*", Kurt Andersen, November 22, 2004. www.newyorkmetro.com/nymetro/news/columns/imperialcity/10424/

- Yearly death totals from various activities. Smoking: 435,000; Poor Diet/Inactivity-400,000; Alcohol-85,000; Microbial Agents (flu, etc)-75,000; Motor Vehicles-43,000; Adverse Reaction to Prescription Drugs-32,000; Sexual Behavior-20,000; Illicit Drug Use-17,000; Anti-Inflammatory Drugs (aspirin)-7,600; Drowning-7,000; Terrorism (4 year average)—750; Bicycle Accidents—730; Terrorism (10 year average)—310; Lightning—73; Tornados—48.

- "Al Qaeda terrorists escaped from Afghanistan and are known to be in Iraq."—President George W. Bush, Speech to United Nations urging disarming of Iraq, Sept. 12, 2002.

- "The (Saddam) regime has a history of reckless aggression in the Middle East. It has a deep hatred of America and our friends and it has aided, trained and harbored terrorists, including operatives of al Qaeda. The security of the world requires disarming Saddam Hussein now."—President George W. Bush, Speech that set a 48-hour deadline for Saddam to leave Iraq or face war, March 17, 2003.

- "The liberation of Iraq is a crucial advance in the campaign against terror. We have removed an ally of al Qaeda and cut off a source of terrorist funding…"—President George W. Bush, Speech announcing the end of major combat in Iraq, May 1, 2003.

- The case for Saddam/Osama connection, based on the Feith Memo, from the Weekly Standard, "*Case Closed*", Stephen F. Hayes, November 24, 2003. www.weeklystandard.com/content/public/articles/000/000/003/378fmxyz.asp?zoomfont=yes/

- Refuting the Feith Memo, from The Hill, "*The Dubious Link Between Iraq and al Qaeda*", Josh Marshall, January 22, 2005. www.thehill.com/marshall/111903.aspx

- Feith resigns from Fox News, "*Pentagon's No. 3 Man, Doug Feith, Resigns*", January 27, 2005. www.foxnews.com/story/0,2933,145525,00.html

- *9/11 Commission Report* CLEARLY states that there is no connection between Iraq and al Qaeda, especially related to the September 11th attack. Washington Post, "*No Evidence Connecting Iraq to al Qaeda, 9/11 Panel Says*", Dan Eggen, June 16, 2004.

- Poll data from The PIPA/Knowledge Networks Poll, "*Americans and Iraq, on the Eve of the Presidential Election*", Steven Kull, October 28, 2004. www.pipa.org/OnlineReports/Pres_Election_04/Report10_28_04.pdf

- Bush Has Had Only 15 Solo Press Conferences, Washington Post, 10/08/2004. Bush has held the fewest solo press conferences in 50 years, holding only 15 to date. At the same point in their presidencies, Bill Clinton had held 42, George H.W. Bush 83, Ronald Reagan 26, Jimmy Carter 59, Gerald Ford 39, Nixon 29, Johnson 88, Kennedy 65 and Eisenhower 94.

- "I wish you'd have given me this written question ahead of time so I could plan for it. John, I'm sure historians will look back and say, gosh, he could've done it better this way or that way. You know, I just—I'm sure something will pop into my head here in the midst of this press conference, with all the pressure of trying to come up with answer, but it hadn't yet…I hope—I don't want to sound like I have made no mistakes. I'm confident I have. I just haven't—you just put me under the spot here, and maybe I'm not as quick on my feet as I should be in coming up with one."—President George W. Bush at a rare Press Conference, April 13, 2004. www.washingtonpost.com/wp-dyn/articles/A9488-2004Apr13_5.html

- Knight Ridder Poll about Iraqis on the planes is from Knight Ridder Newspapers, "*Poll: Majority of Americans Opposed Unilateral Action Against Iraq*", Martin Merzer, January 12, 2003.

- Information on Mark McGwire and Andro from the Baseball Library, "*Mark McGwire*". www.baselllibrary.com/baselllibrary/ballplayers/M/McGwire_Mark.stm

- Information on Major League Baseball banning Andro from the Boston Globe, "*Sportview: McGwire Record Has Blemish*", Tim Dahlberg, June 30, 2004. www.boston.com/sports/baseball/articles/2004/06/30/sportview_asterisk_for_homer_records/

- McGwire info and quote from number 62 from Associated Press, "*It's McGwire's Record Now!*", September 9, 2004. www.hannibal.net/stories/090998/McGwiresrecord.html

- McGwire quote about studying pitchers and working hard from the San Francisco Chronicle, "*The Mac Attack: Strong McGwire Silent About HR Mark*", Henry Schulman, May 22, 1998. www.sfgate.com/cgi-bin/article.cgi?file=/chronicle/archive/1998/05/22/SP92195.DTL

- January 2005 baseball steroid agreement from CBS News, "*Baseball Gets Tougher on Steroids*", January 13, 2005. www.cbsnews.com/stories/2005/01/13/entertainment/main666807.shtml

- Copernicus and Round Earth theories from multiple sources.

- International Square Earth Society really existed, or at least it did in 1980, www.lhup.edu/~dsimanek/fe-scidi.htm

- John 16:13, "Howbeit when he, the Spirit of truth, is come, he will guide you into all truth: for he shall not speak of himself; but whatsoever he shall hear, that shall he speak: and he will shew you things to come."

- John 14:26, "But the Counselor, the Holy Spirit, whom the Father will send in my name, will teach you all things and will remind you of everything I have said to you."

- "The area in the south and the west and the north that coalition forces control is substantial. It happens not to be the area where weapons of mass destruction were dispersed. We know where they are. They're in the area around Tikrit and Baghdad and east, west, south and north somewhat."—Secretary of Defense Donald Rumsfeld, on ABC's *This Week With George Stephanopoulos*, March 30, 2003.

- "We know he's been absolutely devoted to trying to acquire nuclear weapons, and we believe he has, in fact, reconstituted nuclear weapons."—Vice President Dick Cheney, "Meet the Press", March 16, 2003.

- President George W. Bush, *State of the Union Address*, 2003. www.whitehouse.gov/news/releases/2003/01/20030128-19.html

- "Saddam Hussein is a man who told the world he wouldn't have weapons of mass destruction, but he's got them. He's a man who a while ago who was close to having a nuclear weapon. Imagine if this madman had a nuclear weapon."—President George W. Bush, Speech at the White House, November 3, 2002. www.iraqwatch.org/government/US/WH/wh-bush-110302.htm

- Scott Ritter quote from CNN.com, "*Former Weapons Inspector: Iraq Not a Threat*", September 9, 2002. archives.cnn.com/2002/WORLD/meast/09/08/ritter.iraq/

- UN Security Council support problems from USA Today, "*Bush Lacks Votes in U.N., Diplomats Say*", Bill Nichols, January 22, 2003.

- June 2003 Harris Poll from Harris Interactive, "*Most People Believe Iraq had Weapons of Mass Destruction*", June 18, 2003. "Fully 69% of all adults believe that Iraq had weapons of mass destruction, and 35% believe that we have found clear evidence of these weapons."

- "A foolish consistency is the hobgoblin of little minds, adored by little statesmen and philosophers and divines. With consistency a great soul has simply nothing to do."— Ralph Waldo Emerson.

- "See, I'm of the belief that we'll find out the truth on the weapons. That's why we sent up the independent commission. I look forward to hearing the truth as to exactly where they are. They could still be there. They could be hidden, like the 50 tons of mustard gas in a turkey farm."-President George W. Bush at a rare Press Conference, April 13, 2004.

- Four hundred member military team withdrawn from Iraq in early 2004, documented in The New York Times, "*The Struggle For Iraq: Arms Search: U.S. Withdraws a Team of Weapons Hunters From Iraq, Saying That Its Work Is Done*", Douglas Jehl, January 8, 2004.

- "Let me begin by saying, we were almost all wrong, and I certainly include myself here."—Formed top U.S. Weapons

Inspector, David Kay, testifying before the Senate Armed Services Committee, January 28, 2004.

- "Going in we expected to find large stocks of chemical and biological agents, weaponized, ready for use on the battlefield, as well as a fairly substantial nuclear program. We did not find that. We have found it a lot. We have found program activities in those areas. We found a resurgent missile program. But, the large stockpile of actual weapons, chemical and biological weapons simply have not yet been found."—David Kay, Interview with Jim Lehrer on PBS, January 29, 2004.

- March 2004 U.N. Weapons inspectors find nothing. From CNN.com, "*Iraq War Wasn't Justified, U.N. Weapons Experts Say*", March 22, 2004. www.cnn.com/2004/US/03/21/iraq.weapons/

- Duelfer report to Congress from the Washington Post, "*U.S. 'Almost All Wrong' on Weapons*", Dana Priest and Walter Pincus, October 7, 2004. www.washingtonpost.com/wp-dyn/articles/A12115-2004Oct6.html

- Weapons search is over, from BBC, "*US Gives Up Search for Iraq WMD*", January 12, 2005. news.bbc.co.uk/1/hi/world/americas/4169107.stm

- Poll data from The PIPA/Knowledge Networks Poll, "*Americans and Iraq, on the Eve of the Presidential Election*", Steven Kull, October 28, 2004. www.pipa.org/OnlineReports/Pres_Election_04/Report10_28_04.pdf

- "Trust, but Verify"—President Ronald Reagan, during 1987 summit meeting with Mikhail Gorbachev.

- USA Today, "*U.S., World Clearly are Safer*", Condoleezza Rice, 7/15/2004. www.usatoday.com/news/opinion/editorials/2004-07-15-oppose_x.htm

- Pakistan President comment on terrorism and safety from CNN.com, "*Musharraf: Look to Terrorism Roots*", December 6, 2004. edition.cnn.com/2004/WORLD/europe/12/06/musharraf.london/index.html

- Safety survey from University of Maryland, "*Arab Attitudes Towards Political and Social Issues, Foreign Policy and the Media*", May, 2004.

- October, 2004 Harris Poll from Harris Interactive, "*Iraq, 9/11, al Qaeda, and Weapons of Mass Destruction: What the Public Believes Now, According to Latest Harris Poll*", October 21, 2004. www.harrisinteractive.com/harris_poll/index.asp?PID=508

- The Human Rights Watch, as referenced by the State Department's own document, did not condone the Iraq War as a humanitarian invasion, in "*War in Iraq: Not a Humanitarian Intervention*", Ken Roth, January, 2004. www.hrw.org/wr2k4/3.htm

- Poll data from The PIPA/Knowledge Networks Poll, "*Americans and Iraq, on the Eve of the Presidential Election*", Steven Kull, October 28, 2004.

- "Frivolous and junk lawsuits are threatening medicine across the country."—George W. Bush, Baptist Health Medical Center, Little Rock, Arkansas, January 26, 2004.

- Actual cost of malpractice insurance premiums as a percentage of total health care costs. Public Citizen, "*President Bush Dis-*

- *Torts the Truth About Lawsuits' Impact on Health Care and the Economy*", December 15, 2004. http://www.citizen.org/documents/BushDistortionFactSheet12-15-04.pdf

- Jeffrey Barbakow compensation from USA Today, "*How CEO Compensation Compares*", June 4, 2003. www.usatoday.com/money/companies/management/2002-09-30-paylist.htm

- Congressman Bernie Sanders discussed Charles A. Heimbold of Bristol-Myers Squibb on the floor of the House of Representatives on May 6, 2004. "And I am talking about Charles A. Heimbold, Jr., of Bristol-Myers Squibb, who received almost $75 million in 2001 while helping to make it impossible for many seniors in this country to pay the outrageously high prices that his company and other companies are charging for prescription drugs."

- Pfizer income for 2002 from Yahoo Finance. finance.yahoo.com/q/is?s=PFE&annual

Chapter 7: The Dawn of Fear

- "Today we've had a national tragedy…", President George W. Bush, Booker Elementary School, September 11th, 2001, 9:29 a.m. EST. www.americanrhetoric.com/speeches/gwbush911florida.htm

- Timeline of events on September 11th, 2001 from CNN.com, "*America Remembers*" www.cnn.com/SPECIALS/2002/america.remembers/sept11.section.html

- "Lead the world to Victory" quote from Associated Press, "*Bush: U.S. Will 'Lead World to Victory*", September 13, 2001.

- "There is a desire by the American people to not seek only revenge, but to win a war against barbaric behavior,"— President George W. Bush, Radio Address, September 15, 2001.

- "Crusade" and "Evil-doers" quoted in CNN.com, *"Bush Vows to Rid the World of 'Evil-Doers"*, Manuel Perez-Rivas, September 16, 2001. "This crusade, this war on terrorism is gonna take awhile. And the American people must be patient. I'm gonna be patient," archives.cnn.com/2001/US/09/16/gen.bush.terrorism/

- On September 16th, 2001, Vice President Dick Cheney appeared on Meet the Press with Tim Russert, and said, "If you've got a nation out there now that has provided a base, training facilities, a sanctuary, as has been true, for example, in this case, probably with Afghanistan, then they have to understand, and others like them around the world have to understand, that if you provide sanctuary to terrorists, you face the full wrath of the United States of America. And that we will, in fact, aggressively go after these nations to make certain that they cease and desist from providing support for these kinds of organizations."

- "With us or against us" quote from President George W. Bush to a Joint Session of Congress on September 20, 2001.

- Howard Zinn quote from documentary, *"Liberty Bound"*, Blue Moose Films, 2004.

- First night of Afghanistan bombing from CNN.com, *"Afghanistan Wakes After Night of Intense Bombings"*, October 7, 2001. "There was no immediate news on damage assessment. The Pentagon is expected to use spy planes and surveillance satellites to help gauge the success of its first night of bombing."

- Information on bombing of Karam and Kama Ado from "*A Dossier on Civilian Victims of United States' Aerial Bombing of Afghanistan: A Comprehensive Accounting*", Professor Marc W. Herold, March, 2002. www.cursor.org/stories/civilian_deaths.htm

- Tur Bakai quote from The Frontier Post, "*Afghanistan's Female Bombing Victims*", October 17, 2001.

- Khair Khana eight family members information from, XTRAMSN, "*Eight Die From One Family in Kabul Raid*", Sayed Salahuddin, October 22, 2001.

- Bill Maher controversy from E-Online, "*Maher Causes 'Cowardly' Flap*", Mark Armstrong, September 20, 2001.

- Ari Fleischer quote from September 26, 2001 Press Conference. "They're reminders to all Americans that they need to watch what they say, watch what they do. This is not a time for remarks like that; there never is." www.whitehouse.gov/news/releases/2001/09/20010926-5.html

- Karzai Helmand restaurants confirmed at Tour San Francisco, "*The Helmand Afghan Restaurant*". "They didn't even know at that time that Hamid Karzai, the brother of the owner of The Helmand, Mahmoud Karzai, was just named head of the interim coalition Afghan Government!" www.inetours.com/Pages/Dining_Archive/The_Helmand.html

- Feb, 2002 meeting on Trans-Afghan Pipeline from DAWN, "*Islamabad, Kabul Pledge to Forget Past.*", Ihtasham ul

Haque, February 8, 2002. www.dawn.com/2002/02/09/top2.htm

- Unocal Press Release from August 21, 1998. www.unocal.com/uclnews/98news/082198.htm

- May, 2002 meeting to sign trilateral agreement found at DAWN, "*Trilateral Gas Pipeline Agreement Signed*", Faraz Hashmi, May 30, 2002. www.dawn.com/2002/05/31/top11.htm

- December, 2002 meeting to review more detailed framework found at DAWN, "*Jamali, Niyazov, Karzai sign gas pipeline accord*", December 27, 2002.

- Minister of Mines and Industries, Razim, told a tale of Unocal's continued involvement at the BBC, "*Afghanistan Plans Gas Pipeline*", May 13, 2002.

- Unocal Press Release conflicts with Razim statement, June 30, 2004. www.unocal.com/uclnews/2004news/063004.htm

- Meeting planned for early 2005, DAWN, "*Reserves certification termed vital for talks: Turkmenistan gas pipeline project*", Khaleeq Kiani, November 9, 2004.

- The Moscow Times reports that Turkmenistan will begin work on the pipeline in 2006, The Moscow Times, "*Turkmenistan Revives Trans-Afghan Pipeline*", January 19, 2005.

Chapter 8: Fear's Agenda Takes Hold

- Car accident fatalities from National Highway Traffic Safety Administration, cited in Tech Central Station, "*We Like The Odds*", Ralph Kinney Bennett, 4/28/2003.

- Cornell University Muslim Rights poll from Associated Press, "*Gov't Should Restrict Muslim Rights: U.S. poll*", December 18, 2004. "Nearly half of all Americans believe the U.S. government should restrict the civil liberties of Muslim Americans, according to a nationwide poll. The survey conducted by Cornell University also found that Republicans and people who described themselves as highly religious were more apt to support curtailing Muslims' civil liberties than Democrats or people who are less religious.

- London Blitz information from EyeWitness to History.com, "*The London Blitz, 1940*". www.eyewitnesstohistory.com/blitz.htm

- "In the next several days" from CNN.com, "*Investigation: Authorities on Alert*", October 11, 2001. archives.cnn.com/2001/US/10/11/inv.investigation.facts/

- "In the next week" from CNN.com, "*Ashcroft: New Terror Attack Possible*", October 29, 2001. archives.cnn.com/2001/US/10/29/gen.attack.on.terror/

- Tom Ridge warnings around Ramadan from CNN.com, "*Ridge issues new security alert*", December 3, 2001.

- Ashcroft warning about suicide attacks from a video found in Afghanistan, from CNN.com, "*U.S. Asks Help Finding Men in Terror Tape*", January 17, 2002. edition.cnn.com/2002/US/01/17/inv.terror.tape/

- February 12th "imminent threat" from CNN.com, "*FBI Warns Terror Attack Could be Imminent*", February 12, 2002. archives.cnn.com/2002/US/02/11/terror.warning/

- Brooklyn Bridge and Status of Liberty warning from CNN.com, "*FBI Warns N.Y. Landmarks May be Attacked*", May 21, 2002. archives.cnn.com/2002/US/05/21/gen.war.on.terror/

- Color-Coded Warning system information from CNN.com, "*Terror Threat Warning System Unveiled*", March 12, 2002. archives.cnn.com/2002/US/03/12/rec.threat.alerts/

- Terror Level to Orange on September 10, 2002 from CNN.com, "*Sources: U.S. to Raise Terror Level*", September 10, 2002. archives.cnn.com/2002/US/09/10/ar911.threat.level/

- Terror Alert raise on dangers to apartment buildings and hotels from CBS News, "*'High Risk of Terror Attacks*", February 7, 2003. www.cbsnews.com/stories/2003/02/08/attack/main539928.shtml

- "No specific reason" raise of Terror Alert level to Orange, based on fears of attacks caused by U.S. invasion of Iraq. Given recent evidence of lack of connection between Iraq and al Qaeda, I call this "no specific reason". From The White House, "*National Threat Level Raised*", March 17, 2003. www.whitehouse.gov/news/releases/2003/03/20030317-8.html

- Nuclear plant threat from The Phoenix Business Journal, "*State Deploys Troops to Nuclear Plant*", March 18, 2003.

- Threat level raised just before Christmas, 2003, from The White House, "*Threat Level Raised*", December 21, 2003. www.whitehouse.gov/news/releases/2003/12/20031221.html

- Trains and buses, oh my, from CBS News, "*Transit Systems Tighten Security*", April 3, 2004. www.cbsnews.com/stories/ 2004/04/06/terror/main610392.shtml

- May 26, 2004 Plane attack threat warning from CNN.com, "*Transcript: Ashcroft, Mueller News Conference*", May 26, 2004. www.cnn.com/2004/US/05/26/terror.threat.transcript/

- Financial threat and accompanying information about the outdated nature of the information from CNN Interview with Condoleezza Rice. "*CNN Late Edition with Wolf Blitzer*", August 8, 2004. "BLITZER: Last Sunday, a week ago exactly, when Tom Ridge, the secretary of homeland security, announced the higher threat levels in parts of New York, New Jersey, here in Washington, he failed to mention that most of the information is three or four years old, and that caused a lot of angst the next day. Was that a mistake? RICE: Well, I don't think that it really occurred to us to mention it, and I'll tell you why. Al Qaeda does meticulous planning over many years. We know that the material that they used to case the East Africa bombing, which was done in 1998, had been generated probably five years before, and we have just found the information, of course." transcripts.cnn.com/TRANSCRIPTS/0408/08/le.00.html

- Floyd Abrams quote from The New York Times, "*In Patriotic Time, Dissent is Muted*", Bill Carter and Felicity Barringer, September 28, 2001.

- Anti-Terrorism Act of 2001, original draft, from The House of Representatives, "*Administration's Draft Anti-Terrorism Act of 2001*", September 24, 2001. commdocs.house.gov/ committees/judiciary/hju75288.000/hju75288_0f.htm

- PATRIOT Act Text in PDF format available here: www.apfn.org/pdf/hr3162.pdf

- Information about the Patriot Act details from Bill of Rights Defense Committee. bordc.org

- Russ Feingold's Statement on the anti-terrorism bill, can be viewed on Feingold's Senate web site. www.senate.gov/~feingold/statements/01/10/102501at.html "We all also had our own initial reactions, and my first and most powerful emotion was a solemn resolve to stop these terrorists. And that remains my principal reaction to these events. But I also quickly realized that two cautions were necessary, and I raised them on the Senate floor the day after the attacks. The first caution was that we must continue to respect our Constitution and protect our civil liberties in the wake of the attacks. As the chairman of the Constitution Subcommittee of the Judiciary Committee, I recognize that this is a different world with different technologies, different issues, and different threats. Yet we must examine every item that is proposed in response to these events to be sure we are not rewarding these terrorists and weakening ourselves by giving up the cherished freedoms that they seek to destroy. The second caution I issued was a warning against the mistreatment of Arab Americans, Muslim Americans, South Asians, or others in this country. Already, one day after the attacks, we were hearing news reports that misguided anger against people of these backgrounds had led to harassment, violence, and even death."

- Wiretap Statute modification from The Patriot Act, Page 115 STAT. 289. www.patriotact.com/patriot-act-15.html

- Patriot Act details from the American Civil Liberties Union, *"Surveillance Under the USA Patriot Act"*. www.aclu.org/SafeandFree/SafeandFree.cfm?ID=12263&c=206

- Bush made the case for the "renewal" of the Patriot Act many times during 2004, including referenced by CBS News, *"Bush Pushes Patriot Act Renewal"*, April 17, 2004. www.cbsnews.com/stories/2004/04/14/terror/main611781.shtml

- Details about Secret Searches from the Seattle Times, *"Patriot Act Allows Surge of Secret Searches in United States"*, Richard Schmitt, May 2, 2004.

- Tim Michels quote about the Patriot Act from his debate with Russ Feingold, 10/1/2004.

- Russ Feingold quote on "police state" from a speech at Beloit College commencement, from Milwaukee Journal Sentinel, *"Russ Feingold at Beloit College: Take Some Risks"*, June 2, 2002. "There can be little doubt that if we lived in a police state, it would be easier to catch terrorists. If we lived in a country that allowed the police to search our homes at any time for any reason; if we lived in a country that allowed the government to open our mail, eavesdrop on our phone conversations, or intercept our e-mail communications; if we lived in a country that allowed the government to hold us in jail indefinitely based on what we write or think, or based on mere suspicion that we are up to no good, then the government would no doubt discover and arrest more terrorists. But that probably would not be a country in which we would want to live. That would not be a country for which we could, in good conscience, ask our young people to fight and die. In short, that would not be America."

- Ashcroft's Patriot Act report on successes, Boston Globe, "*AG Touts Patriot Act; Opponents Unconvinced*", Brian Bender, July 14, 2004.

- List of cities and states with resolutions critical of the Patriot Act from the Bill of Rights Defense Committee. www.bordc.org/Chronology.pdf

- New York City Council Bill of Rights Resolution, Res. 60-2004 (formerly 0909-2003-A), February 4, 2004. www.nycbordc.org/resolution0060-2004.html

- *The 9/11 Commission Report*, Page 394, July 22, 2004.

- Opening Statement Of Senator Patrick Leahy, Senate Judiciary Committee, Oversight Hearing Attorney General John Ashcroft, June 8, 2004. leahy.senate.gov/press/200406/060804.html

- Description of the Kings Penalty for Treason from Richard M. Ketchum, *The Winter Soldiers*, Henry Holt and Company, 1973, page 147.

- Nathan Hale information from The Connecticut Society of the Sons of the American Revolution, "*Captain Nathan Hale*". www.ctssar.org/patriots/nathan_hale.htm

- John Gilbert information from The Connecticut Society of the Sons of the American Revolution, "*Captain John Gilbert*". www.ctssar.org/patriots/john_gilbert.htm

- Thomas Paine information from Strike The Root, "*Failure Writes Pamphlet, Changes American History*", George F. Smith. www.strike-the-root.com/columns/Smith/smith37.html

- Read the Bill of Rights at the National Archives. www.archives.gov/national_archives_experience/charters/bill_of_rights_transcript.html

- Information on Steve Kurtz from the Critical Art Ensemble Defense Fund. www.caedefensefund.org

- Information on Michael Galardi from the Las Vegas SUN, "*Patriot Act Aided Feds in Probe*", Jace Radke, November 4, 2003.

- Brandon Mayfield information from CBS News, "*DOJ Terror Probe Scrutinized*", September 14, 2004. www.cbsnews.com/stories/2004/04/28/terror/main614335.shtml

- Additional details from The Associated Press, "*'My Heart Hurts'—Oregon Lawyer Speaks Out About His Ordeal Behind Bars*", May 25, 2004. www.bostonherald.com/national/view.bg?articleid=29307&format=

- Carlos Corrales quote from The New York Times, "*Spain Disputes FBI on Bombing Probe U.S. Accused of Ignoring Warning on Suspect*", Sarah Kershaw, June 5, 2004. www.sfgate.com/cgi-bin/article.cgi?f=/chronicle/archive/2004/06/05/MNG1K71FRR1.DTL

- The George W. Bush Endorsement Form similar to the one used at the campaign rallies can be seen on numerous Bush web sites, including Veterans for Bush, Maine. www.veteransforbush-maine.org/endorse.htm

- Information about Nicole Rank, FEMA worker who was arrested at Bush campaign event, from the Associated Press, "*Couple Arrested at Bush Event Sues Federal Officials*",

Jennifer Bundy, September 15, 2004. www.herald-dispatch.com/2004/September/15/LNlist8.htm

- Information about family of three with pro-choice shirts from Feminist Daily News Wire, "*Pro-Choice T-Shirts and Undecided Voters not Welcome at Bush Rallies*", August 11, 2004. www.feminist.org/news/newsbyte/uswirestory.asp?id=8585

- Story of three Oregon teachers with "Protect our Civil Liberties" T-shirts from BEND.com, "*Teachers' T-shirts Bring Bush Speech Ouster*", October 14, 2004.

- "Free speech zones" in Pittsburgh and elsewhere documented by The San Francisco Chronicle, "*Quarantining dissent: How the Secret Service Protects Bush from Free Speech*", James Bovard, January 4, 2004.

- "Little Guantanomo" information from The New York Times, "*Convention Protestors File Lawsuit over Detentions*", Julia Preston, November 23, 2004.

- Domestic Terrorist definition from The Patriot Act, Section 802.

- Effort to block part of the Patriot Act with the 15-minute time limit extension covered by The Associated Press, "*House Refuses to Curb USA Patriot Act*", July 8, 2004. msnbc.msn.com/id/5394518

- Leahy statement on Operation TIPS and Homeland Security Act, "*Statement of Senator Patrick Leahy, The Homeland Security Department Act*", November 19, 2002. Available from his Senate web site: leahy.senate.gov/press/200211/111902c.html

- Critique of the draft version of the Patriot Act II from the American Civil Liberties Union, "*Interested Persons Memo: Section-by-Section Analysis of Justice Department Draft, 'Domestic Security Enhancement Act of 2003,' also known as 'Patriot Act II'*", Timothy H. Edgar, February 14, 2003. www.aclu.org/SafeandFree/SafeandFree.cfm?ID=11835&c=206

- "Victory Act" information from The New York Daily News, "*Ashcroft Tour to Plug Terror Bill*", James Gordon Meek, August 6, 2003. www.nydailynews.com/news/wn_report/story/106872p-96686c.html

Chapter 9: Most of History's Lessons are Never Learned

- Information about the Alien and Sedition Acts from the Wikipedia, "*Alien and Sedition Acts*". en.wikipedia.org/wiki/Alien_and_Sedition_Acts

- "A little patience, and we shall see the reign of witches pass over, their spells dissolve, and the people, recovering their true sight, restore their government to its true principles…"—Thomas Jefferson to John Taylor, June 4, 1798

- Jefferson pardoned everyone convicted under the Sedition Act, from EDSITEMent, "*Certain Crimes Against the United States: Consequences of the Sedition Act*". "When Jefferson became president, he pardoned everyone convicted under the Sedition Act. However, Congress apparently felt the need to apologize for its abuse of power for the next 50 years…The act still called for Congressional action to compensate the victims (posthumously) in the 1832 Bill to refund a fine imposed on the late Mathew Lyon, under the Sedition Law and the 1850 Bill to refund the fine imposed on the late Dr. Thomas Cooper, under the Sedition Law."

- Woodrow Wilson information from The White House, "Woodrow Wilson". www.whitehouse.gov/history/presidents/ww28.html

- George Creel, *How We Advertised America*, 1920.

- Other CPI and Creel details from Disinfopedia, "*Committee on Public Information*". www.disinfopedia.org/wiki.phtml?title=Committee_on_Public_Information

- Rose Pastor Stokes information from Spartacus Educational, "*Rose Pastor Stokes*". www.spartacus.schoolnet.co.uk/USAWstokes.htm

- Eugene Debs information from Spartacus Educational, "*Eugene Debs*". www.spartacus.schoolnet.co.uk/USAdebs.htm

- Robin Hood book banning from the University of Colorado, "*Nightmare in Red*". www.colorado.edu/AmStudies/lewis/film/fried1.htm

- McCarthyism and "Hollywood Ten" details from the Wikipedia, "*McCarthyism*". en.wikipedia.org/wiki/Mccarthyism and "Joseph McCarthy". en.wikipedia.org/wiki/Joseph_McCarthy

- Margaret Chase Smith quotes from Gifts of Speech, "*Declaration of Conscience*", Margaret Chase Smith, June 1, 1950. gos.sbc.edu/s/chasesmith.html

- Definition of Fascism from The Columbia Encyclopedia, Sixth Edition, "*Fascism*", 2001.

- New Deal information from the Wikipedia, "*New Deal*". en.wikipedia.org/wiki/New_deal

- Information about the American Liberty League from the Wikipedia, *"American Liberty League"*. en.wikipedia.org/wiki/American_Liberty_League

- Information about Lawrence Dennis and economic Fascism from LewRockwell.com, *"Economic Fascism"*, Thomas J. DiLorenzo. www.lewrockwell.com/dilorenzo/dilorenzo85.html

- Henry Wallace quotes from The New York Times, *"The Danger of American Fascism"*, April 9, 1944.

- Roger Rosenblatt quote on "Too much patriotism" from CNN Sunday Morning, July 7, 2002.

Chapter 10: On The Front Lines of Class Warfare

- Ronald Reagan 1981 tax cut and quote from The Associated Press, *"Tax Cut Reminiscent of Trickle-down Economics"*, April 10, 2001. http://www.wpi.edu/News/TechNews/010410/taxcut.shtml

- Ronald Reagan 1982 Tax increase from The Heritage Foundation, *"Ronald Reagan: The Heritage Foundation Remembers"*. www.reagansheritage.org/reagan/html/reagan_edwards12.shtml

- Tax savings per return and AMT claims from the Internal Revenue Service, cited by the *Philadelphia Enquirer,* October 21, 1991.

- Xavier Roberts personal tax cut from Forbes Magazine, *"Personalized Taxes"*, Laura Saunders, June 1, 1987.

- Tax gap between the classes from Columbia Journalism Review, *"Pushing for Answers"*, Barlett and Steele, March/April, 1992.

- Reaganomics comparison to Bush Tax policy, CNN Money, *"Reaganomics Lives On"*, Kathleen Hays, June 7, 2004. money.cnn.com/2004/06/07/commentary/column_hays/hays/

- Bush tax cut details from Citizens for Tax Justice, *"Final Tax Plan Tilts Even More Toward Richest"*, May 22, 2003. www.ctj.org/pdf/sen0522.pdf

- Triple the national debt by 2013 information from Citizens for Tax Justice, *"Bush Still on Track to Borrow $10 Trillion by 2014"*. www.ctj.org/pdf/def0104.pdf

- Clinton Vetoes Republican tax cut to protect Social Security and Medicare from CNN.com, *"Clinton: 'This tax cut will not become law'"*, August 7, 1999. www.cnn.com/ALLPOLITICS/stories/1999/08/07/clinton.tax.cuts/

- National Low Income Housing Coalition, *"Out of Reach 2004"*. www.nlihc.org/oor_current/data.php?state[ ]=_all

- *It's a Wonderful Life*, 1946.

- Four counties where a minimum wage earner could afford a one-bedroom apartment from SignOnSanDiego, *"Report: Only Four Counties Where Minimum-Wage Earner Can Afford One-Bedroom Rental"*, Gernaro Armas, December 20, 2004. www.signonsandiego.com/news/business/20041220-1200-affordablerent.html

- Walton family ownership from the Wal-Mart Proxy Statement, SEC, April 15, 2004.

- Other Wal-Mart dividend and wage information from CounterPunch, "*Wal-Mart's Magic Numbers*", Stan Cox, April 20, 2004. www.counterpunch.org/cox04202004.html

- Pfizer has almost $30 billion in unrepatriated earnings from Forbes, "*Eye on Stocks for Wednesday, January 19*", January 18, 2005. www.forbes.com/2005/01/18/cx_pk_0118 eyeonstocks_print.html

- Offshoring Tax Breaks detailed in The Wall Street Journal, "*U.S. Tax Code Provisions Encourage Offshore Jobs*", March 11, 2004. "What we know is that the amount of unrepatriated foreign earnings is growing substantially. The non-partisan Congressional Research Service in a report last year said it had increased to $639 billion in 2002 from $403 billion in 1999."

- WTO trade sanction of $4 billion from The Seattle Times, "*WTO OK's $4 billion in EU Trade Sanctions on U.S.*", Naomi Koppel, August 30, 2002. "The World Trade Organization said Friday that the European Union can impose $4 billion in sanctions against the United States—a figure 20 times bigger than any sanction allowed in the past—because of tax breaks given to U.S. corporations operating abroad. The EU vowed to go ahead with plans to impose the sanctions by working on lists of targeted products, including everything from textiles, foodstuffs and automotive parts to nuclear reactors, unless Washington ends the tax policy. 'The cost of noncompliance with WTO is crystal clear,' said EU Trade Commissioner Pascal Lamy in a statement. 'The path is now clear for the EU to adopt sanctions if the United States does not repeal the…scheme expeditiously.'"

- Call center information and Praful Bidwai quotes from the BBC, "*Call Centres 'Bad for India'*," December 11, 2003. http://news.bbc.co.uk/1/hi/world/south_asia/3292619.stm

- Poverty data from CNN Money, "*Poverty Spreads*", August 26, 2004. http://money.cnn.com/2004/08/26/news/economy/poverty_survey/

Epilogue: Bigger Than You Can Imagine

- "Yes, there were some in our country who doubted the Iraqi people wanted freedom, or they just couldn't imagine they would be welcome—welcoming to a liberating force. They were mistaken, and we know why. The desire for freedom is not the property of one culture, it is the universal hope of human beings in every culture. (Applause.)"—President George W. Bush, April 28, 2003, Ford Community and Performing Arts Center, Dearborn, Michigan.

- Poverty data article text directly from CNN.com, "*Holes in the Net*", Brian Todd, August 26, 2004. www.cnn.com/2004/US/08/26/insurance/index.html

- Powell aid quote from The New York Times, "*Powell says it Plainly: Aid has Image Value*", Scott Shane, January 5, 2005.

- Lee Scott quote from CNN.com, "*Wal-Mart launches P.R. Blitz*", January 13, 2005. www.cnn.com/2005/US/01/13/walmart.pr/index.html

- "Saddam Hussein is a man who told the world he wouldn't have weapons of mass destruction, but he's got them. He's a man who a while ago who was close to having a nuclear weapon. Imagine if this madman had a nuclear weapon. It's a man who not only has chemical weapons, but he's used chemical weapons against some of his neighbors. He used chemical weapons, incredibly enough, against his own people. He can't stand America. He can't stand some of our closest friends."—President George W. Bush, November 3, 2002, Sioux Falls Convention Center, Sioux Falls, South Dakota.

- Patriot Act article text from CNN.com, "*Bush Signs Antiterrorism Bill into Law*", October 26, 2001. archives.cnn.com/2001/US/10/26/rec.bush.antiterror.bill/index.html

- "What does Iraq look like now?" quote from Newtopia Magazine, "*Unembedded, Independent: An Exclusive In-depth Interview with journalist Dahr Jamail*", Charles Shaw, January 27, 2005. www.newtopiamagazine.net/content/issue19/features/DahrJamail.php

- Marriage ban article text from CNN.com, "*Same-sex Marriage Bans Winning on State Ballots*", November 3, 2004. www.cnn.com/2004/ALLPOLITICS/11/02/ballot.samesex.marriage/index.html

- "I see more bloodshed and chaos." quote from Newtopia Magazine, "*Unembedded, Independent: An Exclusive In-depth Interview with journalist Dahr Jamail*", Charles Shaw, January 27, 2005.

- Bush 2005 budget article text from Reuters, "*Bush's $2.5 Trillion Budget Calls for Sweeping Changes*", Caren Bohan and Adam Entous, February 7, 2005.

- Cheney mandate quote from Knight Ridder Newspapers, "*Bush, Democrats differ over whether he has Mandate*", Steven Thomma, November 12, 2004.

- Jerry Falwell said, "If it takes 10 years, let's blow them all away in the name of the Lord" on CNN's Late Edition on October 24, 2004.

- Stem cell article text from CNN.com, "Subcommittee Hears Testimony on Stem Cell Research", September 14, 2000. archives.cnn.com/2000/HEALTH/09/14/stemcell.hearing.02/

- "There was support by most Iraqis for the removal of Saddam Hussein." quote from Newtopia Magazine, "*Unembedded, Independent: An Exclusive In-depth Interview with journalist Dahr Jamail*", Charles Shaw, January 27, 2005.

- Unisured Americans article text from PBS, "*Healthcare Crisis: The Uninsured*". www.pbs.org/healthcarecrisis/uninsured.html

Author Contact

- I can be reached at growingupred@hotmail.com. Please feel free to send a note.

0-595-34613-8

Printed in the United States
27790LVS00001B/166